Imagining Flight

NUMBER SEVEN:

Centennial of Flight Series

Roger D. Launius, *General Editor*

Imagining Flight

Aviation and Popular Culture

A. Bowdoin Van Riper

Texas A&M University Press / College Station

The paper used in this book meets the minimum requirements
of the American National Standard for Permanence
of Paper for Printed Library Materials, z39.48–1984.
Binding materials have been chosen for durability.
∞

Library of Congress Cataloging-in-Publication Data

Van Riper, A. Bowdoin.
    Imagining flight : aviation and popular culture / A. Bowdoin Van Riper.—
1st ed.
        p. cm. — (Centennial of flight series ; no. 7)
    ISBN 1-58544-300-x (cloth : alk. paper)
    1. Aeronautics—Popular works. 2. Aeronautics—History. I. Title.
II. Series.
    TL553.V37 2004
    629.13—DC21

                                        2003007848

Dedicated to the memory of

Anthony K. Van Riper

1926–2001

Contents

Illustrations

Acknowledgments

*N*o book goes from brain to paper as quickly or as easily as the author expects it to. This one was no exception. It was written, then revised, in many hours "borrowed" from other activities. I owe an even greater debt than usual to my family—Julie, Joe, and Katie—for their patience, their understanding, and their cheerful willingness to rearrange the family schedule.

No book, likewise, goes from brain to paper without the help of others. This one's passage was assisted, from conception to publication, by Kevin Brock and the editorial and production staffs of Texas A&M University Press. For observations made, suggestions offered, sources pointed out, details checked, and theories critiqued, I am also indebted to Roger Bilstein, David Courtwright, George Larson, Roger Launius, Susan Mangus, Joe Mundt, Julie Newell, Frederick Ordway, Michael Palmer, Lester Reingold, Timothy Warnock, Margaret Wirth, and two anonymous readers. All have made this book better than it would otherwise have been; any errors or infelicities that remain are my fault, not theirs.

Thanks are also due to those who contributed, even though they did not know at the time that they were doing so: Gene Galanter, Dick Sherman, and the crew at Katama Airport for the rides; Lois Reitzes and the staff of WABE (90.1 FM) in Atlanta for the music; the folks at the Cobb County Public Library System and the Lawrence V. Johnson Library, Southern Polytechnic State University, for the books; and the late Fred Eaton, formerly of the U.S. Army Air Force and Trans World Airlines, for the stories.

My father—private pilot, English teacher, and lifelong airplane lover—touched this project in countless ways, many of them while it was in the earliest planning stages. He did not live to see the book completed, but it is better by far for his involvement. I owe him a greater debt than any paragraph can express.

Note on Terminology

"Airplane," throughout this book, refers to a powered, fixed-wing, heavier-than-air flying machine, anything from an ultralight to a jumbo jet. "Airship" refers to a powered, lighter-than-air flying machine, anything from a World War I zeppelin to Goodyear's famous blimps. "Aircraft" is a generic term encompassing both airplanes and airships as well as helicopters, gliders, autogiros, and free balloons.

References to books are to the first American hardcover edition, where one exists; facts of publication are as given in the online catalog of the Library of Congress (http://catalog.loc.gov). Credits for films are as given in the *Internet Movie Database* (www.imdb.com). Credits for television programs are as given in Alex McNeil, *Total Television*, 4th ed. (New York: Penguin, 1996).

Imagining Flight

Introduction

"During the past year," wrote James Thurber and E. B. White in 1929, "two factors in our civilization have been greatly overemphasized. One is aviation, the other is sex. Looked at calmly, neither diversion is entitled to the space it has been accorded. Both have been deliberately promoted."[1]

Thurber and White wrote with tongues in cheek, but they had a point. Aviation, whether deliberately promoted or not, attracted more public attention in 1928–29 than ever before. Charles Lindbergh, who in May, 1927, had become the first pilot to fly solo across the Atlantic, was at the height of his fame. Enthusiastic crowds had greeted him at every stop of his postflight tour of the United States; his image decorated every imaginable kind of object; and We, his book about the flight, was a bestseller. Amelia Earhart, a Kansas-born Boston teacher, had become in June, 1928, the first woman to fly across the Atlantic as a passenger. Small planes designed for private flying, built by companies like Stinson and Travel Air, began to enter the market in large numbers during 1928–29. The number of passengers carried by U.S. airlines in 1929 was triple that for 1928, catapulting the United States from third to first place among nations with scheduled airline service. Western Airlines hired the first cabin stewards for its Los Angeles to San Francisco flights in 1928, and in 1929 Transcontinental Air Transport began to offer coast-to-coast passenger service using carefully coordinated planes (by day) and trains (by night).[2]

Americans interested in flight did not, however, have to content themselves with reality: flying stories saturated the popular culture of 1928–29. *Wings*, an epic silent film about World War I fighter pilots, took Best Picture honors at the first-ever Academy Awards in May, 1929. Howard Hughes, after seeing *Wings* several times, had begun filming his own aerial epic, *Hell's Angels*, in the skies over southern California. Meanwhile, "air-minded" filmgoers could content themselves (in 1928 alone) with cheaply made features like *Air Mail Pilot*, *Air Legion*, *Air Circus*, and *Won in the Clouds*.[3] Bookstores featured Dorothy L. Sayers's new mystery novel *Clouds of Witness* and Nevil Shute's espionage thriller *The Mysterious Aviator*, both of which had aviation themes.[4] Young readers could choose from the aerial adventures of series characters like Rex Lee, Andy Lane, or Ted Scott, or (if allowed) they could turn to pulp-fiction magazines like *Air Adventures*, *Air Trails*, and the futuristic *Air Wonder Stories*.[5]

Public interest in aviation had been growing steadily for two decades before the peak that Thurber and White commented on in 1929. It fluctuated but remained strong in the seven decades afterward, and it remains strong today. This book is a history of that interest: an exploration of the ways in which people who were not aviators looked at, lived with, and thought about aviation.

Technology, we are told, makes us human. The depth of our ability to devise new tools and improve old ones sets us apart from other animals. Technology also, however, makes us more than human, more than the fragile, weaponless, hairless creatures that evolution produced. We improve old tools and invent new ones in order to do things well that—with existing tools, natural or artificial—we would do badly, inefficiently, or not at all. Toolmaking success has meant, since the days of *Homo erectus*, evolutionary success for humans and their ancestors. Transformed by our tools, we can outrun the antelope, out-dig the badger, and out-muscle the elephant. We can fly higher than any bird, dive deeper than any whale, and—as we have learned at great monetary and social cost—manipulate the Earth's surface to suit our needs.[6] Small wonder, then, that we are fascinated by our tools. Small wonder too that they figure prominently in the stories we tell to instruct, inform, and entertain one another.

Some technologies captivate because they confer extraordinary powers.[7] Dams hold the waters of great rivers in check and dispense them at our command for drinking, irrigation, driving mill wheels, or turning turbines. Antibiotic drugs vanquish, in a matter of days, infections that once brought weeks of pain and often death. Telephones enable any pair of users, no matter how distant, to converse as easily as if they were in the same room. Personal computers can, with the right software, make any teenager's desk into a music studio, any kitchen table into a small printing shop, and any office into a typesetting room. "Buy this product," we are told a thousand or more times a day, "and you too can do the things that the people in this advertisement are doing." Buy this kitchen knife, and you can cut tomatoes or two-by-fours with equal ease. Buy this wrench, and you can easily turn every kind of nut or bolt ever manufactured. Buy this drug (after asking your doctor if it is "right for you"), and your chronic medical condition will be cured or controlled. These ads persist because, presumably, they work—because for every problem there is a group of people ready to leap at the prospect of a technological "fix."

Other technologies captivate because they give access to otherwise inaccessible places. Remotely operated robot explorers show us the wreckage of the *Titanic* and the surfaces of distant planets. Television daily makes millions of viewers virtual witnesses of events and performances on Earth that they could not have seen in person. Computers act (for most users) as a portal to the dream worlds of games and the ever-expanding realms of the Internet. Much of the imaginary hardware in science fiction stories—spaceships, time machines, and interdimensional gateways—exists to take the characters "where no one has gone before." Car manufacturers, selling vehicles that both they and their customers know will be used for commuting and in-town errands, favor advertisements set in a land of spectacular scenery and challenging, wide-open roads. Buy the car, they imply, and you too can enter this world.

Still others captivate because they stand for ideas that are themselves appealing. Medieval and Renaissance visitors to the great cathedrals of Europe responded to them as embodiments, in stone, wood, lead, and glass, of God's majesty and the church's power. The thousands of electric light bulbs that illuminated the buildings of the Chicago World's Fair in 1893 were an affirmation of the city's rebirth after the catastrophic fire of 1888. The opening of the Panama Canal in 1914 marked not only the end of the largest civil engineering project in history but also the emergence of the United States as a world power with interests in both the Atlantic and Pacific Oceans. On a more prosaic level, the telephone has become not just a communication device but also a symbol for the *idea* of communicating, of "reaching out and touching" a distant loved one. Cars are not just a means of traveling but also a symbol of the *possibility* of traveling at will—any time, for any reason, anywhere that a road leads.[8]

Aircraft captivate for all three reasons. They bestow the powers of gods on mere mortals. They give unfettered access to the Earth's surface, to the skies above, and to the vacuum beyond. They symbolize the wonders and the horrors of the modern age, the settlement of old frontiers, and the opening of new ones, the greatness of nations and of individuals.

The gods fly, so do the angels, and so do a host of lesser magical creatures, from fairies to dragons to Pegasus, the winged horse of Greek mythology. Ordinary, mortal humans (according to a centuries-old literary traditions) fly only with magical aid. Perseus flies off to his meeting with Medusa using winged sandals borrowed from the god Hermes. Ebenezer Scrooge takes flight, in Charles Dickens's *A Christmas Carol*, when the Ghost of Christmas Past takes his hand. Wendy, John, and Michael Darling begin their journey to Neverland with the help of ageless Peter Pan and his fairy companion, Tinkerbelle.[9] Aircraft democratize the magic. They bring the power of flight to anyone with the price of a ticket, the address of an airfield, and the name of a pilot, things much easier to come by in the modern world than a visit from a god, ghost, or fairy. Aircraft also offer other godlike possibilities. Once aloft, pilots and passengers alike can take in a town at a glance, a county in a moment, or an entire state in an hour or two. People left behind on the ground shrink into insignificance, and even the most impressive cities seem toylike when seen from altitude. Suitably armed, the occupants of an aircraft can strike at enemies, their property, or their territory at will. There is little difference (to the victim at least) between aerial bombs and the thunderbolts of Zeus, Odin, or Jehovah.

Humans are a mobile species, and even in the settled societies that arose with the invention of farming, travel is part of our cultural life. For the better part of a million years, however, travel was circumscribed by natural barriers. Crossing deserts, ice fields, mountain ranges, or oceans was possible, but it was also difficult, time consuming, and dangerous. Few people made such treks even once, and most of them did it *only* once. The British colonists who crossed the Appalachians into the Ohio River Valley in the 1750s or the Amer-

icans who followed the Oregon Trail to the Pacific in the 1840s engaged in life-defining migrations, not routine travel.[10] Steamships
and railways by the 1840s began to ease the difficulty of crossing natural barriers, but as early as the 1920s, aircraft had begun to obliterate it. The Atlantic and Pacific, the Alps and the Rockies, the North
and South Poles, and the Sahara and Arabian Deserts had all been
crossed by air before 1930. Within a decade, scheduled intercontinental air service would reach every inhabited continent. Within a
generation, jet airliners would make six-hour flights across North
America and the North Atlantic routine. Aircraft also overthrew,
by the end of the 1930s, the tyranny of time and distance that had
isolated Western inhabitants of remote continental interiors. North
and East Africa, the Amazon Basin, and the Alaskan and Australian
bush thus became functionally, if not physically, closer to the centers
of "civilization."[11] Within a generation, helicopters created the possibility of on-demand air service to still-more-remote areas. Western
travelers contemplating a journey now no longer ask "How far can I
go?" but "Where do I want to go?"

Powerful, world-changing technologies need not *look* impressive. The antibiotic drugs that transformed twentieth-century medicine are unremarkable tablets, capsules, and liquids. Aside from a
few striking machines made by Apple and Dell, most personal computers are bland gray boxes. But the technologies that most intrigue
us, those that we most often put on display to symbolize some larger
idea, are those that not only do impressive things but also *look* impressive as they do them. Aircraft, mostly for practical engineering
reasons, routinely display exactly those qualities that the modern
world finds impressive in a machine. Most have, at least since the
early 1930s, a sleek and streamlined shape that suggests speed and
power even at rest. Most have large, clearly visible engines that reinforce the impression of speed and power. Most are impressively
loud in operation, and many are literally deafening. Most are large
enough to dwarf a human observer, even when both are standing on
the ground—an experience that, with the decline of passenger railways and heavy industry, is less familiar to Americans now than fifty
years ago. Finally, all airplanes, though not all aircraft, share a distinctive shape unlike that of any other machine. Many of our tools
are variations on the rectangular box, but only airplanes have wings.

"Any sufficiently advanced technology," wrote engineer and
science-fiction writer Arthur C. Clarke, "is indistinguishable from

magic."[12] We know, because we have seen them evolve, that aircraft are "just" advanced technology. We know, at a basic level at least, how they work. We know that like all machines they require routine maintenance and that, even so, they suffer occasional breakdowns. We can, at the beginning and end of our flight, not only see but also speak to the "man behind the curtain," whose pulling of levers and pushing of buttons makes the machine take flight. Still, for all our knowledge, it is difficult to watch an aircraft leave the ground without a suspicion that some kind of magic is afoot. That intellectual tension shaped the public's perception of aircraft even before the Wright brothers made their first controlled, powered flight in 1903. A century later, it shows no signs of waning. We know that aircraft are "just" technology, but the stories we tell about them are laced with suggestions that they are something more.

This is a small book about a big subject, intended as an introduction to a variety of topics rather than an in-depth study of any of them. It depends (like all such books) on selective exclusion, compression, and rearrangement. Three limits in particular, responsible for the book's intellectual "shape," deserve special notice here.

First, aircraft have meant different (sometimes radically different) things in different times, places, and contexts. Britons, nursing the still-raw memories of wartime German bombing, looked at the steadily increasing ranges and payloads of 1920s aircraft and worried about what the next war might bring. Australians of the same era, surveying their nation's sparse road and rail networks, looked at the same performance figures and saw a way to link isolated backcountry villages to coastal cities. Americans of the 1950s saw the long-range nuclear-armed bombers of the Strategic Air Command both as abstract symbols of national power and as the particular weapons that would, in the event of nuclear war, bring an end to life as they knew it. Those same Americans, however, also celebrated the unprecedented comfort, speed, and range of destinations offered by a new generation of airliners. Some seriously considered acquiring their own small, private airplane. Others dreamed of winged rockets that would offer airliner-style service to Earth orbit. The many, varied, and intertwined ways in which people have responded to aircraft make for a complex story, one impossible to tell while maintaining both clarity and strict chronological order. Forced to choose, I have taken liberties with chronology in the interest of preserving clarity.

Second, again in the interests of clarity, I have written as if "the public" was a single, homogeneous entity. The public is, of course, nothing of the sort; it can be divided by gender, race, class, occupation, religion, national origin, region of birth or residence, and many other factors. I have glossed over those differences not in order to deny their significance, but in order to stay true to the book's stated purpose: a brief overview of how aviation has appeared in mainstream popular culture. The public discussed here is, therefore, more white, more male, more educated, and more prosperous than the population of the industrialized world (or even the United States) as a whole.

Finally, this book touches on perceptions of aircraft as they have been expressed in a half-dozen nations and many forms of popular culture. It is not, however, intended as a *definitive* study of those perceptions in any nation, time period, or cultural form—not even those (the United States, popular fiction, and film) that are covered in comparatively greater depth. Definitive studies of the cultural history of aviation in selected places, times, and media *do* exist, and (as the notes reflect) I am indebted to them. The bibliographic essay that concludes the book is intended as a guide, for those seeking more depth, to the comparatively scattered places where that depth exists.

1
····

Imagining the Air Age

*T*he pace of technological change quickened during the 1780s as the Industrial Revolution began. It has continued to quicken ever since, with profound consequences. Some are obvious: five-pound, inch-thick laptop computers like the one on which this book was written did not exist a decade ago. Others are less obvious: the idea, for instance, that the path of technological change can be forecast and the shape of the future predicted. That concept is commonplace now, but (in historical terms) it has not been around very long. It makes sense only in a world where technological change is continual and rapid—that is, in the kind of world created by the Industrial Revolution.[1]

If technological change is sporadic and major breakthroughs widely spaced, the connections between old and new technologies are often blurred. Each new breakthrough appears to be an independent event, a break with the past rather than a continuation of it. What *has* been invented seems to have as little connection to what *will* be invented as the last roll of the dice does to the next. Attempts to predict the future course of technology can, in such a world, be little better than guesses. If technological change is continuous, however, major breakthroughs occur closer together and the incremental improvements seamlessly bridge the gap between them. Each advance is a link in an orderly chain of causes and effects that firmly connects the past and the present. Such a worldview renders technological forecasting plausible—the predictions become a matter of logical extrapolation rather than guesswork.

If technological change is slow, most people will grow old in a world much like the one they grew up in. An imagined "world of the future" would be of little interest because it would be little different from either the world of the present or the recent past. If advancements are rapid, however, most people can expect to see the world change substantially within their lifetimes. Attempts to imagine the "world of the future" thus become more interesting. Audiences approach them knowing that they may be glimpsing the world of their old age, their children's adulthood, and their grandchildren's youth.

Forecasts of the future, and of technology's role in shaping it, became an established literary genre by the end of the nineteenth century.[2] Powered flight became practical a few years later, ushering in what many saw as a new epoch in human history, the "air age." These two developments quickly merged. Observers both inside and outside the world of aviation speculated on how the technology of flight would develop and on what life in the air age would be like as a result. They expressed their ideas in novels, short stories, poetry, paintings, cartoons, and scores of magazine articles. The latter ran not only in periodicals about flying or outdoor sports—specialized publications with limited audiences—but also in leading weeklies and monthlies: Harper's Weekly, Century Magazine, and the North American Review among others.

Speculations on the future of flight began to appear before the Wright brothers first flew, and they continued to appear long after the First World War ended.[3] Those that came out between 1903 and 1918, however, did so at a unique moment in aviation history. They were written by authors who realized that aircraft had become viable but not yet technologically mature. They were written for audiences who had heard many uses for aircraft proposed but seen few seriously tested. They were reflections were of an era in which aircraft still seemed protean, capable of assuming any form and taking on any function. Prior experiences with electricity primed middle- and upper-class audiences to see aircraft as versatile and capable of transforming society. By 1903 electricity had already transformed the public lives of millions of city dwellers and the private lives of thousands. Infinitely adaptable, it had fostered a succession of wonders: first lights, then fans, irons, washing machines, stoves, and refrigerators.[4] Aircraft took their place alongside electricity as a symbol of the new century, of progress, and of technology's central role in shaping both. Speculations on the future of flight never again ran as wild, or reached as far, as they did in the fifteen years between Kitty Hawk and Versailles.

The forecasts of the 1903–18 era, read nearly a century after they were written, are interesting less for being right or wrong than for being revealing. They provide windows into the early workings of the aviation business, into the minds of the forecasters, and into the workings of the societies that produced *them*.

Insiders and Outsiders

Predictions of the future of flight published before the end of World War I varied in many ways. Those published by serving military officers, for example, differed not only from those published by civilians interested in recreational or commercial flying but also from those published by civilians writing specifically on military issues. The difference in the first case was one of subject matter, while in the second it was one of emphasis. Military officers stressed the tactical aspects of military aviation, while civilians focused on its strategic (or even geopolitical) implications.[5] Forecasts presented as fiction also varied systematically from those presented as serious analysis. They were not only more extravagant but also more detailed, paying far more attention to the texture of everyday life in the just-dawning air age. The political concerns and cultural attitudes of the day produced differences too, with American and British writers foreseeing highly dissimilar futures.

The most consistent and most clearly marked differences, however, were those separating the forecasts of those inside and outside the aviation business. Insiders' forecasts (viewed as a group) tended to be brief, modest, and cautious to the point of dullness. Outsiders' forecasts (again, viewed as a group) offered longer discussions, bolder predictions, and more extravagant visions of the future. Both groups believed that aircraft would change everyday life, but they disagreed on how and by how much. Breadth of vision tended to vary inversely with the writer's day-to-day familiarity with aircraft.

Viewed from the early twenty-first century, this pattern seems odd, even backward. Technology-driven corporations have been marketing their visions of "The _____ of the Future" at trade shows and expositions since the 1930s. Appliance makers tout the

next generation of kitchens, automobile manufacturers proudly un-
veil models of their latest "concept cars," and communication companies promise to deliver an ever greater range of content. Promising the imminent reinvention of life as we know it has been part of
the personal-computer industry since the industry itself was born.
Apple Computer's legendary "1984" television advertisement—
which aired during that year's Super Bowl and presented the new
Macintosh as the reason why "1984 won't be like *1984*"—is only the
most elegant example of a revered Silicon Valley tradition. Con-
sumers, after decades of such promises, have come to see them as part
of what the creators of new technologies *do*.[6]

No such popular expectations existed in the early days of aviation. Inventors, in the public's mind, were still seen as "ingenious
mechanics" who owed their success to steady, determined tinkering
rather than to brilliant, transcendent insight. Extravagant predictions of the future fit awkwardly with that image and with the perceived contrast between the practical-minded men who had built
the first flying machines and the learned theoreticians who had declared such vehicles impossible. Those who spent their working days
in intimate contact with aircraft—builders, mechanics, and pilots—thus had little to lose by avoiding bold speculations about the
new technology they were creating. But speculating entailed serious
risks—of being perceived as a crackpot, of being proved wrong, and
of creating an undesirable image for the fledgling aviation industry.
Insiders also knew, in a way few outsiders did, the complexity of the
technical problems involved in flight and the difficulty of solving
them. Their intimate, day-to-day familiarity with the problems may
have left them less willing to blithely assume that solutions would
soon be found.

Small wonder, then, that the boldest speculations on the future
of aviation tended to come from outside the industry or from those
within it who worked at arm's length from the machines themselves.
Less constrained by technical knowledge than the insiders, and with
less to lose by their boldness, such seers were far more free to specu-
late on how aircraft might evolve and on what changes they might
bring.

Insiders' Forecasts

Insiders made no secret of their distaste for speculation. Wilbur
Wright, responding to a magazine interviewer who claimed to be

"looking for a prophet," was succinct: "Well, I guess you have come to the wrong shop; I'm no hand at prophesying." Pressed by the interviewer, Wilbur admitted that he had "had ideas" on the future of aviation "for a long time" but reiterated that it is "never safe to prophesy." Orville Wright, responding to a 1909 question about aviation's future, was even more brusque: "I am not a prophet. I can't say. I don't know."[7] Record-setting French pilot Louis Paulhan wrote two years later: "One of the most dangerous things to do in flying matters is to set up as a prophet. Men who have done so, have lived to regret it." Offering his own views on the future, he gently chided "enthusiastic people" who, "when talking of the future of flying, are apt to go rather too far in their hopeful prophecies." Commenting on whether or not the airplane would entirely replace ground transportation, for example, he contrasted his own "distinctly negative" view with the glowing speculations of enthusiasts.

The predictions that insiders *did* offer tended to be modest, short-term extrapolations from current realities, not only unlikely to astound but also unlikely to be branded as fantasy. Wilbur Wright, early in 1909, published an article on the *Daily Mail* prize: £10,000 offered by an English newspaper for the first flight from London to Manchester. The award had been on offer since 1906, and Wright (after pages of bet-hedging discussion of the problems involved), concluded, "it is quite reasonable to believe that the prize will be won in the near future." Fourteen months later, in April, 1910, French pilot Louis Paulhan landed in Manchester and claimed the money. Paulhan himself predicted in 1911 that speeds of 150 kph (90 mph) would be attained within a few years. Henri Farman, one of Europe's leading designers and pilots, took the slightly bolder position that such speeds would be reached within the year. Neither was far wrong: the 150 kph mark was broken in January, 1912. Speculating on scheduled intercity air travel, Paulhan ventured that it would begin by 1920, a decade hence. Farman was less specific, postponing it to an indefinite future of more powerful engines and more robust airframes.[8]

Insiders' forecasts of the future of aviation assumed that the future would see no great leaps in aircraft performance. They focused instead on the potential for steadily improving safety and reliability. Farman, writing less than a decade after the Wright brothers made their first tentative flights in 1903, assured readers that bold experimentation had given way to the consolidation of technological breakthroughs. Advances in performance would come more slowly

Figure 1. Henri Farman, in a plane of his own design, set a world aerial-endurance record in 1910 with a flight of more than eight hours. Farman and fellow aviation insiders were already arguing at the time of this flight that the future development of aviation would take place in small, unspectacular steps. *Courtesy Library of Congress, LC-USZ62-100562.*

now, he argued, but that was a sign of maturity rather than decline. Paulhan also defended the idea of technological progress made in small cautious steps. "The lines upon which the airplane will perfect itself," he wrote, "must be governed by our experience, and nothing else." The Wright brothers themselves spoke out repeatedly on the value of small incremental advances and the folly of any headlong pursuit of performance. "All maker[s] agree on this point," Wilbur cautioned in a 1911 article on the air races for the Gordon Bennett trophy, "No one dares build the fastest machine he knows how to build." The following year he spoke out against speed competitions for airplanes and in favor of carefully planned reliability—flights of one thousand miles or more broken into daily runs of one hundred to two hundred miles. Orville argued in 1914 that, while a nonstop flight across the Atlantic might (just barely) be possible, it should not be attempted until time and experience rendered airplane engines more reliable. Like other insiders, he emphasized that practical knowledge, not extravagant dreams, would define aviation's future.[9]

Insiders worked the intertwined themes of safety and reliability into virtually everything they wrote about the future of aviation. Renowned British exhibition pilot Claude Grahame-White argued: "The machine of 1911 will be a very much more practical and all-around craft than any of its predecessors," stronger, faster, more readily controlled, and more comfortable to fly. Paul Beck, a U.S. Army lieutenant assigned to investigate aviation on behalf of the Signal Corps, wrote in 1910 that the problem in most crashes was not bad design but slipshod maintenance. The real problem, he told readers sternly, lay in pilots' "carelessness, recklessness or inability to foresee possible dangers." American flier Samuel Cody estimated in 1911 that careful experimentation would render flying much safer within four or five years. Mervyn O' Gorman, director of Britain's Royal Balloon Factory, wrote that same year that engines and structural elements would soon cease to be sources of anxiety. Airplanes would be so reliable within a few years that pilots would no longer need to be mechanics as well. Paulhan ventured that within a decade, passenger-carrying airplanes would be designed in ways that made them naturally stable. "[We] have almost reached the stage," pilot and designer A. V. Roe said with evident satisfaction, "where a really safe machine is possible."[10]

The automobile, already seen as safe and familiar, was a favorite point of comparison. British pilot F. K. McClean, writing in 1910, argued that the airplane of 1911 "will certainly be as easily manipulated and as safe as a motor car, provided that continuous care is taken, and only well-tried machines are used." J. T. C. Moore-Brabazon, a fellow pilot, concurred. "One can easily obtain an aeroplane," he wrote, "which can be handled, easily, by a motorist of experience." Farman declared that designers should strive to produce a machine "that will be as reliable as a motor-car, and will require no more skill and nerve to fly it than does the driving of a car." Paulhan looked forward to a not-too-distant day when a four-seat airplane would cost no more to purchase, and less to run, than a four-seat car.[11]

Few insiders imagined, however, that aircraft would compete with automobiles, much less railways or shipping lines. McClean predicted that the prospect of airplanes carrying freight was "very distant" at best. He believed that large passenger-carrying aircraft would appear (if they appeared at all) only in the long-term future. American pilot and designer Glenn Curtiss insisted, "we can hardly expect to see railroads, steamboats, and motor cars entirely displaced by flying machines as has been expected by some." Farman saw aerial tours of the countryside, rather than scheduled intercity passenger and cargo service, as the best commercial application for the airplane in the foreseeable future. The commercial prospect of the airplane lay, according to most insiders, in specialized niches where aircraft could complement existing technologies. Airplanes might carry the mail, but only in areas inaccessible to trains and large steamers. They might also carry small cargoes for which speed was essential and money no object—those that, as Federal Express would advertise decades later, "absolutely, positively, had to be there overnight." The airplane, Wilbur Wright declared, "will always be a special messenger, never a load carrier." Applications like these might be profitable, but they were no basis for a major industry or a major alteration of everyday life.[12]

Insiders acknowledged the twin pillars of the post-1918 aviation industry—military flying and scheduled airlines—but envisioned no great progress in either one. Orville Wright was typical. Interviewed in 1915, he speculated that airplanes might replace "special trains" and on the battlefield might take over the scouting and harassing missions once reserved for light cavalry units. Airplanes, he suggested, would make war obsolete not by crushing would-be aggressors with their firepower, but by rendering surprise impossible and reducing any armed conflict to a politically unsustainable stalemate.[13]

The future of aviation would, they believed, look more or less like its present. The machines would be safer and more numerous, but most would be owned and operated by private individuals for personal purposes. Even then, however, few imagined a world where all (or even most) financially secure households owned an airplane. Paulhan, although he predicted that private airplanes would soon become no more costly than automobiles, wrote at a time (1910–11) when car ownership had yet to be democratized. "I see a definite market," he wrote, "for aeroplanes among rich travelers. The aeroplane will afford them a new amusement and, once enjoying its fascination, they will become enthusiastic." The wealthy, Paulhan implied, would own (and perhaps pilot) their own planes. The middle-class, though, might buy tickets for occasional "pleasure voyages through the air" as they would for an afternoon's voyage on an excursion steamer.[14] It was a vision of the future in which airplanes, like the

IMAGING THE AIR AGE

cars of 1910, would be peripheral to the everyday business of getting from point A to point B.

Insiders had varied reasons to be cautious in their predictions.
One, ironically, was their deep familiarity with the technology.
No one knew better than they how many problems remained to be
solved and how difficult finding solutions might be. Paul Beck wrote
in 1910, with an insider's characteristic caution, that "*unless* some
new method of producing power with relatively lighter engines is
discovered, there will be no aircraft equivalent to railway trains or
steamships."[15] Having immersed himself in the world of aviation and
watched leading pilots and designers at work, he was not willing to
reject the possibility entirely. Nor, however, was he willing to simply
assume (as many outsiders did) that the invention of such engines
was natural and inevitable.

Many insiders also wrote with future business interests in mind.
The audience for the books and magazines in which they aired their
views was the educated middle class, the pool of customers on whom
any future expansion of the aviation business would depend. Insiders had realized by World War I that it was not enough to sell airplanes (or rides in them) to a few brave, wealthy adventurers. Even
those in the modest-sized aviation industry envisioned that they
would have to tap the middle-class market in order to prosper. A future full of bold advances in aircraft performance would, inevitably,
be a future full of new experimental machines. Some of those machines would, inevitably, be potentially dangerous—good for advancing aircraft performance, though not for advancing aviation's
image among potential customers. Stable, reliable aircraft made no
headlines, but they would attract the kind of buyers and paying
passengers on whom the aircraft industry would, in the long run,
depend.

Outsiders' Forecasts—Transport

Commentators who worked outside the aviation industry or at
arm's length from the aircraft it produced took a more expansive
view of its future. Less constrained by technical knowledge and by
business concerns, they saw the future not in terms of limits but in
terms of possibilities, assuming things that detail-oriented insiders
could not afford to assume. Their visions of the air age took much
for granted: the availability of reliable, powerful engines; ubiquitous

landing fields; a pool of skilled pilots; and organizations willing to embrace aircraft quickly and wholeheartedly. Unencumbered by the need to actually make this future *happen*, they took for granted rapid improvements in aircraft performance. Their forecasts focused on the changes flying machines would bring to everyday life.

Outsiders believed that aircraft would play a central role in travel and commerce during the twentieth century. They routinely imagined, as few insiders dared to, the wholesale replacement of ships, trains, and other vehicles by aircraft. Outsiders tended, however, to see the resulting social changes as evolutionary, not revolutionary. They envisioned futures that differed from their present in dozens of small ways but few large ones.

With the Night Mail, a 1905 novella by British writer Rudyard Kipling, offers a striking example of this essentially conservative vision.[16] Kipling presents the tale as a young journalist's account of crossing the Atlantic aboard a steel-hulled dirigible (the *No. 162*) that operates as a "fast mail packet" between London and Montreal. Along the way, the unnamed narrator tours the ship and watches as the crew deals with a series of crises. Kipling set the story in the year 2000, but his elaborately detailed future is really the England of 1905, outfitted with futuristic costumes and new technology. Dirigibles have replaced steamers, but skippers still steer by the coastal lights, and the routines of shipboard life would be familiar to any merchant seaman of 1900. The unflappable captain and the earnest young officer standing watch on the bridge could have stepped straight out of a Joseph Conrad novel or Kipling's own tales of the sea. When the narrator reaches the *162*'s engine room, the chief engineer is (in keeping with steam-age tradition) a dour Scotsman who loves his engines as though they were his children.

An appendix added to the 1909 book edition of *Night Mail* reinforces this sense of familiarity by printing "extracts" from the twenty-first-century magazine in which the journalist-hero's narrative appears. An advertisement from the imaginary magazine extols the virtues of a new type of "aeroplane starter" very suitable for installation outside the home. An official government notice reminds pilots that a particular lighthouse has changed its pattern of flashes. Last of all comes a classified advertisement for "a competent, steady man wanted for slow speed, low level Tangye dirigible. No night work, no sea trips. Must be member of the Church of England and make himself useful in the garden"—those interested in the position

Figure 2. Many pre-1918 commentators on the future of aviation assumed that airplanes would replace existing forms of transportation without fundamentally changing society itself. C. K. Berryman's cartoon, published in 1909 or 1910, shows "modern" witches who (except for the fact that they are flying airplanes) are identical to their "ancient" broom-riding sisters. *Courtesy Library of Congress, call number CD 1—Berryman (C. K.), no. 1131 (B size).*

are advised to apply at the Rectory, Gray's Barton, Wiltshire. Even in an aircraft-filled future, Kipling implies, England would still be England, right down to its eccentric parsons living in rose-covered cottages.

Other British outsiders followed Kipling in viewing aircraft as the natural successors to oceangoing ships. "The greyhound of the sea is well-nigh obsolete," wrote T. R. MacMechen and Carl

Dienstbach in September, 1912, for *Everybody's Magazine*. "For yet a little time the *Olympics* and the *Mauretanias* will continue their boastful voyages. . . . But the end is near." The zeppelin-type airship, they told their readers, "is as true a ship as any that floats on the ocean." Indeed, they continued, zeppelins had already proved themselves superior: faster, more stable, and (in an explicit comparison to the *Titanic*, lost five months earlier) more likely to remain intact and maneuverable if badly holed by a collision. Transatlantic airship service would, the authors concluded, become a reality within a few years. "Aerial navigation that will bring Europe and America within three days of each other," they wrote at a time when the fastest liners took five days, "waits, chiefly, not upon a suitable ship, not upon new steering or propelling apparatus, but on more and better weather reports!"[17]

A year later, in 1913, Harold Frazer Wyatt made similar claims for airplanes in the monthly *The Nineteenth Century and After*. He assumed, with an outsider's typical optimism, that airplanes would steadily increase in size and carrying capacity. Within five years, he predicted, airplanes would be capable of flights of eight hundred miles, long enough to cross the Atlantic in stages, from northern Scotland to Iceland, southern Greenland, Newfoundland, and then to mainland Canada. Not long after, when airplanes achieved ranges of sixteen hundred miles, direct flights from Ireland to Newfoundland would become possible. Airplanes could then reach New York from London in thirty to thirty-five hours, and (as MacMechen and Dienstbach had argued) the ocean liner would become obsolete.[18]

Not all forecasts of the future of aviation focused on Atlantic crossings. Alberto Santos-Dumont, a Brazilian airman living in Paris, found aerial yachts more intriguing than aerial ocean liners. Already famous for flights around the city in dirigibles of his own design, he described such a yacht in one section of a 1905 article, "The Future of Air-Ships." Its control car would be a "floating house," lightly but strongly built and well-insulated against the cold of higher altitudes. The "house" would be designed to keep the pilot and a few passengers in perfect comfort for periods of several days. "We shall dine. We shall watch the stars rise. We shall hang between the constellations and the earth. We shall awake to the glory of the morning. So day shall succeed to day. We shall pass frontiers. Now we are over Russia—it would be a pity to stop—let us make a loop and return by way of Hungary and Austria. Here is Warsaw! Let us set the propeller working full speed to change our course. Perhaps we shall fall in with a current that will take us to Belgrade?"[19] Santos-Dumont's vision of leisurely cruising in his aerial yacht, "watching the great map of Europe unroll beneath," was clearly inspired by his own aerial jaunts around Paris. It also suggests the life of the leisured rich aboard seagoing yachts, touring the ports of the Mediterranean. Only the technology—and the view—is different.

Many American commentators followed Wyatt and Santos-Dumont. They imagined aircraft replacing existing transportation and changing the surface, though not the underlying structure, of everyday life. Explorers, traveling salesmen, and real estate agents would use airplanes to do their work more efficiently, but the nature of the work itself would not change. Criminals might, as Charles Loomis suggested in *Century* magazine in 1912, use airplanes for ambushes and quick getaways, but the crimes themselves—robbery, kidnapping, and so forth—would be the same. The annual Harvard-Yale boat races might become air races, but the rivalry behind them would remain intact. Santa Claus might, as a cartoon from Christmas, 1912, suggested, abandon his sleigh and reindeer for a plane, but he would still be Santa and still be eagerly awaited on Christmas Eve.[20]

Outsiders' Forecasts—War

Death and destruction have always been prominent in visions of aviation's future. Alfred Tennyson's 1842 poem "Locksley Hall" includes a couplet describing "nations' airy navies grappling in the central blue," Jules Verne wrote of a giant flying war machine in *Clipper of the Clouds* (1886) and *Master of the World* (1904), and H. G. Wells's *War of the Worlds* (1899) takes place amid the invasion of Britain from the air—albeit by Martian rather than human enemies. Beginning around 1908, however, visions of the future of military aviation became more numerous, more concrete, and more urgently written. They took on, for the first time, the tone of prophecy rather than fantasy.

This new wave of forecasts was triggered, in part, by the first signs that aircraft had become reliable machines capable of useful work. It was boosted by the public's growing awareness of aviation, which reached critical mass in 1908.[21] It was finally shaped by changes in the diplomatic and military relations between the major industrial nations. The Russo-Japanese War of 1904–1905 had damaged Russia and established Japan as a force to be reckoned with. By launching the revolutionary battleship *Dreadnought*—so advanced that no older warship could stand against it—in 1906, Britain had precipitated a naval arms race with her emerging rival, Germany. The United States advertised its new interest in world affairs by sending its "Great White Fleet" of sixteen modern battleships on a two-year, six-continent world tour in 1907–1909. A new weapon that rendered existing armies and fleets obsolete—as *Dreadnought* did existing battleships—in such a tumultuous age could completely reshape international relations.[22]

Aircraft, many commentators believed, collectively constituted such a weapon, nearly invincible and capable of destroying targets effortlessly. "Nothing alive on the ground can escape the fire of an airship," wrote Carl Dienstbach and T. R. MacMechen in August, 1909. "[It] will annihilate infantry and cavalry beneath it as surely as the hand of God. It will not be directed long at any coherent body which could be called troops. Human nature forbids the possibility of men remaining to be shot down like rats in a pit." Henry B. Hersey, writing in the same year for the American monthly *The Century*, described "silent cruisers of the air, hovering like vultures over cities, harbors, and fortifications, dealing, with hawk-like swiftness, death and destruction, and then disappearing as suddenly." Airships might, for example, "sail over the skyscrapers of New York, dropping bombs or torpedoes into the very light-shafts of the proud structures and wrecking them completely." Harold Frazer Wyatt, in a two-part article for *The Nineteenth Century and After* in 1908, argued that in future wars, "there will not be one dweller in any town of any size upon whose roof the . . . bolt of death may not descend while he sleeps. Each night, as he goes to his rest, he will realize that he may be blown into eternity by a bomb from the dark heights of the air before the break of another dawn."[23]

Fiction writers, describing similar attacks, embellished them with concrete details and spectacular—even lurid—descriptions of the results. Rudolf Martin, in his 1907 novel *Berlin-Baghdad*, imagined the pacification of rebellious Central Asian villages by the dropping of "two or three" aerial bombs and a Russian aerial attack on Berlin in which airships sweep over the city "like a flight of fantastic dragons," leaving in their wake forty thousand dead and seventy thousand injured. Bert Smallways, the British hero of H. G.

Wells's *The War in the Air* (1908), witnesses the destruction first of an American fleet and then of New York City itself by German dirigibles. Wells, unlike Hersey, left no doubt that the destruction would involve people as well as structures, describing the scene in Manhattan as the dirigibles prepare to depart: "Below they left ruins and blazing conflagrations and heaped and scattered dead: men, women, and children mixed together as though they had been no more than Moors, Zulus or Chinese. Lower New York was soon a furnace of crimson flames, from which there was no escape. Cars, railways, ferries, all had ceased, and never a light led the way of the distracted fugitives in that dusky confusion but the light of burning." Jack London's story "The Unparalleled Invasion" (1910) took aerial warfare to its logical conclusion. Not content with the destruction of individual cities, he described (approvingly) America's systematic extermination of "the Asiatic Race" with poison gas released from airships.[24]

Writers of fiction and nonfiction alike believed that the military use of aircraft would transform international relations. Belligerent states like Japan and Germany could now threaten not just their neighbors but also states halfway around the world. Minor players could become major powers once they realized that aircraft were cheaper to build and maintain than battleships or infantry divisions. Westerners could move easily by air across vast stretches of Asia and Africa that were difficult to penetrate by land or water. Above all the writers warned of the terrible fates awaiting Britain and the United States once the seas that had long protected them could be crossed easily by air. They painted dark portraits of cities set aflame, fleets rendered helpless or sent to the bottom, and populations fleeing in panic. Interwoven with these dark prophecies came dire warnings about both nations' woeful neglect of their own air fleets. Prepare defenses now, the writers warned, against the aerial attacks that are sure to come soon.

Edmund Clarence Stedman wrote in a 1908 article in *The Century Magazine* that, by making watery barriers irrelevant, the advent of air power would cost Britain the unique status that (as an island) she had long enjoyed. Aviation "must reduce [Britain's] pride, her vaunted superiority, and her prerogatives, to the common international denominator." Harold Frazer Wyatt offered a stronger prescription. Once an advocate of a strong navy, he argued in his 1908 and 1913 articles that the battleship was obsolete and only airships could protect the British Isles. The empire, Wyatt continued, was equally at risk. Australia and New Zealand would be open to attack from China, Canada would lie within striking distance of Japan, and the Royal Navy could no more defend them against air attack than defend the British Isles themselves. Henry Hersey warned that the enemies of the United States could establish airship bases in Canada and Mexico and strike her major cities at will. Aviation magazine publisher Alfred W. Lawson, in a 1913 article urging Congress to appropriate money for an American air fleet, warned that airships already built and tested by Germany could "float over Washington and lay its magnificent public buildings in waste. They could pour down shot and shell, in fact, tons of ignitable explosives right over the Halls of Congress themselves, and the strangest part of the whole affair would be our absolute helplessness to prevent it."[25]

Seen in retrospect nearly a century after they were written, these forecasts seem eerily prescient. Their descriptions of armies routed, fleets sunk, and cities demolished anticipated the dominant role of airplanes in World War II and the smaller wars that followed. They were without question the most accurate predictions of the future of aviation to appear before 1920. The authors did not, however, pull their forecasts out of thin air or a convenient crystal ball. The air-war fiction of Wells, London, and others belonged to a tradition of "future war" tales begun by George Chesney's The Battle of Dorking (1871). Wyatt and Lawson, calling upon their governments to build large air forces, used the same arguments as those who urged the building of more battleships. Wyatt, in fact, saw both kinds of advocacy as part of a single continuum. More battleships today, he urged, and more airships tomorrow.

Forward looking as they now seem, the writers who saw great military potential in aircraft were also deeply conservative. They shared the worldview of earlier "future war" writers and of those who wrote nonfiction articles calling for a strong national defense. They identified the same enemies, worried over the same inadequate defenses, and issued similar warnings that only substantial military spending would avert disaster.[26] These men believed that the inevitable replacement of battleships with bombers would change the conduct of war but not its political context. Regardless of whether the threat came by sea or by air, Germany and Japan remained the enemy, and preparedness remained vital.

A Shared Vision—Flight as the Road to Utopia

Most insiders presented the future of flight as a slow, steady march along routes already established. Most outsiders assumed that aviation would change the surface of society but leave its core values and institutions untouched. Some, however, imagined the future of flight in more extravagant terms. They dreamed a world in which old social and political institutions had been swept away and new ones erected in their place—a world whose social fabric had been rewoven. These visions were consistently utopian and their writers overwhelmingly American. The forecasts reflected a faith in the transforming power of flight, which historian Joseph Corn later dubbed "The Winged Gospel," and a deep-seated belief in the perfectibility of social and political institutions. They were products of the same optimism about the human condition that, in the decades around 1900, drove the Progressive movement in American politics.

The specific ideas of Progressive reformers often colored utopian visions of the future of aviation. They involved changes far more radical than the simple replacement of cars, horses, or carriages by airplanes. Some writers, for example, predicted not just that the airplane would supplant the railroad but also that it would sweep away the social evils associated with the railroad. There would be no more graft orchestrated by city officials who controlled vital rights-of-way since aircraft are not bound to fixed routes. There would be no more railway companies to monopolize trade, control schedules, and inflate prices because the airplane's supposed ability to operate without extensive infrastructure would make such companies (and the capital they controlled) irrelevant. Aircraft, according to a recurring theme, would make all Americans pilots, individuals in charge of their own transportation and thus of their own destinies. Women, in particular, would benefit. Aviation was a brand new field with no long-established tradition of sex discrimination; women could enter it, as they wished to enter politics and the older professions, on equal terms with men. Journalist and pilot Harriet Quimby modeled this idea as well as promoted it. She used her own flying career—cut short by a fatal accident in 1912—as material for a series of magazine articles suggesting that men and women were equally qualified to take to the skies.[27]

The most popular of all utopian ideas about aircraft and the future had no specific Progressive roots, however. This was the belief that flight would make war obsolete. Maj. G. O. Squiers of the U.S. Army Aeronautical Board found a hopeful note in H. G. Wells's nightmare vision of cities set aflame by aerial bombing. Those who declared and directed wars, he argued in 1908, would "now be in the thick of it and inclined to think twice before launching a war." A writer in the American periodical *The Independent*, surveying the situation in 1909, viewed aircraft as a democratizing agent in international relations. Planes would be so cheap that even the smallest states could empower themselves by building large air fleets. So armed, they would be safe from any (rational) larger state because it would be too difficult and costly to launch an attack.[28]

Hiram Maxim, an inventor more famous for his machine guns than for his one attempt at a flying machine (1891–94), suggested in 1911 that soldiers faced with attack from the air would "lay down their weapons" and refuse to continue fighting. The machine gun, presumably, was familiar enough to cope with, but the airplane was a terrifying novelty. The *Independent* author made a similar point two years earlier. Only "fools," he suggested, would fight an army that could attack from the air as well as on the ground.[29] If trained Western soldiers refused to fight against such odds, the morale of conscripts and native tribesmen would, presumably, collapse even faster. If even large forces could be expected to melt away under the threat of an air attack, armies would cease to be useful or even necessary. Aircraft, cheaper to create and maintain, would replace them.

Arguments like these took the visions of more-conservative military commentators to their logical conclusion. The destructive power of aircraft was so great, the arguments implied, that the mere *threat* of its employment would accomplish what could once have been achieved only through battle. Some commentators went even further. They looked beyond visions of a universal "armed peace" and imagined a world in which warfare was not just unprofitable but also literally inconceivable. Henry Woodhouse, editor of the magazine *Flying* at the outbreak of World War I, confidently predicted in 1915 that the current conflict would be the last great war in history. That it had happened at all was an accident of timing. The dawn of the Air Age meant that, within a decade, the airplane would usher in "a new period in human relations" and a lasting global peace.[30]

These forecasts—visions of war not just checked but eradicated—rested on the idealistic assumption that unity, rather than division, was humanity's natural state. Air travel need only erase the

Figure 3. The prospect that the airplane would end war forever appealed to many commentators in the years just before World War I. Herbert Johnson's 1917 drawing shows Uncle Sam looking with fierce satisfaction at an airplane soaring over the tools of modern warfare—a battleship, a submarine, a machine gun, and a mine—which many believed it would make obsolete. The idea that aircraft would bring world peace was one of the intellectual casualties of World War I. *Courtesy Library of Congress, call number CD 1—Johnson (H.), no. 78 (B size).*

barriers that held people apart, believers argued, and the "Golden Age" would begin. The idea had widespread appeal. Philander Knox, who immersed himself in the complexities of international affairs as secretary of state under Pres. Howard Taft, argued that aircraft would eliminate war by bringing nations closer together. Poet Rhoda Hero

Dunn wrote in 1909, "Hearts leaped to meet a future wherein un-fenced realms of air have mingled all earth's peoples into one and banished war forever from the world." Charlton L. Edhold, writing in the same year, offered a similar vision in his poem "Wings":

> What narrow space holds man today apart from brother man,
> A range of rock, a river or a span of Channel?
> Our wings shall overleap
> These dwarfish landmarks, *Then* what king shall keep
> His folks from merging with humanity
> As waters intermingle in the sea?

Feminist writer Charlotte Perkins Gilman and publisher Alfred W. Lawson pursued, further still, the idea of aviation remaking the world. Each foresaw the evolution of a wholly new type of human. Gilman called the new being "aerial man" and Lawson "alti-man," but both envisioned him as superior to ground-dwelling humans. He would be at home in the air; Lawson saw him eventually "swimming" in it more easily than people now do in water. He would also be mentally and spiritually superior. Gilman, for example, imagined "aerial man" free of the prejudice, parochialism, and limited vision of "earthy man"—if not an angel, then physically and spiritually closer to the angels than earthbound folk.[31]

Looking back at the forecasts of aviation's future made between 1900 and 1915, it is easy to see where they missed the mark. Most un-derrated the importance of scheduled air travel, overrated the value of the dirigible, and failed to realize the extent to which more pow-erful aircraft would require more advanced ground facilities. Most also underestimated the extent to which conservatism (both indi-vidual and institutional) would slow the changes they believed to be inevitable. The predictions are interesting, however, less for their accuracy (or lack of it) than for the hopes, fears, and ideals they embodied. The utopian writers' dreams of a world transformed are rooted in the optimism of the Progressive Era. Wells's and Wyatt's apocalyptic visions of the Royal Navy rendered impotent and Brit-ain rendered vulnerable reflect anxieties generated by the Anglo-German arms race that raged around them. American writers' garish tales of Japanese aerial attacks and American vengeance are steeped in the worries created by America's emergence as a world power after the Spanish-American War (1898). Kipling's cozy vision of England in the year 2000 was the work of a man born and raised in the Victorian Era and looking for reassurances that technological change would alter the surface, but not the substance, of his world.

These forecasts of the future of aviation were typical of the genre they helped establish. Like countless later predictions (including today's breathless visions of computer-rich utopias), they reflected the places and times that produced them. Indeed, as in later years, they revealed their writers' present far more clearly than they did the future.

2
• • • •

Pilots as National Heroes

*T*he word "hero" has been dulled by too-frequent and too-broad use. It has become a synonym for "protagonist," "star," or simply "admirable person"—the last giving rise to the "gridiron heroes" of newspaper sports pages, the "guitar heroes" of 1970s rock music, and the "everyday heroes" of elementary-school essay contests. The older, narrower definition of "hero" still survives, however, and still retains its potency. It paints heroes both as human and as more than human: rare individuals who stand a few steps closer to the gods than ordinary folk. It is a role that, from the beginnings of the air age, pilots were uniquely qualified to fill.

Pilots acquired their heroic image not just because they did extraordinary things but also because of the *kinds* of extraordinary things they did. They separated themselves from the earth and rose into the sky at will. Once aloft, they could leap mountain ranges, span oceans, race the sun across the sky, or lose themselves among the clouds. Aviators could see behind the highest walls, take in an entire town with a glance, or rain death on those who opposed them. All those activities had been depicted in literature and art for thousands of years as the province of the gods or (as in the ancient Greek myth of Perseus or Charles Dickens's *A Christmas Carol*) of those whom the gods briefly favored. Aircraft allowed those with the skill and nerve to fly them to enter the realm of the gods at will. Prometheus, the god-hero of another Greek myth, gave the secret of fire to all of humankind, but the Wright brothers gave the gift of flight to a tiny elite—the pilots.

The culture of flying, as it developed over the first half of the twentieth century, reinforced the status of pilots as an elite group, a gathering of heroes. Business suits gave way to leather jackets, starched linen collars to silk scarves, and backward-turned cloth caps to close-fitting helmets and goggles. Pilots' working clothes soon became both a practical response to the demands of the job and a "uniform" instantly recognizable to aviators and nonaviators alike. Rapid-fire technological changes lengthened the list of skills essential to pilots but not to ordinary folk, adding practical meteorology, navigation, and radio operation to the stick-and-rudder skills necessary to control an aircraft. A new technical vocabulary (aileron, camber, stall) and a new vocabulary of three-dimensional maneuvering (slow roll, Immelman turn, outside loop) put ever more distance between pilots' speech and ordinary conversation. By about 1916, a year or two into World War I, pilots stood visually and audibly apart from everyone else.

The identification of particular pilots—both individuals and small groups—as "national heroes" began in World War I, flourished during the 1920s and 1930s, and found new life during the 1940s thanks to World War II. Though in slow decline since the late 1940s, this practice has never entirely ended. "National hero" status is nearly always conferred informally by public acclamation. It is a recognition less of the pilot's skills and achievements (though both are usually substantial) than of a perception that such people embody their homeland's distinctive "national character." Take, for example, the case of Douglas R. S. Bader. He compiled a distinguished World War II record as a fighter pilot and squadron leader, but so did many of his Royal Air Force comrades. What made Bader unique was that he did so after losing both legs in a 1931 crash and grimly working his way back to flight status, overcoming both his disability and the skepticism of senior officers. He became for Britons, struggling with wartime adversity and postwar austerity, not just a hero but a distinctively *British* hero, triumphing over adversity through stoic endurance and quiet determination.[1]

Bader's heroic reputation was a product of a particular place and time. So it is with most national heroes, and pilots are no exception. It is hardly surprising, then, that the first pilots to emerge as national heroes did so during World War I, a time when nationalist senti-

Figure 4. Pilots began to appear as national heroes during World War I. This 1917 recruiting poster by Charles Livingston Bull uses the bald eagle as a symbol of U.S. Army Air Service pilots and in its traditional role as a symbol of the United States itself. The airmen, the poster suggests, do not just defend America, they *are* America. *Courtesy Library of Congress, LC-USZ62-19936.*

ments ran high and the stalemated ground war offered few opportunities for conventional heroism.

World War I: Aces as National Champions

The popular image of World War I fighter pilots equates them with medieval knights, elite warriors for whom combat was personalized and meaningful. This image was created during the conflict, has been burnished in virtually every decade since 1918, and has been portrayed in every possible medium: novels, biographies, popular histories, pulp adventure magazines, comic books, popular songs, films, television programs, and even cereal boxes.[2] The World War I air shows staged on summer Sunday afternoons at New York's Old Rhinebeck Aerodrome feature immaculate restorations and replicas of vintage fighters along with "several zany characters such as Trudy Truelove, the Evil Baron of Rhinebeck, and Sir Percy Goodfellow."[3]

The popular image of knightly fighter pilots contrasts the chivalrousness and "purity" of the air war with the brutal, mechanized slaughter of the ground war. "The heavens are their battlefield," wrote Britain's wartime prime minister, David Lloyd George. "High above the squalor and the mud, so high in the firmament that they are not visible from the earth, they fight out the eternal issue of right and wrong."[4] The popular image suggests that, in the air, glory and honor mattered more than military expediency and that there was still a place for individual judgment and heroism. Above all, it implies that fighter pilots treated one another with unfailing respect and consideration. The most famous story of the air war, based on a real encounter between Georges Guynemer and Ernst Udet but retold many times as fiction, involves a pilot who breaks off a dogfight when he realizes that a mechanical problem has left his opponent unable to defend himself.[5] Out of such incidents—unusual, though often portrayed as if they were typical—came the image of a "brotherhood of the air" transcending nationality. That idealized image coexisted, however, with a strongly nationalist view of fighter pilots, one that made them not just representatives of their countries but also embodiments of national character.

Georges Guynemer was France's "ace of aces," the air service's highest-scoring fighter pilot, when he was shot down and killed on September 11, 1917. He was a fragile-looking young man with the face of a Romantic poet, but he fought like a demon and delighted in blasting his opponents out of the sky at pointblank range. Although an efficient killer—fifty-four victories in just over two years—to the French people he was also something far more significant. Félix Brocard, his former squadron commander, wrote in an open letter to the Chamber of Deputies that Guynemer had "the qualities native to the soil he so well defended: tenacity, perseverance in effort, indifference to danger, to which he joined the most generous heart. His short existence knew neither bitterness, nor suffering, nor disillusionment." Moved by the commander's letter and by their own awe of Guynemer, the Chamber of Deputies acclaimed the pilot a "symbol of the aspirations and enthusiasms of the Nation." The letter, which went on to describe young Guynemer stepping from the classroom to the cockpit, was read aloud in schools throughout France. The implication was clear: What Guynemer had been, all Frenchmen should aspire to be. Rather than succumb to despair and resignation in the third year of a seemingly endless war, Frenchmen should emulate his enthusiasm for war and his devotion to France.[6]

Henry Bourdeaux made this theme explicit in his best-selling biography of Guynemer, published only a few months after the ace's death. "France loved herself in loving Guynemer," Bourdeaux wrote. She recognized in him "her élan, her generosity, her ardor, a blood line undiluted by the passing of centuries." Guynemer's successes thus became triumphs in which all Frenchmen could take pride. His prowess as a warrior became a reflection of the warrior-spirit that all true Frenchmen possessed and could call on in times of need (like 1917–18). "In the name of Guynemer," Bourdeaux concluded, "one must hear the battle cry of all French youth . . . just as one hears in a seashell the noise of an entire ocean with its innumerable waves."[7]

The British public bestowed a similar brand of adulation on their own favorite ace: Capt. Albert Ball of the Royal Flying Corps.[8] Ball, like Guynemer, was a skilled, aggressive flier and a superb marksman. He shot down forty-four enemy aircraft in a career that lasted less than two years. It was his persona as much as his martial skills, however, that gave him a nearly cultlike following among his countrymen. Only days past his twenty-first birthday when he died, Ball had the face of an innocent schoolboy. Reserved, deeply religious, and devoted to his family, he wrote long letters to his mother and sister in England, wishing for a speedy end to the war. Off-duty, he tended a small vegetable garden, kept a pet rabbit, and played the violin.

The most famous photograph of Ball shows him dressed in an immaculate uniform, looking past the photographer with an expression of fierce determination on his boyish, clean-shaven face. The engine and propeller of his Nieuport fighter are visible behind him, but little else in the picture identifies him specifically as an aviator. The innocent schoolboy who goes to France and never returns was a central figure in Britons' memories of World War I. They responded to Ball in those terms, not just as a man or as a warrior, but as the symbol of an entire self-sacrificing generation.

Germans also viewed aces as national heroes. Two in particular stand out. Oswald Boelcke amassed forty victories between August, 1915, and his death in a midair collision in October, 1916. He literally wrote the book on fighter tactics for the German air service and established the squadron rather than the single plane or two-plane element as the basic unit of air combat. Manfred von Richthofen, a protégé of Boelcke, doubled his mentor's score before his own death in combat in May, 1918. His eighty victories made him the highest-scoring pilot of the war, and his all-red planes gave him a visual trademark and a nickname: the Red Baron. The two aces had similar backgrounds and—not surprisingly, given their master-pupil relationship—used similar tactics in combat, but their public images were fundamentally different.

The public embraced Boelcke, who achieved his fame relatively early in the war, as an individual.[9] Books, magazines, and newspapers celebrated his victories and featured portraits of him: a serious young man with close-cropped hair, piercing blue eyes, and the Blue Max, Germany's highest decoration for valor, at the throat of his high-collared uniform. The opening lines of his biography describe him as a man of "tenacious strength and a firm will, a cheerful temperament, and a sunny nature" and portray him as the son of "true German parents," raised in a home "dominated by a spirit of piety and patriotism," where "simple, old customs held sway." Passersby stared at him in awe on the street; autograph-seekers mobbed him in public places. Informed that Boelcke was in the audience, a singer with the Frankfurt Opera performed an impromptu serenade in his honor between acts of E. T. A. Hoffman's *Undine*. A poet writing in honor of Boelcke's visit to their shared hometown of Dessau imagined the large audience of local well-wishers consumed by a single dream: "to be as brave as Boelcke!" A fellow airman, Lt. Hermann Thomsen, echoed the sentiment when he spoke at Boelcke's funeral. "Today," he said, "there is no vigorous young German whose heart does not burn with the secret desire: 'I want to be a Boelcke.'" It was that spirit, Thomsen argued, that would keep Germany strong.[10]

Richthofen's fame was greater, but his public image was more austere. His reputation as a supremely efficient destroyer of the enemy overshadowed any sense of the man as an individual. "Half knight and half scythe," one contemporary called him, invoking the tool used to "mow down" wheat and associated with the cloaked-and-hooded personification of Death. Floyd Gibbons, the American journalist who wrote the first biography of Richthofen in 1927, began his book with these lines: "To kill and kill and kill was the cry. To burn, to destroy, to devastate, to lay waste." Richthofen was, to German commentators, the perfect symbol of a new and characteristically German style of war: aggressive, efficient, and uncorrupted by romance or sentimentality.[11] Richthofen's austere image extended even to his name. To the admiring German public, Boelcke was always "Lieutenant (or later Captain) Boelcke." Richthofen was known as well or better as "the Red Baron," with its echoes of the medieval "Black Death," Edgar Allan Poe's "Red Death," and other deadly forces of nature. The weekly magazine *Simplicissimus* commemorated Boelcke's death with a delicate, detailed cover illustration of a hawk swooping down to lay a wreath at the tomb of its "brother," the fallen ace. Eighteen months later the cover illustration for Richthofen's death showed, in stark black silhouette, a hawk perched in a barren tree above a simple wooden cross.[12] Where Boelcke had inspired love, Richthofen inspired awe.

The common thread that endeared both Boelcke and Richthofen to the public was their embodiment of middle-class German virtues. Both were taciturn, vigorous, physically fit, and aggressive in combat. Both were methodical and efficient at their work. Boelcke and his disciples, including Richthofen, disdained aerobatics and relied on speed, surprise, and superior numbers to give them an advantage over their enemies. They held fire until there was little chance of missing, then poured bullets into the enemy plane's most vulnerable components: the engine, the fuel tank, and the pilot. Boelcke routinely followed his victims down to ensure that they crashed. Richthofen preferred to destroy an enemy plane by setting it afire, which all but assured its destruction and (since few aviators had parachutes) the death of those on board. Both believed in the power of the group and the absolute necessity of cooperation. They scored most of their victories not in one-on-one combat, but as leaders of highly trained, tightly disciplined squadrons.[13]

Like Boelcke and Richthofen, top-scoring American pilot Edward V. Rickenbacker distinguished himself as a squadron leader.[14] Like them, he valued efficiency over chivalry, famously referring to aerial combat as "scientific murder." Like Ball, he had a short but brilliant career, amassing twenty-six victories (admirers suggest that the real total approached forty) in the last eight months of the war. He was, however, a distinctively *American* hero: the living embodiment of a host of cherished American ideals.

The son of an immigrant day laborer, Rickenbacker dropped out of school at fourteen, taking a job in a glass factory in order to help support his family. He parlayed his aggressive nature, fondness for machinery, and ruthless drive to succeed into a career in the brand-new automobile industry. By the time he turned twenty (in 1910), Rickenbacker had experience as a mechanic, engineer, salesman, and manager and was developing a reputation as a top race driver. He drove in the first Indianapolis 500 in 1911 and was soon earning fifty thousand to sixty thousand dollars a year at a time when Henry Ford made history by paying his assembly line workers five dollars a day. Acutely conscious of his grammar-school education and working-class speech patterns, Rickenbacker made a fetish of self-improvement. He took correspondence courses, worked to expand his vocabulary, and cultivated the broad smile and hale-fellow-well-met persona of a successful middle-class businessman. He succeeded brilliantly. His brother officers (many of them products of elite eastern colleges) gradually accepted him, and his best-selling war memoir, *Fighting the Flying Circus*, expertly mimics the genteel "literary" style expected of an educated writer in those days. Even so, he stayed close enough to his roots to work alongside (and give technical advice to) his squadron's enlisted mechanics. Rickenbacker thus personified the American dream: a son of poor immigrants finds wealth and fame through hard work but remains a "man of the people" at heart. He also embodied a classic American personality: the tough, fiercely competitive warrior who, between battles, greets friends and strangers alike with a broad smile and a friendly manner. It may be no coincidence that Rickenbacker rose to prewar fame at the same time that Theodore Roosevelt—a politician with a very similar public persona—captivated Americans with his "Bull Moose" campaign for the presidency.[15]

The aces of World War I were not interchangeable. Ricken-backer's rough-edged, working-class manner played differently in Europe than it did in America. Richthofen's steely efficiency im-pressed the British but did not move or inspire them. The swash-buckling, danger-seeking exploits of Charles Nungesser, which de-lighted his fellow Frenchmen, left most Germans cold. Maj. Edward "Mick" Mannock shot down at least fifty enemy planes and was cred-ited with seventy-three—more than any other British pilot of the war.[16] He won his countrymen's respect, but they saved their love and adulation for others. Mannock was too old (at thirty-five), too world weary, too brutally efficient in combat, and too unsentimental about war to appeal to the same nation that preferred Albert Ball's pious innocence. Britons recognized Mannock as a great combat pilot but not as a national hero. There was, perhaps, too much of Richthofen in him.

The 1920s: Glider Pilots and German Pride

The Treaty of Versailles, imposed on Germany by the victorious Allies at the end of World War I, stirred deep feelings of resentment among the German people. The dismantling of the German air force, part of the demilitarization program imposed by the treaty, was especially painful. Military aviation had been a source of great wartime pride. The systematic destruction of aircraft, abandonment of airfields, and grounding of airmen became a source of equally great postwar anguish. The Allies also imposed, in the first half of the 1920s, a separate set of limits on civil aviation, including restrictions on aircraft performance and a brief ban on the construction of new machines.[17]

Rumors about the Allied-imposed restrictions on civil avia-tion—erroneous but widely believed—portrayed them as even more stringent. The stories also conflated the limits on civil aviation with the treaty-imposed limits on military aviation. Many Germans be-lieved, therefore, that the despised Versailles Treaty had imposed a ban on all powered flight. The Nazis, who rose to power by exploit-ing resentment of the treaty and the Allies, erected a monument to the Allies' perceived attempt to destroy all German aviation. Placed at the Hamburg airport, it consisted of a stone pedestal with an air-plane engine bound to the top by heavy chains. A plaque on the side read "Versailles, 1919."[18]

German interest in gliders and gliding emerged, in 1920, independently from these feelings. A small group of glider enthusiasts began flying home-built machines from the Wasserkuppe, a hilly section of central Germany near the town of Fulda. Their first season's efforts produced glides of only a few minutes. Within two years, however, the best pilots, many of them former military aviators, were making flights lasting several hours. The discovery of thermals (rising currents of warm air) in the mid-1920s allowed pilots to extend the ceiling and range of their glider flights still further: flights that began in central Germany now ended as far away as Czechoslovakia and France.

Gliding began to attract wide public attention in 1922. From that moment on it became an explicitly patriotic activity, a sign that the German people's spirit was still alive despite the Allies' best efforts to crush it. When a German pilot broke the world gliding endurance record in 1922, German papers touted him as a new national hero, one whose greatness even the French could not deny. According to one paper, thousands of spectators who had gathered to watch the attempt spontaneously burst into singing the German national anthem when it succeeded. Over the course of the 1920s, gliding became more than just a spectator sport. Thousands of Germans joined gliding clubs, acquired a basic familiarity with the machines, and made brief ground-hugging downhill flights. Thousands more, too poor to take up the sport, read about it and dreamed of attending the "gliding camps" that sprang up on hilltop areas like the Wasserkuppe.

The broad public appeal of gliding lay in the belief, inaccurate but heartfelt, that it annoyed and frustrated the Allies. Enthusiasts saw themselves as practicing a form of civil disobedience. Finding and exploiting a "loophole" in the Versailles "ban" on civil aviation gave them a way to celebrate their nation's cleverness and resilient spirit as well as their own daring. The Allies might have beaten Germany, but gliding—to those who practiced it anyway—was proof that they could not keep her in chains. A monument to German aviators killed in World War I, erected in 1923 on the slopes of the Wasserkuppe, overlooked the glider flights of the fallen pilots' "heirs." The wording on the monument's plaque made explicit the connection between wartime and peacetime struggles against the Allies:

We dead fliers
remain victors
by our own efforts.
Volk, fly again
and you will become a victor
by your own efforts.[19]

The wording on the memorial is significant: the individual "dead fliers" of wartime are passing their torch to the German people (*Volk*) as a group. The memorial quickly became a site for dramatizations of that transition. Mass rallies and ceremonies held there drew surviving wartime pilots, who came to pay their respects to fallen comrades and to exhort (or join) their successors in learning to glide.

Many gliding enthusiasts saw their sport as more than an extension of past glories. They believed that it developed in its participants the very qualities that would make Germany great again: physical strength, mechanical aptitude, self-discipline, self-confidence, and a sense of purpose. They also praised the way in which their sport both demanded and rewarded group effort. Gliding clubs worked together to gather materials, acquire tools, and build their machines. Each member, while waiting for his turn to fly, joined in the hard work that made the flights possible: carrying the glider back uphill, making minor repairs, and pulling ropes to provide forward speed for takeoff. Each member worked and sacrificed for the good of the group, and each member eventually benefited from the group's success. Commentators throughout the 1920s and early 1930s viewed the glider pilots as ideal Germans: self-sacrificing and filled with a sense of purpose.

Hermann Göring, a wartime ace and leading member of the Nazi party, praised gliding in just such terms in a 1934 magazine article. "I have seen Germans gliding at the Rhön," he announced, "worker and student, artisan and professor, . . . tirelessly, repeatedly haul their glider up the hill, all pulling on the rope together."[20] It was, he concluded, the essence of the Nazis' vision for Germany—the individual subordinated to the group and the group struggling tirelessly in pursuit of its goal. His conclusion also echoed a familiar refrain from the 1920s: gliding, by bringing out the best qualities of the German people, would help make Germany great again.

The Nazis, who saw both symbolic and practical value in the

Figure 5. Germans of the 1920s saw gliding as both a source of national strength and a symbol of defiance. The Nazis supported and encouraged gliding on both grounds during their rise to power in the late 1920s and early 1930s. And, as in this flyover during the Nuremberg party conference of 1938, they lauded air power as a symbol of Germany's return to great-power status. *Courtesy Library of Congress, Hermann Göring Collection, LC-USZ62-96768.*

sport, supported it with party (and later state) funds and kept many clubs afloat during the depression of the early 1930s. They also praised the early glider enthusiasts of the 1920s, linking their sly "defiance" of the Versailles Treaty to the Nazis' outright flouting of it. When the Nazis came to power, they enthusiastically exploited the equation of gliding with national strength, defiance, and renewal. They folded most existing gliding and flying clubs into the official German Airsport League and disbanded those that remained outside it. The fourteenth annual glider rally at the Wasserkuppe (in 1934) was open only to competitors accredited by the league. Two years later the Nazis redefined the glider rallies as military reviews in which the strength of the German people was put on display. Competitors wore military-style uniforms, operated under military discipline, and were treated as pilots-in-training for the emerging Luftwaffe. The Nazis thus linked the spiritual strength of the German people (symbolized by the gliding movement) to the growing military strength of the German state.

The 1930s: Lindbergh, Earhart, and the American Ideal

Dozens of aviators captured the attention of the American public in the 1920s and 1930s. None, however, captured it so fully or so intensely as Charles Lindbergh and Amelia Earhart. Many Americans saw in them the qualities that they most valued in their countrymen and most hoped to find in themselves. They looked like Americans' image of themselves and acted the way that Americans saw themselves acting. The aviators' triumphs became the country's triumphs, and they became, respectively, embodiments of the ideal American man and woman.

Lindbergh had already been air show performer and a mail pilot when, in 1926, he decided to compete for the Ortieg Prize: twenty-five thousand dollars to the first person or team to fly nonstop from New York to Paris. Lindbergh entered the competition more or less on his own, with money raised from private backers and a plane built to his specifications by Ryan in California. Having flown across the country to arrive at his take-off point on Long Island, he quickly made preparations for the trip. Bad weather delayed him, and waiting for it to clear cost him sleep. Lindbergh had already been awake for twenty-three hours when his chance came. He took off, barely coaxing his fuel-laden plane off the muddy runway, and disappeared into the clouds. Twenty-eight hours later, having successfully coped with ice, low visibility, and creeping exhaustion, he sighted the coast of Ireland. Six hundred miles farther on, he landed at Le Bourget field in Paris, claiming the Ortieg Prize, setting a new record for the longest nonstop flight, and becoming the first pilot to fly the Atlantic solo.[21]

But the public's fascination with Lindbergh stemmed from not only what he did but also who he was. Had he been a fictional character invented for the purpose, Lindbergh could not have been closer to Americans' idealized image of themselves. He was born and raised in a small Midwestern town with the too-good-to-be-true name of Little Falls, Minnesota. The grandson of immigrants, he was close to his mother, admiring of his father (an attorney turned politician), and awkward around girls. Minnesota was no longer the frontier in the early twentieth century, but Lindbergh had a boyhood worthy of

Davy Crockett or Tom Sawyer. Indifferent to school, he preferred the outdoors: riding, hiking, swimming in the headwaters of the Mississippi, and building rafts and tree houses. Given his first .22-caliber rifle at age six, he was an expert marksman with both pistols and long guns by the time he reached his teens. When he was ten, his father acquired a Ford Model T, and though he could see over the dashboard only with difficulty, he quickly became a skilled driver and mechanic. A rapidly urbanizing America had already begun, by 1927, to mourn the passing of small-town life and to draw the gauzy blanket of nostalgia around the memory. Lindbergh, a product of that disappearing world, seemed to embody everything that was admirable about it.

And Lindbergh looked the part. His name and his features reflected his Scandinavian ancestry and rendered him unthreatening at a time when middle-class anxieties about immigration and "racial purity" ran high. He was handsome, though in a blandly conventional way. No one, for example, would mistake his boyish good looks and broad grin for the dark, smoldering sexuality that had caused women to swoon over film star Rudolf Valentino earlier in the 1920s. Lindbergh's public face—the one on display in countless photographs—was always well-scrubbed, clean-shaven, and composed. It implied (accurately) a man equally fastidious in his behavior, one who did not smoke, drink, gamble, or flout sexual conventions. Americans who despaired over what they perceived as the country's moral and spiritual decline saw Lindbergh as a shining beacon of decency. He was a living, breathing answer to flappers and prizefighters, to F. Scott Fitzgerald's liquor-soaked playboys and Dashiell Hammett's amoral detectives. Lindbergh even dressed the part, wearing the middle-class "uniform" of white shirt and dark tie under the pilot's "uniform" of leather coat, flying helmet, and goggles. His clean-cut image remains so powerful that it is almost impossible to imagine him arriving in Paris in need of a shave or even a comb.

Lindbergh's personality added another dimension to his appeal. He possessed bold, even reckless, courage but in person was modest and self-effacing rather than flamboyant. His first words to the crowd that swarmed around him after his arrival in Paris were the pedestrian (and superfluous) "My name is Lindbergh." He went out of his way to acknowledge French aviators Charles Nungesser and François Coli, who had died attempting to cross the Atlantic from Paris

Figure 6. With his white shirt, black tie, clean-cut Midwestern looks, and self-deprecating manner, Charles Lindbergh embodied what many Americans of the 1920s and 1930s saw as distinctly "American" virtues. *Courtesy Library of Congress, LC-USZ62-93443.*

to New York. Their flight, west to east against the prevailing winds, had been a far greater challenge than his "easier" journey, he insisted. Awarded 150,000 francs by a French flying club, Lindbergh asked that the money be given instead to the dead pilots' families. Elaborately honored in Washington after his return to the United States and awarded the very first Distinguished Flying Cross by Pres. Calvin Coolidge, the self-effacing aviator's first reaction was to wonder to himself "whether I deserved all this."

Preferring to acknowledge the contributions of those who had helped him prepare for the famous flight, Lindbergh downplayed his own role. Using a plural pronoun to describe the most famous solo flight in history, he titled his 1927 book about the flight *We,* a reference to the partnership between himself and his backers.[22] Lindbergh's personality, like his clean-cut looks and sober habits, gave him a special status in the public's eyes. Self-promotion is an American tradition, and the 1920s saw it raised to an art form, but

Lindbergh, by scrupulously avoiding it, appealed to an older and more valued tradition of soft-spoken modesty.

The flight itself was central to the public's recognition of Lindbergh as not just a hero but a distinctly American hero. He flew alone, though the terms of the Ortieg Prize competition did not require this, and thus satisfied Americans' love of individual achievement. Lindbergh tried for a characteristically "American" constellation of reasons: money, fame, and the chance to pioneer a new route through a barely charted wilderness (the skies over the North Atlantic). He pitted himself simultaneously against the wilderness and a large field of competitors, most of them better equipped, better funded, and better known than he was. Lindbergh's "underdog" status and the fact that he was virtually unknown beforehand made his triumph even sweeter to the American public. He stepped into the starring role in the most enduring of all American legends, that of the ambitious young man who wins fame and fortune through his daring and dedication.

Lindbergh's contemporaries, hailing his accomplishment, proclaimed him the perfect embodiment of America's distinctive national character. Myron T. Herrick, the U.S. ambassador to France, told a Parisian audience, "this young man from out of the West brings you better than anything else the spirit of America." President Coolidge called him a "genial, modest American youth" who represented "the best traditions of this country." Lindbergh, said Chief Justice Charles Evans Hughes, "represents to us, fellow Americans, all that we wish—a young American at his best."[23]

Amelia Earhart first stepped into the public eye in 1928, when she crossed the Atlantic aboard a Fokker F-7.[24] Earhart, though a licensed pilot herself, did none of the flying, instead traveling as a passenger and, more than that, as a symbol. The flight had been conceived by Amy Phipps Guest, who had bought the Fokker (used by Richard Byrd in his 1926 flight over the North Pole) with the idea of crossing the Atlantic in it herself. When her family (she was heir to a Pittsburgh steel fortune and wife of former British cabinet official Frederick Guest) recoiled from that plan, she began to search for a replacement—a woman who, in the words of one Earhart biographer, "could represent the United States with charm, intelligence, and ability." New York publisher George Palmer Putnam, whose firm (G. P. Putnam's Sons) had published Byrd's memoir *Skyward* and Lindbergh's *We*, learned of the planned flight and was instrumental in connecting Guest's agent, Capt. H. H. Railey, with Earhart. Meeting her for the first time, Railey quickly concluded that she was ideal. "Her resemblance to Colonel Lindbergh," he recalled later, "was extraordinary. Most of all I was impressed by the poise of her boyish figure. Mrs. Guest had stipulated the person to whom she would yield must be 'representative' of American women. In Amelia Earhart I saw not only their norm but their sublimation."[25]

Like Lindbergh, Earhart had a biography to match her newfound status as an American celebrity. Born and raised in the heartland (Kansas and Iowa), she descended from families that had immigrated before the Revolutionary War. She grew up loving books and the outdoors with equal fervor, devouring the works of Dickens but also learning to ride, shoot, climb trees, and play football. She pursued both sets of interests into adulthood: studying at Columbia and Harvard's summer school on the one hand, but learning to drive, fly, and repair engines on the other. Amenable to marriage in the abstract, she devoted most of her attention to pursuing a career, considering medicine before settling on teaching—a profession she had been pursuing for several years, with diminishing satisfaction, when Railey caught up with her in 1928.

Earhart also looked and acted the part—not only as the quintessential American but also as the quintessential American *woman*. Her independence of mind and career-before-marriage goals, as much as her slender body and short hair, echoed the look and lifestyle of the flappers. Beyond that echo, however, she projected the same air of wholesomeness and propriety that Lindbergh did. Her makeup was modest, her clothes (when away from the flight line) conventional, and her use of tobacco and alcohol limited to nonexistent. If Lindbergh was middle America's answer to Rudolph Valentino, then Earhart was its answer to the movies' "It Girl," Clara Bow. Like other independent, unconventional women of the era (actress Katharine Hepburn, newspaper columnist Dorothy Thompson, photographer Margaret Bourke-White, and athlete Babe Didriksen), she showed that "modernity" was compatible with traditional virtues like industry, dedication, and seriousness of purpose.[26]

Earhart went on to a decade-long career in aviation that deserves the overused adjective "meteoric." Blazing into prominence with her 1928 crossing of the Atlantic, she thereafter went from success to success in aviation. She became the first woman to fly the Atlantic solo in 1932 and the first pilot of either sex to fly solo from

Hawaii to the mainland United States in 1935. She flew in cross-country air races; set women's speed, altitude, and distance records; and helped found the "Ninety-Nines," an association of women pilots that in 1931 included well over half of those licensed in the United States.[27] Believing that the cause of gender equality was better served by expanded opportunities than by legislation, Earhart tirelessly worked to broaden opportunities for women and girls in aviation. She disappeared over the Pacific in 1937 while trying to become the first pilot in history to circle the world at the equator.

Despite these formidable achievements, she never entirely lost the iconic reputation or the nickname "Lady Lindy" that had attached itself to her after the 1928 Atlantic crossing. She remained, to her annoyance, inextricably paired with Lindbergh in the public's mind. One reason for the pairing is obvious—each was the first of their sex to fly the Atlantic solo. Its origins and longevity depended, however, on a deeper and more meaningful parallel between the two fliers: They were, for countless Americans in the 1930s, idealized examples of American manhood and womanhood.

The 1940s: The Group as Hero

Britain's geographic isolation from continental Europe for centuries has made foreign invasion difficult and therefore unlikely. The last invading army to touch British soil arrived under Duke William of Normandy (William the Conqueror) in 1066. That history, combined with Britons' traditional pride in their cultural separation from the rest of Europe, makes the prospect of an invasion uniquely horrifying to most Britons. The defeat of a Spanish invasion fleet (the Armada) in 1588 remains widely remembered and widely celebrated, as does the Battle of Trafalgar, when Adm. Horatio Nelson ended Napoleon's hopes of adding Britain to his empire. Novels and stories, from George Chesney's *The Battle of Dorking* (1871) to Len Deighton's *SS-GB* (1978), have induced shivers in their readers by depicting Britain defeated and conquered.

The fighter pilots who defended southern England from German bombers in the summer of 1940 for this reason are among Britain's most revered twentieth-century heroes. British leaders saw the bombing campaign, which initially focused on military airfields, as an attempt to destroy the Royal Air Force (RAF) in preparation for a German invasion. Poland, Norway, Denmark, Holland, Belgium, and France had all fallen in 1939–40, and British leaders feared their nation was likely to follow them if Germany was able to mount an invasion unopposed from the air. The pilots of the RAF's Fighter Command thus became—particularly in British eyes and especially in retrospect—all that stood between Britain and German occupation. The survival of the British nation and its unique cultural identity depended on its airmen's ability to stop the bombers. The passage of time deepened Britons' sense that national survival was at stake, and the RAF's struggle for survival, which lasted from July 10 to September 15, 1940, became known as the Battle of Britain.[28]

Winston Churchill, speaking of the pilots in a speech on August 20, 1940, proclaimed, "Never in the field of human conflict was so much owed by so many to so few." His words have shaped all subsequent public memories of the battle, and the pilots have been known ever since as "The Few." Like the sailors who beat the Spanish Armada or ensured Nelson's victory at Trafalgar, these airmen are revered as a group rather than as individuals. They have also been credited ever since with preventing the German conquest of Britain. Churchill's phrase "so much owed by so many" is read as—for he clearly meant it to be—a reference to the invasion apparently preempted by Britain's victory in the contest. "The Battle of Britain," a thirty-two-page propaganda pamphlet produced by the Air Ministry the following year, enshrined Churchill's heroic vision of the battle as the "official" version. One million copies of the government's record of "The Great Days from 8th August–31st October 1940" were sold in Britain alone, and the narrative "shape" that it imposed on the battle has been the basis of countless later works.[29]

Since the summer of 1940, the battle has been refought countless times in books, articles, documentary films, feature films, television programs, and scores of novels. The tide of re-creations began to flood while memories of the battle were still fresh. The first of the documentaries (a short film titled *Britain's RAF*) appeared in 1940, the first major novel (Keith Ayling's *RAF: The Story of a British Fighter Pilot*) in 1941, and the first feature films (*Spitfire* and *Eagle Squadron*) in 1942. Sixty years later the tide of interest shows no signs of ebbing. *Flight of Eagles*, a novel by Jack Higgins, made the best-seller lists in 1998, and the 2001 film *Pearl Harbor* includes a long and improbable digression about an American fighter pilot who goes to England and helps fight off the Luftwaffe.

Fictional and semidocumentary re-creations of the battle (for example, the 1969 all-star film *Battle of Britain*) generally follow Churchill's interpretation.[30] They exalt The Few as supreme national heroes and tacitly assume that Britain's survival was at stake. They also follow well-established visual and dramatic conventions and as a result tend to strongly resemble one another.

The setting, for example, is nearly always the same: an airfield, nestled somewhere in the countryside of southern England, and a town just up the road. The airfield is modest: a runway, a control tower, a few barracks for the men, and a few hangars for the planes. The countryside is composed of fields, hedgerows, and low hills, and it is a lush, deep, beautiful green. The town is small—really only a village—with a few houses, a shop or two, and (always) a pub. The air battles themselves take place amid crystal-clear blue skies and towering white clouds, with more green fields or the deep blue waters of the English Channel beneath the dueling airplanes. The pilots also vary little from one portrayal of the battle to another. They are uniformly young, handsome, well scrubbed, and well mannered. They speak with accents that suggest, at least, a middle-class upbringing and an education that included some time at a university. They are calm and reserved, and their speech is measured, even in combat or in the face of life-threatening danger.[31]

These representations—like the image of chivalry that clings to World War I fighter pilots—are not inaccurate, only incomplete. They are a carefully selected, lovingly embellished slice of the reality of the battle presented as typical of the whole. The result is an idealized version of both The Few and of Britain itself. The island-nation, in most recreations of the Battle of Britain, is a rural paradise. The dominant tones are the bright blue of the sky, the deep green of the fields, and the crisp white of the clouds, and Shakespeare would instantly recognize it as the "green jewel set in a silver sea" that he celebrated in *Richard II*. The human aspects are equally idealized: small towns, friendly townspeople, cozy pubs, and neatly kept cottages. There are no sooty factory towns in the Britain The Few are so gallantly saving. The gray-and-black palette, harsh sounds, and sharp-edged ugliness of the industrial age enter the picture only when German planes darken the skies. This, the visual contrast seems to suggest, would have been the result if The Few had failed in their mission—Britain's lush beauty permanently despoiled by the ugliness of the German invaders.

The pilots who are saving this idealized Britain are themselves equally idealized. They are a distinctly British sort of hero: dedicated amateurs who, without obvious practice or preparation, distinguish themselves in competition. Popular images of the Battle of Britain routinely portray the Germans as grim-faced, humorless professionals who are completely dedicated to their work. There is never a question that they are formidable adversaries. The British pilots, in contrast, seem far less formidable. In the evenings, off-duty, they delight in drinking beer, singing humorous songs, flirting with the local barmaid, and playing practical jokes. During the day, anticipating action, they wait casually by their planes. Pilots read, smoke pipes, listen to records, or play chess, looking but for their flying clothes like university students on vacation at a seaside resort. Once called to battle, however, the men are transformed. Climbing into the cockpit, they become highly skilled pilots and deadly marksmen. The "scramble" scene, in which that transformation takes place, is part of virtually every movie depiction of the Battle of Britain.

The Few represented wartime Britons' image of themselves as a nation at their best, relaxed, pleasant, and carefree when among friends and neighbors but capable of fierce attacks and resolute defense if threatened by a foreign enemy. The Tuskegee Airmen, African American fighter pilots who fought over Europe in 1943–45, had a different but equally significant role in American culture. Within the African American community, they served, as boxer Joe Louis had before the war, as a symbol of accomplishment and a focus for African American pride. Their distinguished service record also sent a clear message to white observers, that all-black military units could be as disciplined on base, as brave in battle, and as skilled in the ways of modern war as all-white units. At a time when the South was segregated by law and the rest of the nation (including the military) by custom, it was a deeply, powerfully subversive message.

Whites who supported segregation in the 1940s justified it in the same way that their predecessors had justified slavery in the 1840s: as a necessary social response to the "natural" inferiority of blacks to whites. Images of black inferiority pervaded mainstream (that is, white) American culture of the time, from science textbooks and museum displays to advertising and popular entertainment. They reflected time-honored prejudices and simultaneously reinforced them. Blacks, according to mainstream culture, excelled at routine manual labor and little else, they lacked the intelligence, ambition, and discipline to do more. Modern technology baffled them, "polite"

(that is, white) society mystified them, and unexpected events instantly reduced them to gibbering terror. The Tuskegee Airmen re-
futed those stereotypes and in the process helped erode the ideas
about black inferiority on which they rested.[32]

The Tuskegee Airmen went to war in the most advanced high-
performance aircraft in the American arsenal: first P-40 Warhawks,
later (briefly) P-47 Thunderbolts, and finally (from mid-1944 on)
P-51 Mustangs. They manned, eventually, all four squadrons of the
332d Fighter Group, flying from bases in Italy on missions throughout southern and central Europe (and on one occasion as far north
as Berlin). In the course of nearly sixteen hundred missions, they
flew more than fifteen thousand sorties and earned hundreds of dec-
orations, including fourteen Bronze Stars and ninety-five Distinguished Flying Crosses. They carried out virtually every type of mission assigned to fighter squadrons in the European theater: dive
bombing, ground strafing, coastal patrol, air superiority, and bomber
escort. Their official record of "kills" totaled 111 enemy aircraft,
among them 13 of 18 attackers in a single engagement near Linz,
Austria, on March 31, 1945. The airmen also accounted for a wide
range of military targets destroyed and damaged on the ground—
trucks, trains, barges, buildings, and, in one celebrated instance, a
German destroyer sunk with machine gun fire by two pilots of the
302d Fighter Squadron.[33]

Medal citations for individual pilots gave color and dimension
to these dry numbers. A typical one, for Capt. Joseph Elsberry, read
in part, "Against heavy opposition from both aggressive and persis-
tent fighter aircraft and intense, heavy, and accurate enemy antiaircraft fire, he has battled his way to his targets, defeating the enemy
in the air, and destroying his vital installations on the ground." A
Presidential Unit Citation awarded to the 332d just after the end of
the war commended the entire group in similar terms, praising the
"outstanding courage, aggressiveness, and combat technique" the pilots had displayed while breaking up an attack by twenty-five German fighters during a bomber-escort mission. The airmen had, the
citation noted, destroyed or damaged nine of the enemy aircraft—
eight of them jet-powered Me-262s—while sustaining no losses of
their own. It concluded, "by the conspicuous gallantry, professional
skill, and determination of the pilots, together with the outstanding
technical skill and devotion to duty of the ground personnel[,] the
332d has reflected great credit on itself and the armed forces of the
United States."[34]

Figure 7. The Tuskegee Airmen compiled an impressive combat record, demon-
strating that the matter of their race was irrelevant to their ability to fly and fight.
White bomber crews who depended on them for protection gradually came to see
them as fighter pilots first and blacks second, a change of perspective speeded by
the fighter pilot's face-hiding "uniform" of helmet, goggles, headphones, and
oxygen mask. *Courtesy Library of Congress, Office of War Information Collection,
LC-USZ62-107498.*

The 332d Fighter Group compiled a record that any unit would
have been proud to claim. Its pilots would have been famous even if
their race had been of no consequence. In the America of the mid-
1940s, however, their race was of enormous consequence. What
made the Tuskegee Airmen not just famous but legendary—made
them important not only in the war against fascism but in the war
against racism—was the contrast between white society's low expectations and the black pilots' extraordinary achievements. Far
from being baffled by modern technology, the pilots of the 332d had
mastered it, and they took intense pleasure in flying a "hot ship" like
the P-51. Far from lapsing into sloth and slovenliness, they had
adopted (in both dress and attitude) the same blend of rakishness
and crisp precision affected by other fighter pilots. Far from fleeing

at the first sign of danger, they relished missions that put them in the thick of the action and aggressively sought out "targets of opportunity." The keystone of the 332d's reputation reflects that willingness to hold their ground in battle—no American bomber was ever lost while under their protection. A widely retold story (which likely happened more than once during the war) involves an all-white bomber crew that admires the cool professionalism of the fighter pilots escorting them and is stunned to discover, after returning safely home, that their "guardian angels" are black.[35] Proud of their reputation, the men of the 332d aggressively defended it, both formally and informally, against white detractors within the military. Reporters for African American newspapers wrote extensively about their achievements, establishing them as heroes within the black community while the war was still in progress.[36]

These men not only became heroes to African Americans but also a direct challenge to white Americans' assumptions about blacks, for they acted not as "black fighter pilots" (whose behavior was determined by their race) but simply as fighter pilots. *The Tuskegee Airmen*, a fictionalized movie produced for the HBO cable network in 1995, thus paid them a backhanded compliment by telling their story in plot devices familiar from dozens of earlier fighter-pilot movies.[37] The young, smart-aleck pilot played by Cuba Gooding Jr. could have been James Cagney's character from *Captains of the Clouds* (1942) or Tom Cruise's from *Top Gun* (1986). Andre Braugher, though playing a real person (Col. Benjamin Davis Jr., commander of the 99th Fighter Squadron), echoes the fictional squadron leaders played by Gregory Peck in *Twelve O'Clock High* (1949) and John Wayne in *Flying Leathernecks* (1951). Braugher, Gooding, and much of the rest of the cast play stereotyped characters, but they are *fighter-pilot* stereotypes rather than *black* stereotypes. *The Tuskegee Airmen* was, in this respect, a product of the America that the real-life Tuskegee Airmen helped create, a society where skin color mattered less and character mattered more than it had in the early 1940s.

The Jet Age: Return of the Cowboy-Pilot

Nationalism faded in the West as World War II gave way to the Cold War. Faced with a new set of challenges, Western European countries relinquished some of their jealously guarded autonomy and joined international organizations like the United Nations, NATO, and the Common Market (predecessor of the European Community). They also emphasized the ties of culture and political ideology that bound them to the United States. The United States, long accustomed to defining itself in terms of its differences from European countries, embraced them as fellow democratic societies and allies in the struggle against the Soviet Union and communism. Shared ideology seemed to matter more in the Cold War world than cultural differences.[38]

The new emphasis on shared values and ideologies muted nationalist sentiments in the West, but it did not eliminate them. Charismatic leaders periodically stirred them to the surface in order to serve what they saw as the nation's interest, as French president Charles de Gaulle did when he pulled France out of NATO in 1966 and British prime minister Margaret Thatcher did during the Falklands War with Argentina in 1982. Ronald Reagan, in his 1980 campaign for the presidency, assured the American people that they were unique in the world and that in that uniqueness lay the capacity for greatness. He continued to emphasize those themes throughout his two terms in office, and popular culture enthusiastically echoed them. Even *Stripes*, a 1981 film about two misfits who join the army, wore its nationalism proudly: "We're all Americans," the hero tells his platoon, "it means our forefathers were kicked out of every decent country in the world. We're mutts . . . but there's nothing more loveable than a mutt!"[39]

Pilots figured prominently in the revival of American nationalism during the 1980s. The helicopter aces of the television series *Airwolf* (1984–86), the hotshot fighter pilots of the 1986 films *Top Gun* and *Iron Eagle*, and the bomber crew featured in Dale Brown's 1987 novel *Flight of the Old Dog* all embody traditional "American" strengths and virtues.[40] They relish improvisation, disdain conventional ways of doing things, and value results over regulations. They also master the highest of high technology with ease—not through study or practice, apparently, but because they have a characteristically American "feel" for machines. The hero of *Iron Eagle*, for example, successfully flies an F-16 fighter into combat even though he is only sixteen and has virtually no experience with high-performance jets.

It was real-world pilot Chuck Yeager, however, whom the public embraced as the ultimate symbol of characteristically American virtues and values. Yeager's service record was impressive. Born in the hills of West Virginia, he joined the U.S. Army Air Force in World War II, flew P-51 fighters over Europe, and became an ace. After the war he became a test pilot and, high over the Mojave Desert in October, 1947, the first person to exceed the speed of sound in level flight. He made further supersonic test flights, then moved on to other flying jobs, and eventually to the command of fighter squadrons and finally fighter groups. He went on to fly more than one hundred missions over Southeast Asia during the Vietnam War and retired as a brigadier general. Yeager remained, for all that, little known outside the world of aviation. Most Americans knew him as little more than a name, someone who decades earlier had made a record-breaking flight. Then around 1980 he suddenly became a living legend.[41]

Tom Wolfe's book *The Right Stuff* (1979) was the key to Yeager's emergence as a national hero. Nominally a history of the earliest years of the U.S. space program, it is also an exploration of how test pilots and astronauts thought about themselves, their work, and the danger involved. The "right stuff" of the title is the mystical quality that separates the very best jet fighter pilots from the merely talented. The idea behind it, Wolfe writes, is that "a man should have the ability to go up in a hurtling piece of machinery and put his hide on the line and then have the moxie, the reflexes, the experience, the coolness, to pull it back in the last yawning moment—and then to go up again *the next day*, and the next day, and every next day even if the series should prove infinite—and, ultimately, in its best expression, to do so in a cause that means something to a people, to humanity, to God." Wolfe argues that all the early astronauts—recruited from the ranks of military test pilots—possessed this mystical quality but that Yeager (barred from astronaut training because he lacked a college degree) was the ultimate exemplar. Yeager was the bravest of the brave and the coolest of the cool—the test pilot who even other test pilots stood in awe of.[42]

Wolfe puts special emphasis on Yeager's public persona, especially his drawling, matter-of-fact voice that suggests that no midair crisis could rattle him. The "cockpit voice" eventually affected by everyone from astronauts to airline pilots was, Wolfe suggests, an imitation of Yeager. Yeager's attempts, in his 1982 autobiography, to downplay his heroism and to suggest that Wolfe might have exaggerated impressed readers as evidence of that mystical quality Wolfe describes. The 1984 movie adaptation of *The Right Stuff* completed Yeager's transformation into a national hero. Sam Shepard portrays him as an island of stillness in a world of people and airplanes in ceaseless, noisy motion. Taking cue from Wolfe's book, the film shows the seven astronauts of Project Mercury constantly competing with one another and arguing with NASA officials. Yeager (still "just" a pilot) stands apart from the commotion they create on-screen. He goes on quietly doing his job, secure in the knowledge that *he* is the very best of the best.[43]

U.S. audiences saw in these three portraits of Yeager the image of "the perfect American." He was cool and laconic (like the cowboys and lawmen of countless westerns), preferring to let actions rather than words speak for him. He was immensely knowledgeable, but his knowledge was solidly practical (like that of Fulton, Edison, and the Wrights), not the abstract "book-learning" of intellectuals. He was not only brave but also had razor-sharp judgment and the ability to escape from a crisis at the last possible second before escape became impossible. He possessed, finally, a characteristically American mixture of respect for the system and disdain for troublesome rules. One of the stories common to all three depictions of Yeager's life involves a fall from a horse, which left him with two cracked ribs, the day before his supersonic flight. Rather than disqualify himself from the attempt (as regulations required), he confided in a fellow pilot, Jack Ridley, who served as the project's flight engineer. The flight itself, Yeager told Ridley, was not the trouble. The problem was how, after climbing into the X-1 through the bomb bay of its B-29 "mother ship," Yeager could exert enough force with his injured body to swing the X-1's hatch shut. The solution devised by Ridley and manufactured by an anonymous janitor was brilliantly simple: a sawn-off broom handle, nine inches long, that gave Yeager the leverage he needed to close the hatch.[44]

Both the book and film versions of *The Right Stuff* present all these qualities in their final, myth-making image of Yeager. Test-flying a rocket-boosted F-104 fighter, Yeager finds that the aircraft, an experimental hybrid of spaceplane and conventional aircraft, has become uncontrollable. He stays with the plane as it falls from 104,000 feet to less than 10,000 feet, trying every trick he knows to save it, and finally ejects in the last split-second before it hits the ground.[45] Members of the ground crew see the crash and hurry toward the burning wreckage, assuming that Yeager is dead. They are astonished to find him alive—badly burned, but still standing and still preternaturally calm. The film shows Yeager walking out of the fire toward two men who have just witnessed the crash. The younger member of the pair, unable to believe what he is seeing, exclaims, "Is that a man?" The older one, looking on in admiration and speaking in a slow drawl reminiscent of Yeager's, responds, "It sure as hell is."

3
• • • •

Death from Above

eapons capable of striking hard and accurately from a distance have always appealed to military leaders. Warriors so equipped can weaken or even rout the enemy before engaging them hand to hand. Spears, thrust or thrown by human muscle power, were the first such weapons. Arrows, propelled by muscle power stored for a moment in a bent wooden bow, offered greater range and accuracy. First employed in prehistory, their use turned the tide of battles as late as 1415, when English archers decimated the French cavalry at Agincourt.[1] Gunpowder and its substitution of chemical energy for muscle power revolutionized the battlefield. Musket balls and cannonballs propelled by it hit harder than arrows shot from muscle-powered bows or rocks thrown by muscle-powered catapults. Even crude firearms could pierce steel armor at close ranges and batter down masonry walls. Technological improvements gradually eliminated firearms' limitations—short range, low accuracy, and slow rates of fire—while innovative tactics compensated for those shortcomings. The gunpowder revolution was complete by 1900, and World War I revealed the full extent of its power. Most of those who died in action fell, riddled by small-arms fire or blown apart by artillery shells, without ever seeing the faces of the men who killed them.

Aircraft promised to trigger a new revolution in long-range weaponry. Limited only by the fuel in their tanks, their range rivaled and would soon exceed that of the most powerful cannon. Their load-carrying ability, limited only by the power of their engines (for airplanes) or the size of their gas bags (for airships), would soon allow them to carry bombs more powerful than the largest artillery round. Their flight paths, controlled by a human pilot rather than the laws of ballistics, would be infinitely more flexible than those of bullets or shells. Aircraft could attack warships before the vessels could reach the coast, leapfrog enemy armies and destroy the roads and factories supporting them, or terrorize enemy civilians by leveling their homes with high explosives and carpeting the ruins with fire and poison gas.

THE FLEET THAT WILL FINALLY SCORE

Figure 8. Well before it was first employed in World War I, aerial bombing was hailed as the ultimate weapon, capable of destroying cities, armies, and fleets at will. This 1918 cartoon by C. K. Berryman shows Uncle Sam watching an American air fleet depart for France, where (implicitly) it will end World War I. *Courtesy Library of Congress, call number CD 1—Berryman (C. K.), no. 417 (A size).*

Aircraft played all those roles in dozens of "future war" tales published between 1900 and 1920. Scenes of destruction from above typically led toward world-altering climaxes in such tales. Aerial bombing obliterates major cities in H. G. Wells's *The War in the Air* (1908). Flying machines armed with "electro-bombs" allow Christendom to triumph in a global war between the "white and yellow races" in J. Hamilton Sedberry's *Under the Flag of the Cross* (1908). An American air fleet uses poison gas to exterminate the entire "Asiatic race" in Jack London's *The Unparalleled Invasion* (1910). The aircraft of a Russian-Asian-Muslim-Martian alliance nearly conquers the United States in Frederick Robinson's *War of the Worlds: A Tale of 2000 A.D.* (1914). On a more hopeful note, the heroes of Hollis Godfrey's *The Man Who Ended War* (1908) and Arthur Cheney Train and Robert Williams Wood's *The Man Who Rocked the Earth* (1914–15) use their superpowerful aircraft to force the abolition of war. The armies of would-be combatants are attacked from the air and wiped off the face of the Earth in short order.[2]

Tales like these created two public images of long-range bombers. The first was strongly positive: the bomber as an invincible weapon—a "terrible swift sword" with which the just could smite the unjust. The second was just as strongly negative: the bomber as an implacable destroyer—a force as relentless as the wrath of God but wielded by the forces of evil. The two images were intimately related. Both depicted the bomber as a superweapon, and both emphasized its ability to strike powerfully at targets far behind enemy lines. These dual images persisted, little altered, throughout the twentieth century.

Bombing in Theory, 1914–39

Britain and the United States had long considered the sea their first line of defense. Thousands of miles of ocean separated the United States from its only likely enemies; the North Sea and English Channel isolated Britain from the rest of Europe. The difficulties of invading an enemy's homeland from the sea made such barriers virtually impenetrable by hostile armies. Even the channel—only twenty-two miles wide at its narrowest point between Dover and Calais, France—had been enough to protect Britain from Napoleon. Aircraft altered those realities forever. The channel stopped Napoleon, but Louis Blériot, Harriet Quimby, and many other pilots crossed it with ease in the years just before World War I. Count Ferdinand von Zeppelin's hydrogen-filled airships readily crossed the North Sea in peacetime, and few Britons doubted that they could do it just as easily in wartime.[3] Americans, whose watery frontiers had yet to be crossed, faced fewer immediate worries but the same long-term problem.

Future-war tales, with their scenes of destruction and invasion from the air, dramatized those fears. They also shaped readers' expectations of what the next major war might be like. When war *did* come in the summer of 1914, Britons in particular watched it arrive with H. G. Wells's nightmarish visions of a bomb-blasted London looming at the backs of their minds. Many expected that the zeppelins would appear overhead within days—an expectation reinforced by earnest instructions from local officials on how to deal with uncontrolled fires or poison gas attacks. Newspapers' stern calls for vigilance and preparedness also made attack seem more likely. By the fall of 1914, Britain was suffering from widespread anxiety about possible German air raids. Some commentators, likening the condition to a disease, dubbed it "Zeppelinitis."[4]

The seamless transition from prewar fantasy to wartime reality entered its final phase in early 1915, when zeppelins began to appear over London, release their bombs, and motor away. The attacks tapered off after mid-1916 as British defenses improved, but in May, 1917, Germany renewed its bombing campaign with multiengine Gotha and Zeppelin Staaken airplanes. The planes bombed by daylight at first but sought the protection of darkness when losses to British fighters and antiaircraft guns became intolerable.[5]

The raids' material effect was slight. They killed sixteen hundred Britons in three years and (according to historian Robin Higham) caused property damage amounting to less than 1 percent of that caused by rats. Their psychological effect, however, was great. The German air fleets were small, disorganized, and ineffective compared to those of prewar fiction, but the fact that they were *real* gave them a shock value far out of proportion to their size. A year of anticipation multiplied the effect of the raids. The death of retired cricket hero W. G. Grace and the partial destruction of London's Liverpool Street Railway Station did the same, creating a tangible sense of loss among millions who had lost neither family nor friends to the bombs. Even the bombers' limitations worked in their favor. The difficulty of identifying targets and aiming bombs meant that the destruction they wrought often seemed random. The shift from day to night raids meant that many victims died in their homes—even in their beds. Reports to the War Cabinet in the summer of 1917 told of declining productivity in factories due to workers' loss of sleep, growing anxiety among the residents of bombed cities, and panicked crowds in the streets of London.[6]

The reports may have been exaggerated descriptions of atypical events, but they drew widespread interest. British leaders pledged to create an independent Royal Air Force capable of bombing German cities from bases in England. Military observers already convinced of aerial bombing's power to destroy and demoralize seized on the German raids as evidence that they were right. Britain emerged from the war with public order and most public buildings intact, but many Britons (military and civilian, citizens and leaders) saw the damage that *had* been done as a sample of things to come. The next war, fought with larger and more capable air fleets, would surely be far worse.[7]

Americans received their first introduction to the realities of aerial bombing under far more pleasant, less threatening circumstances. Brig. Gen. William (Billy) Mitchell returned from the just-concluded war convinced that airplanes—bombers in particular—would dominate the next conflict. Determined to sell the idea to skeptical superiors and a largely uninterested Congress, Mitchell organized public demonstrations of the bomber's power. Determined that the demonstrations should sway the public as well as official observers, he arranged for them to be photographed from the air with both still- and motion-picture cameras. The demonstrations were a brilliant success, and the pilot's-eye photographs a brilliant public-relations coup. Mitchell's photographic record ensured that, in the summer of 1921, millions of Americans became virtual witnesses to the destruction of the captured German battleship *Ostfriesland.* The images were eloquent testimony to the apparent power of the bomber: twenty minutes after the first one-ton bombs fell alongside the big ship, she was gone.[8]

Other demonstrations of the bomber's power—some staged, others part of the era's "small wars"—followed Mitchell's 1921 spectacles. Mitchell himself led his bombers in mock air raids against East Coast cities and described the "damage" they had done in articles written for local newspapers. U.S. Marines flew bombing missions against Sandinista rebels in Nicaragua. Britain's newly

independent Royal Air Force bombed rebellious Iraqis, Afghans, and others in "air police" operations throughout the British Empire. U.S. Army bombers received heavy newspaper and radio coverage when they intercepted the New York–bound Italian liner *Rex* in the Atlantic. One New York paper, echoing the army's characteri-
zation of the exercise, proclaimed, "Flying Forts, 630 Miles Out, Spy Enemy Troop Ship." As peace slipped away in the late 1930s, demonstrations of the bomber's power took on a new significance. The climax came in 1937, when German bombers supporting Gen. Francisco Franco's armies in the Spanish Civil War devastated the city of Guernica. This was once a city, a British newsreel announcer intoned over footage of the ruins, "and these were homes, like yours!"[9]

A steady stream of books, articles, and speeches reinforced the lessons of these demonstrations and solidified the public's belief in air power. Mitchell, for example, wrote a widely read series of ar-
ticles for *The Saturday Evening Post* in 1925, arguing that sustained bombing of key targets could force an enemy to surrender. Hector C. Bywater used another of Mitchell's pet ideas—the bomber as the scourge of the battleship—as the basis of his 1925 book, *The Great Pacific War*. In it, Japanese air strikes devastate the U.S. Pacific Fleet as a prelude to Japanese conquest of the Pacific region. "I think it is well," British prime minister Stanley Baldwin cautioned in a widely quoted 1932 speech, "for the man in the street to realize that there is no power on Earth that can protect him from bombing, whatever people may tell him. The bomber will always get through, and it is very easy to understand if you realize area and space." Winston Churchill, who would assume the office in 1940, referred to London in a speech in July, 1934, as "the greatest target in the world, a kind of tremendous, fat, valuable cow tied up to attract the beast of prey."[10]

The bomber's reputation by the late 1930s was taking on myth-
ical qualities. As portrayed to the public, these aircraft were capable of effortlessly penetrating enemy territory and wreaking havoc on an unimaginable scale. Neither cities nor battleships could with-
stand their power, and no one on the ground was safe. Baldwin, though not Churchill, saw Britain's vulnerability as inevitable—the result not of poor defense policy but of the impossibility of defending "hundreds of cubic miles" of airspace. The bomber's fearsome reputation was enough to influence national policy—it was one fac-

tor in the Anglo-French decision to appease rather than resist Germany in 1938—but it was also fragile. Large parts of the bomber's reputation rested on theories, eloquent rhetoric, and selective memories of World War I. World War II, with its systematic air attacks on cities, brought this reputation into full contact with reality for the first time.

Bombing in Wartime, 1939–45

The pre-1939 image of the bomber emphasized its invincibility and its capacity for destruction. Wartime experience quickly demonstrated that the situation was more complicated. The air-power theorists, politicians, and popular writers of the 1920s and 1930s had underrated the bomber's vulnerability and overrated the ease with which it could damage the enemy. Most of the air attacks of the those decades had been carried out against virtually defenseless targets, a condition unlikely to persist during a full-scale European war. Baldwin had been half-right: some bombers from an attacking force would "always get through," but many others would fall to defending fighters and antiaircraft guns along the way. Mitchell had also been half-right: bombers could cause enormous material devastation, but city dwellers would display surprising resilience in the face of such devastation.[11]

The bombs that Britons had anticipated for twenty-one years began falling on London on September 7, 1940. The raids continued daily until November 2 and regularly from then until May 11, 1941. London was the primary German target but far from the only one. Most of Britain's major industrial cities suffered multiple raids. Several, like Plymouth and Coventry, had their town centers almost totally destroyed. The seven months of bombing, which became known as the Blitz, took a staggering human toll: more than fifty thousand dead, more than sixty thousand injured, and millions more left homeless. Three thousand perished in London alone on the last night of bombing—twice the number killed, nationwide, by all the raids of World War I.[12]

The Blitz was seven months of sustained effort by one of the world's most advanced air forces. Its failure to demoralize the British public flew in the face of prewar expectations. This was a gratifying result (for the Allies at least) but one that needed to be explained. Britons quickly identified two causes: extensive civil defense measures and their own indomitable will to "carry on" despite the bombing. The common theme that linked the two—the collective action of thousands of individuals—became a potent symbol of a democratic society at war.[13]

The Blitz generated thousands of stories that emphasized, to varying degrees, the power of coordinated individual efforts to blunt the effect of bombing. A few—for example, the Windmill Theater's proud claim, "We never closed!"—became nationally known. Far more were passed down as oral traditions within families, neighborhoods, or groups of friends. American journalists Quentin Reynolds and Edward R. Murrow made the theme of collective effort central to their coverage. Mrs. Miniver, a 1942 Hollywood film about a "typical" British family, was an early, highly polished example of the emerging view that democracy beat the Blitz. The final scene gathers the surviving characters in their roofless, bomb-ravaged parish church. They are engaged, the vicar tells them, in "a war of the people, of all the people, and it must be fought not only on the battlefield, but in the cities and in the villages, . . . in the home, and in the heart of every man, woman, and child who loves freedom!"[14]

Germany's Luftwaffe endured mounting losses in order to carry out the Blitz. The Allies, in their bombing campaigns against Germany, faced a similarly stiff resistance and paid a similarly high price. Britain's Royal Air Force lost at least one hundred bombers per month between March, 1942, and April, 1945; many times the total exceeded two or even three hundred per month. Each plane lost carried between three and seven fliers, and over the course of the war, RAF Bomber Command lost more than 47,000 men. American bomber crews faced similar dangers. Of a sample group of 2,051 studied by U.S. Army doctors, 58 percent died in combat before completing a standard tour of duty, 25 missions. Another 16 percent died in accidents or were grounded by disease, severe wounds, or mental breakdown. Only one bomber crewman in four completed his tour. The average number of completed missions for the group was 14.7— a little more than half a tour.[15]

The Allied bombing offensive against Germany, like the Blitz, generated stories with a strong democratic subtext, revolving around groups of individuals whose collective will and combined efforts allowed them to triumph over a powerful enemy. The victors in such stories were usually the crew of a particular bomber. Their triumph lay in completing their mission, penetrating enemy territory and bombing a specific target in the face of overwhelming enemy resistance. The heroes of these stories, even more explicitly than those in the Blitz stories, symbolized democracy in action. John Steinbeck used the theme in his nonfiction treatise *Bombs Away* (1942), as did William Wyler in his documentary film *Memphis Belle* (1944), but it was aired most extensively in fictional films. The bomber crew in the documentary *Target for Tonight* (1941) is a carefully chosen cross-section of British society, and the crew in *Air Force* (1943) is America in miniature. *Desperate Journey* (1942) takes the metaphor a step further, with a multinational crew (led by Errol Flynn and Ronald Reagan) that mirrors the Anglo-American alliance.[16]

Wartime stories about bomber crews, unlike prewar works, depict bombers as vulnerable. All three films above end with the

Figure 9. British and American stories of World War II bombers often emphasized the skill and dedication of their crews. The ten men of the U.S. B-17 *Memphis Belle* completed a twenty-five-mission tour and became famous as the subject of a 1944 documentary film and a fictionalized 1990 film about their final mission. *Courtesy Library of Congress, LC-USZ62-104224.*

heroes' aircraft destroyed or badly damaged, as do numerous others. The films follow prewar convention, however, in depicting bombers as devastatingly powerful weapons. When the heroes' plane reaches the target—as it nearly always does, damage and crashes tend to happen on the return journey—it releases its bombs with perfect accuracy and to great effect. The target, whether the factory in *Target for Tonight* or the enemy fleet in *Air Force,* is nearly always destroyed or badly damaged.

Tales about Britons during the Blitz and Allied crews on missions added a dimension to the public image of the bomber that had been absent in the 1920s and 1930s—people. In these stories the bomber was no longer an implacable, inhuman, unstoppable force, the mechanical equivalent of the wrath of Nature or even God. It remained powerful, but its power was mediated by the actions of humans. Bombers' ability to reach their target depended (bomber-crew stories implied) on their crew's ability to combine their talents, put aside their differences, and form a cohesive team. Bombers' ability to break down a people's will to fight depended on the people's willingness to band together and resist.

These shifts were subtle but significant. They removed the bomber from the class-unto-itself status it had occupied during the interwar period and made it just another weapon: powerful, though not all-powerful. The image of the bomber as an inhuman, invincible destroyer might have faded away permanently had not the last year of the war invested it with new meaning.

The Allied bombing raids of 1945 faced only limited opposition from German and Japanese defenders. The missions employed new weapons and tactics that expanded their destructive power. The massive Anglo-American attack on Dresden on February 13–14 set a precedent as its bombs kindled a firestorm that burned out the heart of the city, killing tens of thousands—perhaps as many as one hundred thousand—in a single day and night. American planes armed with incendiary bombs kindled a similar inferno in Tokyo on the night of March 9–10, leaving (again) as many as one hundred thousand dead and more than one million homeless. Over the next four months, similar raids burnt out more than sixty Japanese cities, though a few were spared—Kyoto, because of its rich cultural heritage, and five others that comprised the list of possible targets for the new atomic bomb. The destruction of central Tokyo in March had taken hours of bombing and involved hundreds of bombers.

Five months later, on August 6, a single plane with a single bomb brought similar devastation to central Hiroshima in a matter of seconds.[17] The second atomic bombing—Nagasaki, August 9—confirmed the new weapon's destructive power. It also marked the point at which the bomber finally caught up with its public image, becoming capable of literally wiping manmade structures off the face of the Earth.

Bombers in the Atomic Era, 1945–65

For Europeans, the bomber had always been a double-edged symbol: it not only promised victory but also threatened destruction. Americans, until about 1950, had the luxury of a simpler perspective. Isolated by oceans no airplane could cross and return, they were free to embrace the bomber's offensive power with no fear that it might be turned against them. The beginning of the Cold War, the Soviet Union's acquisition of nuclear weapons, and the development of the first intercontinental bombers ended that sense of security. The knowledge that "World War III" would involve attacks on American as well as Soviet cities set the stage for a rethinking of strategic bombers and bombing. The reassessment focused on the twin icons of wartime stories about bombers, the resilient community and the stalwart crew.

Bomber-crew stories continued to appear, virtually without interruption, as World War II gave way to the Cold War. Some, like the 1948 film *Command Decision*, the 1948 novel *Twelve O'Clock High* (filmed in 1949), and the 1952 film *Above and Beyond*, took place in World War II. A few others, like the 1953 novel *The Bridges at Toko-Ri* (filmed in 1955) were set in the Korean War. Still others, like the films *Strategic Air Command* (1955) and *Bombers B-52* (1957), took place during the uneasy peace of the 1950s.[18] Whatever their setting, however, they offered a different message than their wartime counterparts, which had focused on the bonding of individuals into a cohesive unit—the crew. They also emphasized individuals pledging their loyalty to one another. The postwar stories, however, focused on the individual, crew, or unit learning to play its assigned role in "The System." Ex–bomber pilot "Dutch" Holland rejoins the U.S. Air Force in *Strategic Air Command*, not because his peers need him, but because the air force needs him. The pivotal scene in *The Bridges at Toko-Ri* involves demoralized naval aviator Harry Brubaker being lectured by his admiral on his small but crucial place in America's (Korean) war effort.

The bomber crew—depicted in World War II stories as a powerful force that reinforced their aircraft's power—became, in Cold War stories, something less grand. Now they were only cogs in the machinery of modern warfare, expected, like the planes they flew, to perform as designed. It is this image of the bomber crew that, by the end of the 1950s, was being questioned in works like *The War Lover*, *Fail-Safe*, *Doctor Strangelove*, and *Catch-22*.

All four of these stories present bomber crewmen in varying degrees of mental unbalance. John Hersey's 1959 novel *The War Lover* (filmed in 1962), set in World War II, is the story of Capt. Buzz Rickson, a B-17 pilot who is truly happy only in combat and cannot form normal human relationships. Col. Jack Grady, a bomber pilot in Eugene Burdick and Harvey Wheeler's 1963 novel *Fail-Safe* (filmed in 1964), is sent by mistake to attack Moscow. He dismisses every human plea to turn back because his orders—part of "The System" to which he has pledged his loyalty—do not allow him to listen. Another pilot, Gen. Warren Black, is tormented throughout the story by disturbing dreams and (after carrying out his final mission) finds release only in suicide. The insanity on display in the 1964 film *Dr. Strangelove* is darkly comic: a bomber pilot straddles a nuclear bomb like a bucking bronco as it falls toward its target, and a squadron commander justifies an attack on the Soviet Union by muttering about fluoridated water polluting his "precious bodily fluids." Joseph Heller's 1961 novel *Catch-22* (filmed in 1970) goes still further. The "catch" of the title is that anyone who would want to fly in combat is, by definition, insane and therefore prohibited from flying in combat. *Not* wanting to fly in combat is, on the contrary, evidence of sanity and therefore of fitness to fly in combat.[19]

Stories of survival during the Blitz disappeared from mainstream popular culture after 1945, but stories of survival during and after nuclear war took their place. Pamphlets, posters, and films promoting civil defense—one major type of after-the-bomb stories—carried the lessons of the Blitz more or less unaltered into the nuclear age. They implied that careful attention to warning signals, prompt action in the face of attack, and orderly evacuation to private or public shelters were the keys to survival. Furthermore, the lasting effect of nuclear bombs would be minimal. Patience and a positive mental attitude were, therefore, essential tools for coping with the immediate aftermath of an attack. Determination to "carry on" would, as it had during the Blitz, enable the preservation of public order and a rapid return to normal life. After-the-bomb dramas like the film *Panic in the Year Zero!* (1962) and Robert A. Heinlein's novel *Farnham's Freehold* (1964) present similar ideas. Not even nuclear bombs, they suggest, could break the human spirit.[20]

Different, less sanguine views of the effects of nuclear bombing began to appear soon after World War II ended. The first, also among the most influential, was John Hersey's *Hiroshima,* which recounts the first atomic bombing of a city through the experiences of six individuals. Hersey's work, which comprised the entire issue of *The New Yorker* for August 31, 1946, examines the aftermath of the bombing in spare, precise prose that throws the horrors he describes into sharp relief. Issued as a book later that year, *Hiroshima* sold millions of copies. *Collier's,* another widely read general-circulation magazine, ran an illustrated article in its issue of August 5, 1950, detailing the effects of an atomic bomb on Manhattan. Neither the article's conclusions nor its title, "Hiroshima USA," were optimistic. Later still, Kurt Vonnegut wove his wartime memories of the destruction of Dresden into his 1969 novel *Slaughterhouse Five.* Like Hersey and the *Collier's* staff, he gave readers a taste of what it might be like to experience bombing from ground zero. All three works paint much grimmer postbombing portraits than stories from the Blitz and subtly ask if there are limits to human resilience.[21]

The possibility that the destruction wrought by nuclear-armed bombers would cause a long-term decline in civilization also received a thorough airing. George R. Stewart's 1949 novel *Earth Abides* chronicles the inexorable erosion of society and culture after a plague kills most of the human race. It was not strictly an after-the-bomb story, but many readers drew strong parallels between the two situations. Walter M. Miller's 1959 novel *A Canticle for Leibowitz* takes place in an America plunged, by successive nuclear wars, into a new Dark Ages. The 1969 British film *The Bed-Sitting Room* is a surreal dark comedy of life after the bomb. The survivors of the nuclear war "carry on" in the best British tradition, disturbed neither by the bomb-blasted urban landscape they inhabit nor by the fact that radiation has turned one of them into a parrot and another into the living space of the title. Nevil Shute's 1957 novel *On the Beach,* filmed in 1959, chronicles the last days of the last survivors of a global nuclear war. It offers them no hope of living—only a choice between death by radiation or death by suicide.[22]

The after-the-bomb story most devastating in its pessimism,

Figure 10. The shadow of a bomber superimposed on an outline image of Alabama in this Work Projects Administration War Services poster from 1942 reminded civilians of the potential threat from enemy bombers. The possibility of an aerial attack on the United States was seriously proposed even before World War I. Civil defense measures—coastal blackouts, appointments of air raid wardens, and instruction in spotting enemy planes—were instituted during World War II as a precaution. The advent of nuclear-armed bombers in the 1950s, however, raised doubts about whether civil defense measures would be effective. *Courtesy Library of Congress, LC-USZC2-1178.*

however, is Peter Watkins's film *The War Game*.[23] Made for the British Broadcasting Corporation in 1965, it uses a cast of mostly nonprofessional actors to dramatize the aftermath of a nuclear attack on a typical British town. *War Game* is an angry refutation of the idea that nuclear war would be like the Blitz, only a bit worse. It shows burnt, dazed, psychologically shattered survivors and the utter breakdown of normal life, raising the possibility that, as Soviet leader Nikita Khrushchev observed in the 1950s, "the living would envy the dead." The ferocity with which *The War Game* tramples on cherished ideas about British resilience contributed to the BBC's refusal to air it for twenty-one years. Finally broadcast in 1985 amid renewed Cold War tensions, it retains much of its original power.

Public attitudes toward the bomber and the atomic bomb between the late 1940s and the early 1960s cannot be separated from one another. Nuclear weapons made the bomber so destructive that, for many civilian observers, even using it against a wartime enemy might be morally unjustifiable. The bomber became, in the politically charged 1960s, a symbol of governments' willingness to gamble with tens of millions of innocent lives and perhaps even the future of civilization.

The Bomber's Decline and Resurrection, 1965–2000

Beginning in the early 1960s, the intercontinental ballistic missile replaced the bomber as the superpowers' principal means of targeting each other with nuclear weapons. Missiles also replaced bombers as the focus of public anxieties about nuclear war. *The Day After*, an after-the-bomb film made for U.S. television in 1984, signals the start of World War III with a scene of Minuteman missiles rising from their silos beneath the Kansas prairie. Bombers quietly faded into the background of American popular culture and remained there, with two exceptions, until the late 1980s. The first exception was formula adventure stories set during World War II—the television series *Twelve O'Clock High* (1965–67) and Frederick E. Smith's *633 Squadron* novels, for example. The second, more significant exception was television coverage of the Vietnam War.[24]

The early stages of the Cold War deeply polarized American attitudes toward the bomber. Vietnam, deeply polarizing in its own right, did little to reduce those divisions. Several of the enduring visual symbols of the war—jungles set afire by napalm, 500-pound bombs pouring from the bomb bays of B-52s, and terrified Vietnamese children fleeing an air attack—were closely linked to American bombing. To supporters of U.S. intervention, the images showed bombing's power to shorten the war by forcing North Vietnamese leaders to the negotiating table. To critics, they showed a grotesque mismatch of force and target: city-killing weapons unleashed on a predominantly rural nation. Revelations of a secret bombing campaign against Cambodia reinforced these differences. Supporters of the war saw a desirable alternative to a ground invasion. Opponents saw the indiscriminate massacre of combatants and noncombatants alike. Signs reading "Stop the Bombing" became common at antiwar rallies by the early 1970s.[25]

The last years of U.S. involvement in Southeast Asia marked the low point of Americans' long-running fascination with the bomber. Much of the public believed that the bombing of Vietnam and Cambodia had been both morally repugnant and militarily ineffective. Those same years, however, marked the first use of precision-guided munitions that routinely hit within ten feet of their aiming point. The "smart bombs" used experimentally in Vietnam allowed U.S. pilots to successfully attack small, valuable targets that could only be damaged by direct hits. They were crucial to the success of the Linebacker and Linebacker II air offensives of 1972, destroying key bridges—like the one at Than Hoa—that unguided bombs had left intact.[26] Refined and diversified in the years after Vietnam, smart bombs made possible the rehabilitation of the bomber's public image in the 1990s.

Smart weapons, by the mid-1980s, had begun to appear in "techno-thrillers"—the future-war tales of the late twentieth century. American pilots use them to good effect in Tom Clancy's *Red Storm Rising* (1986), Dale Brown's *Flight of the Old Dog* (1987), and Larry Bond's *Red Phoenix* (1989). It was the Persian Gulf War of 1991, however, that marked smart bombs' real public debut. The Gulf War was in many ways the conflict that novelists and air-power theorists had been imagining since the beginning of the century. It was fought primarily from the air, and destruction wrought from above made the final ground offensive quick, decisive, and low in casualties. The Iraqi army, rated the fourth-strongest in the world by prewar intelligence estimates, collapsed because its support infrastructure—supply, communication, air defense, and command systems—had been destroyed by weeks of systematic air attacks. Smart bombs (which became, in casual usage, the term for all precision-guided munitions) contributed to this strategy in two crucial ways. First, they increased the efficiency of the air war by increasing the chances that a chosen target would be hit and destroyed the first time it was attacked. Second, they reduced the number of civilian casualties by allowing pilots to target a single building in a crowded city.[27]

Precision bombing was a recurring theme in American news coverage of the Gulf War. Michael Kelly, writing in the magazine *New Republic*, described an early raid that demolished the Ministry of Defense building in Baghdad without touching the hospital next door or the homes nearby. Milton Viorst, who visited Iraq two months after the war, found Baghdad little changed from his prewar visits, except that strategic targets had been destroyed "with meticulous care—one might almost call it artistry" by coalition bombers. Baghdad's central post office had been completely gutted, for example, but three of its four walls remained standing. Joost R. Hiltermann, in a report published in *Mother Jones*, remarked on how little damage had been done in civilian areas. Peter Arnett, the onsite war correspondent for the Cable News Network (CNN), observed that Iraqi civilians soon lost their fear of coalition air raids, having concluded that they were not the intended targets. The defining images of the Gulf War for many Americans were those taken by television cameras in the guidance systems of smart weapons. A target—not just a building but its air shaft or front door—would steadily fill the screen until, at the last moment, the screen went blank.[28]

The Gulf War transformed, in a matter of weeks, the American public's image of aerial bombing. U.S. planes suffered few combat losses and achieved almost complete success in destroying their assigned targets. They did so, moreover, while keeping civilian casualties and damage to nonmilitary targets to a bare minimum. The bomber's reputation as a uniquely powerful and flexible weapon was enhanced, and its reputation (among critics) as a brutal and imprecise weapon virtually erased. The American public and their political leaders, wary since Vietnam of protracted, costly ground wars, embraced the bomber as a way around such fighting. The new image of bombing also affected popular culture. The hero of Frederick Forsyth's 1995 novel *The Fist of God* is a British commando sent into Iraq during the Gulf War to destroy a giant Iraqi cannon. He is armed not with explosives but with a portable target-marking laser with which he can "paint" the target and identify it to the bombers

that will then obliterate it. *Saving Private Ryan*, Steven Spielberg's
epic 1998 film about the Allied invasion of France in 1944, is even
more revealing. The real invasion was accompanied by a massive Allied bombing campaign, but the only airplane shown in the film is a
P-51 fighter that, in the best Gulf War style, destroys a German tank
with a single, perfectly aimed bomb.[29]

One measure of how quickly and completely the bomber's reputation changed is the response to the U.S. bombing of the Chinese
embassy in Belgrade in May, 1999. The bombing, which killed three
and injured twenty-seven, took place during a NATO air campaign
against Serbian forces in Kosovo. The U.S. government called the
bombing accidental and attributed it to faulty intelligence—specifically, an out-of-date map. The Chinese government, many foreign
observers, and some skeptical Americans concluded that it had been
deliberate. The possibility that the embassy had been hit by a bomb
aimed at a different building was never even raised; once the obvious
answer, it seemed utterly implausible by the late 1990s.[30]

September 11: Airplanes as Weapons

Arrows, though not easy to make well, are easier to make than
the bows that propel them. Powder and shot for muzzle-loading
firearms, or cartridges for breech-loading versions, are easier (and
cheaper) to manufacture than the firearms themselves. The chance
to throw easy-to-replace objects rather than hard-to-replace soldiers at the enemy accounts for much of projectile weapons' appeal.
Bombers are, in the broadest sense, also projectile weapons. The
expensive part of the system (the aircraft and crew) is reused, and
the inexpensive part (the bombs) is hurled at the enemy. The loss of
more than a few bombers on a mission is traditionally cause for concern, and sustained high losses cause for withdrawing a particular
type of aircraft from service or abandoning attacks on a particular set
of targets.

Intentionally using an aircraft *itself* as a weapon violates these
traditional ideas. It also requires the knowing sacrifice of the crew's
lives, negating what many see as a key reason for preferring bombing
raids to infantry assaults. Americans have traditionally embraced
with great fervor the idea that bombing can save money and lives.
They have traditionally rejected with equal fervor the premeditated
use of piloted aircraft themselves as weapons. The U.S. military seri-

ously experimented with the idea only once, in 1944, packing worn-out heavy bombers with tons of high explosive with the intention of crashing them into targets that had resisted conventional bombing. Human pilots in Project Aphrodite were responsible only for the takeoff and initial guidance of their explosive-laden planes. The approach to the target, the dive, and the crash were to be handled by remote control after they had bailed out.[31] The project was cancelled after initial tests on the grounds that it was too risky. Most popular histories of the U.S. war effort treat it as a freakish aberration.

American antipathy to the use of airplanes as weapons is not rooted in a general distaste for suicidal courage. Soldiers who knowingly advanced into heavy enemy fire—at Gettysburg in 1863, the Argonne in 1918, Omaha Beach in 1944, and the Ia Drang Valley in 1965—are widely (and rightly) regarded as heroes. The American torpedo bomber squadrons that fought at the Battle of Midway in June, 1942, flew what amounted to suicide missions: attacking well-defended enemy ships in lumbering, obsolete airplanes. They suffered horrific losses—ten of fourteen planes in one squadron, ten of twelve in another, and all fifteen in a third—and were (again rightly) hailed for their bravery and dedication. Other fliers have been similarly honored for similar, virtually suicidal missions. Cold War–era pilots trained to deliver low-altitude attacks with nuclear bombs joked with one another about their all-but-nonexistent chances of survival but accepted the risks as part of the job.

Taking off in an airplane with the premeditated intention of crashing it into a target is, for most Americans, something fundamentally different. It is also an act literally beyond comprehension—impossible to grasp and thus shocking and disorienting when it happens.

Many novelists and screenwriters have used the shock value for dramatic effect. An early scene of the 1977 movie Telefon, for example, shows the pilot of a small floatplane deliberately crashing into an oil-tank farm. He is, the film later reveals, a Soviet agent planted in the United States years before and brainwashed to carry out the despicable act when he hears the proper code phrase. The desperate hero of The Running Man, a 1982 novel by Stephen King, takes his final revenge on a corrupt corporation by flying an explosives-laden airliner into its high-rise headquarters building. The paperback edition of Dean Ing's novel Soft Targets shows a small plane smashing (intentionally) into the Statue of

Liberty. The Japanese-American war chronicled in Tom Clancy's novel *Debt of Honor* ends with a disturbed Japanese airline pilot crashing his (empty) Boeing 747 into the U.S. Capitol during the State of the Union address. Similar terrorist attacks—averted at the last minute by the heroes—drive the plots of Ridley Pearson's *Hard Fall* and Dale Brown's *Storming Heaven*.[32]

Airliners, hijacked soon after takeoff and laden with fuel for cross-country flights, proved on September 11, 2001, to be highly efficient weapons. The terrorists chose their targets carefully and calculated well in advance the physical effects of crashing airliners into large buildings. Whether the terrorists also considered the psychological effects of using airliners as flying bombs remains an open question. Planned or not, however, the psychological effects of their choices were as substantial as the physical. In the chaotic hours and uncertain days immediately following the attacks, images of the second airliner striking the second tower of the World Trade Center were everywhere. The images—incongruous as a red ace of spades—reinforced Americans' sense that their world had been turned upside down. The images also reinforced their belief that those behind the attack could not be reasoned with or even understood. People who would deliberately fly an airplane into a building were madmen capable of committing any act, no matter how horrific, at any moment. The attacks of September 11 thus achieved, at least in the short term, both of the standard goals of long-range bombing: they destroyed structures the attackers regarded as vital targets and sowed confusion among those whom the attackers considered their enemies.

The continental United States had, until the attacks of September 11, never been attacked using piloted aircraft. The only bombs to fall on the U.S. mainland had been those carried across the Pacific by Japanese "bombing balloons" in 1945, intended to set the forests of the Pacific Northwest ablaze. Aerial attacks on American landmarks remained the stuff of fiction—from H. G. Wells's *The War in the Air* (1908) to the alien-invasion movie *Independence Day* (1997)—or speculative nonfiction like the works of Alfred Lawson, Henry Hersey, and Billy Mitchell. The only enemy with the power to strike U.S. cities from the air—the post-1945 Soviet Union—disintegrated without ever doing so. The United States on the morning of the attacks was the only great power of the modern era that had *not* suffered serious damage from aerial bombardment. When the twin towers fell, that longstanding distinction collapsed with them.

Devastating as it was, the damage done to New York City and Washington, D.C., by the terrorist attacks was only a fraction of that done by sustained raids carried out in wartime. The public's reaction to it, however, followed patterns familiar since the first German raids on London during World War I. Among both survivors and onlookers, shock gave way to anger and—very quickly—to resolve. Subsequent comments by Osama bin Laden, the apparent architect of the attacks, suggests that the terrorists accurately predicted the physical effects of their attacks (at least in New York) but overestimated the psychological effects. It appears that they expected their air attacks to produce panic, crippling fear, and social dislocation, and it seems likely that they were surprised by their enemy's (that is, Americans') resilience. If so, they were following in a well-established tradition, making a mistake that German, British, and American air power theorists all made before them.

The retaliatory U.S. air campaign in Afghanistan was, in contrast, presented by military leaders and perceived by the public as another triumph for modern precision bombing. Like the air campaigns in Iraq (1991) and Yugoslavia (1998), it was quick, decisive, and (for the U.S. forces involved) virtually bloodless. Media coverage, as in the Gulf War, focused on the technological dimensions of the campaign and the differences between (for example) JDAMs and "Daisy Cutters." The ability of massive air strikes to destroy an enemy's ability to fight (rendering their *desire* to fight moot) was taken for granted by the military, the media, and the public alike. So, as in every bombing campaign since the Gulf War, was the ability of U.S. planes and pilots to deliver bombs with pinpoint accuracy. Instances where U.S. bombs hit the wrong targets—a Red Cross food warehouse, a wedding party, or a convoy carrying Afghan tribal leaders to an official meeting—were treated as failures not of the technology but of the humans behind it.

During the winter of 2001–2002, the Bush administration and its critics sparred over the total number of civilians accidentally killed by U.S. bombs. Critics pointed to a study of foreign press reports by economist Mark Herold that suggested nearly 3,500 civilians had died in the last two months of 2001 alone. Administration officials countered that the real civilian death toll numbered only in the hundreds and insisted that the bombing campaign had been the most accurate in history.[33] Both sides, significantly, assumed that virtually pinpoint accuracy was not only possible but desirable—even in raids against an enemy more reviled than any that Americans had fought since 1945. The technology of aerial bombing has changed profoundly, and the public image of aerial bombing—once built around aircraft armadas capable of darkening the skies and leveling entire cities—has changed with it.

4
····

The Allure of Air Travel

*I*nterest in paying to fly is almost as old as powered flight itself. There have been people since the beginning of the twentieth century willing to put down money for a ride, an airline ticket, or even an airplane of their own. They are, at one level, all buying the same thing: a chance to leave the ground and travel through the air. At another level, however, each of them is also buying other things: adventure, speed, convenience, comfort, or a chance to project an image they find appealing. Aviation, at various times and in various ways, has offered all those things—for a price.[1]

Convenience

Convenience, in the world of air travel, is a composite of several things. One is the range of possible destinations. Another is the number and timing of flights. A third is the efficiency with which passengers move through the terminals at each end of their flight. A fourth is the accessibility of the airport; small, center-city airports like Chicago's Midway and Washington's Reagan National flourish in the shadow of larger, better-served airports like O'Hare and Dulles for precisely this reason. Speed, however, is the key to convenience in air travel, often sufficient to balance limitations in the other areas. Speed is preeminent because public perceptions of convenience do not exist in a vacuum. The question, for potential passengers and airlines alike, has always been whether flying was *more* convenient than traveling by other means: cars, trains, or ships. Speed has been crucial to making it seem so.

Speed has been commercial air travel's ace in the hole from the beginning. The airliners of the 1920s and 1930s could not match the range, reliability, frequency of service, or passenger comfort offered by trains and ships. Nor could private aircraft compete, on those same grounds, with cars. Speed was the one area where the aircraft *did* have a clear advantage, and people interested in selling flight promoted it heavily. A 1929 advertisement for Transcontinental Air Transport's pioneering New York–Los Angeles service promises passengers a forty-eight-hour trip by rail and air instead of seventy-two hours or more by rail alone. Its choice of adjectives is telling: "By night . . . luxurious trains. By day . . . safe, swift planes."[2]

The speed advantage air travel had over other forms of transportation was greatest on long, complex, or lightly served routes. Aircraft were at their best, in other words, where ships and trains were at their worst. Handley Page, one of Britain's leading aircraft manufacturers, promoted its first generation of purpose-built airliners using precisely this idea. "Once you have flown to Paris," promises a 1922 booklet produced by the manufacturer, "you will never go by boat again." The text outlines a traditional London–Paris journey in horrifying detail: Leave London by train at the crack of dawn, board a ferry to cross the English Channel, then board another train in France, arriving in Paris at dinnertime with your day "spoilt" and your evening "ruined." The railway journey was "dull and uncomfortable," the channel-crossing "a torture to many," and the transition between them filled with "confusion and irritation." The speed of air travel, however, allows the traveler to "gain a useful morning in London and arrive unjaded in Paris rather early for afternoon tea, in time, may be, to pay an important business call, or with leisure to do a little sightseeing before dinner."[3]

Qantas, now the national airline of Australia, began in the 1920s as the Queensland and Northern Territory Air Service—an air-taxi company linking the towns and cities of northeastern Australia. "Flights on any section of the route," it informed customers in a mid-1920s advertising brochure, "show a large savings [of time] over other means of transport." The savings were especially great, it noted, in remote Western Queensland, where rail service was "slow

CITY OF NEW YORK
MUNICIPAL AIRPORTS
NO.1 FLOYD BENNETT FIELD · NO. 2 NORTH BEACH
EAST RIVER SEAPLANE BASES   WALL STREET — 31ˢᵀ STREET
F.H.LaGUARDIA   JOHN McKENZIE
MAYOR   COMMISSIONER OF DOCKS
MADE BY WORKS PROGRESS ADMINISTRATION · FEDERAL ART PROJECT NYC

Figure 11. The sleek, art deco lines of the airplanes surging powerfully across this
Work Projects Administration Federal Art Project poster of the late 1930s suggest
speed and efficiency. The seaplane bases it advertises were on the shores of lower
Manhattan, only a few blocks from the financial district. *Courtesy Library of
Congress, LC-USZ62-91801.*

and disconnected" and roads impassible after heavy rains. A table comparing travel times by rail and air reinforced the point: traveling the 577 miles from Charleville to Cloncurry took a week by rail but less than a day by air.[4]

Aircraft offered similar advantages for travelers moving between the more- and less-developed parts of the world, and the advantages multiplied on longer routes. Flying from France to its North African colonies, from Britain to India, or from the Netherlands to the Dutch East Indies (now Indonesia) involved multiple days and multiple stops, but the trip was faster and more direct than going by sea. Air travel thus became the preferred means of transit for civil servants, senior military officers, engineers, and others whose overseas postings meant that trips home to Europe covered thousands of miles. One pilot estimated that, on Britain's Imperial Airways in the 1930s, such people accounted for 90 percent of his passengers. The same held true in the Americas, where Pan American Airways found a ready market for the U.S.-Caribbean routes it began serving in 1931. Frequent travelers were more than willing to abandon the small, slow, often ill-kept ships that served the region for the speed and reliability of Pan Am's multiengine seaplanes. NYRBA Airlines, an abortive operation bought out by Pan Am in 1930, captured this appeal in one of its few advertisements. "Weeks faster to South America," it promises extravagantly, "by the route of the giant flying yachts."[5]

U.S. airlines operating over domestic routes also used speed as a selling point. Some of the dozens of new companies that emerged in the late 1920s advertised it in their names: Varney Speed Lines, Rapid Air Transport, and the vaguely redundant Southern Air Fast Express. Others put it in their slogans: "Speed—Courtesy—Safety" for Martz Airlines or "Safe Scenic Swift Service" for Rapid Air Transport. Still others emphasized their speed symbolically, an approach shared by many European lines of the period. The baggage labels for Interstate Airlines, which linked Chicago and Atlanta, juxtaposed a small image of a plane in flight with a slightly larger silhouette of Mercury, the fleet-footed messenger of the Roman gods. A late-1920s poster for KLM, the Dutch national airline, shows a twin-engine Fokker crossing paths with a sailing seventeenth-century sailing ship. "The Flying Dutchman," reads the caption, "The Legend Becomes Fact."[6]

The revolutionary Douglas DC-2 and DC-3 raised cruising

speeds to nearly 200 mph in the mid-1930s, opening new opportunities to sell speed. Focusing their attention on business travelers, they equated speed with efficiency, productivity, and increased sales. "Your Competitors Fly TWA" warns the headline of one 1940 advertisement in the *New York Times*. "They're hot after business . . . after your customers. Beat them to the dotted line by going TWA airline."[7] The following year, Pan Am warned readers of *Time*: "'Roll-Top Desk' Thinking Won't Do in Selling Latin America!" Flying Pan Am, however, means that "you can get there and back . . . while your competition is still on the way." Other TWA ads, run in the *New York Herald Tribune* in 1941, urge businessmen with interests in Chicago to "Be There Today!" and promise "Commuter Convenience to Cincinnati and Dayton." Both ads—typical of the era—quote specific departure times, numbers of flights, and flight times. The third went a step further, pointing out that a 9:00 A.M. departure time from New York left ample opportunity for early afternoon meetings in Ohio.[8]

A new generation of airliners, designed during World War II and put into service immediately afterward, made convenience a more attractive selling point than ever before. The Lockheed Constellations, Douglas DC-6s, and Boeing Stratocruisers of the late 1940s could cruise at close to 300 mph and cross the United States or the North Atlantic with only a single refueling stop. Their successors—the Super Constellations and DC-7s of the mid-1950s—offered cruising speeds over 300 mph and still-longer ranges. They were the first aircraft capable of covering transcontinental and transatlantic routes nonstop and the first capable of flying them in under eight hours. The technological breakthroughs of the late 1940s and early 1950s made air travel decisively faster than either rail or ship travel, and the airlines took full advantage in their marketing campaigns.

Postwar advertisements aimed at business travelers continued to emphasize speed as an essential business tool. Capital Airlines, in a 1951 ad, showed a smiling businessman walking jauntily toward his car at the end of a one-day, thousand-mile business trip. Flying Capital, the ad urges readers of *Business Week*, would allow them "to save time, energy, and money," all traditional corporate goals. British Overseas Airways Corporation (BOAC), the descendent of Imperial Airways and predecessor to British Airways, made the same argument on a grand scale in a 1952 ad. "Called to Calcutta?" it asks readers of the *New York Times*, naming a destination that (even for residents of that most cosmopolitan city) probably seemed alarmingly distant. Quickly, however, the ad's text turns reassuring: "It's only 3 days from New York when you fly," making it "good business to fly BOAC." Moreover, it promises, BOAC's extensive route system makes it possible to make the outbound trip via London, Rome, and Cairo and the return via Singapore, Sydney, and Honolulu—a business trip *and* a whirlwind world tour all (the ad promises) in only a week.[9]

The higher speeds and shortened transit times made possible by technological advances, combined with a new post–World War II "cult of domesticity," also gave airlines a powerful new way to sell their services. Business travelers, they suggested, could now reap the benefits of flying at home as well as at the office. A trio of magazine advertisements used by Trans World Airlines in the early 1950s reflects this strategy. Drawn in a style reminiscent of the then-popular "Dick and Jane" grade school readers, they focus readers' attention not on columns of departure and arrival times but on richly colored scenes of idealized middle-class families. "Daddy will be back tonight," proclaims the headline of one, above a picture of a smiling businessman hugging his two young children at the airport gate while his wife looks on fondly. Another carries the headline "Here today . . . there today . . . *home* today, too." The copy goes on in the same vein: "Time was when the man who traveled for a living enjoyed precious few hours of home life. But that was before TWA became such a good family friend." Now the businessman is rarely more than "a few pleasant hours" from his loved ones. A third ad shows a businessman relaxing in his airplane seat, which the headline refers to as "Dad's favorite chair." It is his favorite, the copy goes on to explain, not only because it allows him to cover more territory and reach potential clients ahead of the competition (the standard 1930s arguments) but also because it allows him to spend "most evenings" in his "*other* favorite chair . . . at home" with his family.[10]

The airlines' postwar marketing efforts were not, however, directed solely toward business travelers. The advent of the DC-3 in 1936 had cut airlines' passenger-mile costs from 12 cents (in the days of the Fokker and Ford Trimotors) to a little over 5 cents. The new postwar airliners, with their larger cabins and lower operating costs, cut passenger-mile costs to 4.5 cents—only one cent higher than top-of-the-line railroad service and up to four times faster. These relatively low operating costs led airlines to introduce the first cut-rate fares. Pan Am's ever inventive Juan Trippe started the trend in September, 1948, introducing "coach" service between New York and San Juan, Puerto Rico, with DC-4s converted to carry sixty-three passengers instead of the usual forty. Capital introduced its own New York–Chicago coach service in November, allowing passengers to fly in less comfort for two-thirds the standard fare. Other lines followed in 1949, and by the end of that year, TWA and American offered a one-way coach fare from New York to Los Angeles for $110 (along with the $159 standard fare).[11] These cheaper rates were aimed primarily at recreational travelers for whom prewar air travel had been too expensive: individuals, couples, and families who before would have gone by car or train.

Postwar advertisements aimed at this new class of travelers naturally emphasized low prices. They devoted equal enthusiasm, however, to speed and scheduling. Ads aimed at tourists, like those aimed at business travelers, equated speed and frequent departures with efficiency—specifically, the efficient use of precious vacation time. A 1951 TWA ad, for example, shows two men fishing in a pristine Rocky Mountain lake. "It's a long way from the office," the headline teases, "or is it?" The copy assures readers that "five-mile-a-minute Skyliner magic" would make "even a week end time enough for days at a remote spot." American Airlines, in a 1949 ad, offered "business girls" the chance to fly to Europe in "practically no time," giving them the opportunity to "almost do Europe inside and out in just two weeks." Another, from 1954, plays more forthrightly on the theme of "working girls" making the most of their annual two weeks of freedom. It shows an attractive young woman relaxing beside the pool at a sun-drenched resort and enjoying the attention of three attractive young men. "Time," the copy reads, "is a girl's best friend . . . two full weeks to *play!* Make the most of every vacation moment by flying Capital Airlines." None of the travelers (or prospective travelers) in these ads are people of wealth and leisure. They are, instead, ordinary middle-class folk—part of the flood of new passengers that doubled airline passenger traffic (from 13 to 29 million) between 1948 and 1953.[12]

The last generation of piston-engine airliners to enter service— the Douglas DC-7 and upgraded models of the Lockheed Constellation, for example—did so in the mid-1950s. Airlines quickly exploited their extended range, introducing nonstop flights westbound across the United States and eastbound across the Atlantic. Westbound transatlantic flights, against the prevailing winds, were more problematic and often involved a refueling stop at Gander,

Newfoundland, or Goose Bay, Labrador. When El Al, the Israeli national airline, introduced the Bristol Britannia 300, the first airliner capable of reliably flying the Atlantic nonstop in either direction, it famously advertised its transatlantic service with the slogan "No Goose, No Gander."[13] El Al, like other airlines before it, recognized the value of convenience—here, shorter trips and reliable arrival times—as a marketing tool.

The introduction of long-range jetliners in the late 1950s brought another revolution in convenience. These aircraft cruised at close to 600 mph, an enormous increase over the piston-engine planes that they quickly began to replace, and so cut travel times drastically. A 1958 magazine ad commissioned by Boeing to introduce the 707 showed a woman passenger with a corsage of fresh flowers pinned to her dress. The flowers, Boeing promised, would end the trip as fresh as they began it thanks to the speed of the new jet.[14] The 707s and DC-8s also doubled the passenger capacity of their predecessors, just as the postwar DC-6s and Constellations had done to the prewar DC-3s. Their hundred-passenger cabins expanded the airlines' opportunities to appeal to the 90 percent of Americans who, as of 1958, had never flown on a scheduled airliner. During the early 1960s, the development of smaller jets like the Boeing 727 and 737 and the Douglas DC-9 completed the revolution by bringing high speeds and cheap tickets to short- and medium-range routes throughout the developed world.

One tell-tale sign of the revolution is the emergence in the mid-1960s of the jet airliner as a presence in popular songs. Peter, Paul, and Mary's 1969 pop standard "Leaving on a Jet Plane," written by John Denver, casually uses one to separate two lovers—a role once reserved for trains and ships. Glenn Campbell's "By the Time I Get to Phoenix" (1967), the Monkees' "Good Clean Fun" (1969), and Cat Stevens's "Oh Very Young" (1974) all use variations on the same lyrical theme. John Stewart could, by 1979, begin his song "Lost Her in the Sun" with the observation that in Los Angeles, at any hour of the day or night, *some* jetliner is preparing to push back from the gate and begin its journey to a distant city. The song itself is a lament for a lost lover who, without a warning, a note, or a backward glance, boarded one of those jets and vanished into the wider world.

Another sign of the revolution was the advent of regional airlines that promoted themselves in terms usually associated with bus lines and commuter trains. Texas-based Southwest Airlines, for example, in the first issue of its own in-flight magazine, published its entire timetable, arrival and departure times for every one of its twenty-six daily flights between Dallas and Houston and its twelve between Dallas and San Antonio. The resulting page, dense with numbers announcing short and frequent trips, could easily have been the schedule of a metropolitan bus or commuter rail network; only a single black-and-white outline of a Boeing 737 marked it as an airline advertisement. Six years later, a much-expanded Southwest touted its range of destinations in another ad. Now, along with major cities like Dallas and Houston, it also promoted service to purely regional economic centers like Corpus Christi, Lubbock, El Paso, and Midland. Pacific Southwest Airlines, a California-based carrier, used a similar approach in the 1960s and early 1970s. "Now You've Got Us Where You Want Us," promises one ad, emphasizing the airline's frequent service to second-tier California cities like Burbank, Ontario, and Sacramento. "We Don't Even Wait for the President!" proclaims another, emphasizing the line's commitment to on-time departures with a story about leaving the company president standing on the runway.[15]

Once jets became standard equipment on all but short, low-traffic routes, the speed of air travel ceased to be a promotional tool except in the specialized niche market served by the supersonic Concorde; so, for the most part, did scheduling matters, that is, numbers of cities served and numbers of daily departures. The traveling public, by the late 1970s, could take convenience as a given in air travel. They could assume that multiple airlines would offer 500–600 mph jetliner service to any major city they wished to visit and that even the longest journeys (New York–Sydney, for example) would require less than a day's travel. Ships and (in the United States) trains had ceased to be viable modes of long-distance transportation. Travelers no longer chose between airplanes and something else but between different airlines. Price then became—and has remained— the principal basis for selling air travel to the public. The Concorde's failure to attract passengers from outside its narrowly defined niche market reflects this growing emphasis on pricing and the traveling public's complex understanding of "convenience." The Concorde's high speed and shortened transatlantic trips make it more convenient than its subsonic competitors, though not to a degree that—for most travelers—justifies the price of a seat.[16]

Comfort

Aircraft, from the beginning, offered speed far superior to that of trains or ships. Comfort was another matter. First-class cabins on ocean liners and Pullman cars on trains set a standard of comfort and service that few airlines could hope to match, much less surpass. Even those airlines that in the 1920s tried to match the gracious appointments of trains and ships were only adding window dressing to an almost inevitably uncomfortable experience. Airline passengers faced more noise, more vibration, greater weather-related turbulence, less (and less palatable) food, and more limited personal attention than rail or ship passengers.[17]

Airlines could, and did, take steps to increase the quality of their cabin service and the comfort of their passengers. In-flight box lunches began to appear in the mid-1920s, cabin attendants in the late 1920s, and the first stewardesses in the early 1930s. The Douglas DC-2s and DC-3s of the 1930s offered, in addition to higher speeds, better insulation against noise and vibration, more comfortable seats, and better onboard bathroom facilities than the machines they replaced. The DC-3, originally called the Douglas Sleeper Transport, also offered the option of converting its seats for twenty-one passengers into beds for fourteen. The resulting bunks, though they reduced passenger capacity and would not have been mistaken for railway berths, made overnight coast-to-coast flights more tolerable. United Airlines, in 1936, established its own kitchens at airports to supply food for their planes—enhancing both the quality and the speed of delivery. Air travel could, nonetheless, be a long way from comfortable. Ernest K. Gann, who flew DC-2s and DC-3s in the 1930s, recalled airplanes that smelled of "hot oil and simmering aluminum, disinfectant, feces, leather, and puke" and stewardesses, "short-tempered and reeking of vomit," seeking momentary relief near the open windows of the cockpit.[18]

The only real exceptions to this pattern were giant airships like Germany's Graf Zeppelin and Hindenburg and Britain's R-100 as well as the long-range flying boats operated by companies like Pan American Airways and Imperial Airways. More spacious than land-based airplanes and capable of carrying larger payloads, they gave cabin designers more freedom to add luxurious touches. Passenger accommodations spread over two decks connected by spiral staircases and included not only cabins but also washrooms, lounges, dining areas, and kitchens capable of preparing multicourse meals to be served on china and linen accompanied by vintage wine.[19] A mid-1930s Pan Am advertisement touts the virtues of the new Martin M-130: "spacious, airy cabins," a fifteen-passenger lounge "as large as a good-sized living room," and room enough for passengers to "move about the ship at will." All of it, moreover, was soundproofed "so effectively . . . that a normal conversational tone may be used at all times."[20] The airships went further still. They offered windowed promenades and, despite being lifted by highly inflammable hydrogen, smoking rooms. An elaborate ventilation system, immovable lighters, and sharp-eyed attendants kept the smokers (and the ships) safe. The *Hindenburg* offered in its main lounge the ultimate symbol of luxury air travel—a piano (specially made from aluminum to save weight).

The heyday of airships and flying boats as standard-bearers for luxury air travel lasted little more than five years, from the fall of 1935 until 1940. The Boeing 307 Stratoliner and Douglas DC-4, which began flying just in time to be overtaken by America's entry into World War II, heralded the coming of land-based planes big and powerful enough to match their ranges and payloads. The new airliners offered passengers a level of comfort similar to that of the airships and flying boats—spacious, soundproofed, climate-controlled cabins; elaborate meals; and comfortable seats that converted into beds—but they cost less to run and could operate from a far wider range of airports. Flying boats periodically carried VIPs across the Atlantic during the war, but Pres. Franklin D. Roosevelt used a converted DC-4 (nicknamed *Sacred Cow* by the press corps) as the first quasi-official presidential airplane.[21]

Delayed (but also improved) by World War II, the successors to the Stratoliner and the DC-4 began entering service in 1946. The Boeing 377 Stratocruiser and the Douglas DC-6, along with the Lockheed Constellation, offered not only profound increases in speed but also substantial advances in passenger comfort. The most important was cabin pressurization. With this, the new postwar airliners could cruise at altitudes where turbulence was minimal and rides smooth, minimizing airsickness and facilitating more elaborate cabin service.

Airline advertisements of the 1920s and 1930s, for good reason, seldom raised the issue of passenger comfort, but those of the 1940s and 1950s emphasized it. Delta promised in 1949 that "no queen, nor any prince, president, or millionaire" could travel in greater luxury than the passengers on its new DC-6 fleet. Travelers would fly "in

Figure 12. The new airliners developed during World War II offered extended ranges and set new standards for passenger comfort when they entered service in the late 1940s. President Franklin D. Roosevelt, shown in this official U.S. Navy photograph from 1942 or 1943 aboard his DC-4 *Sacred Cow*, benefited from, and helped popularize, the new machines. *Courtesy Library of Congress, LC-USZ62-97736.*

a spacious, comfortable cabin decorated in the finest taste," sit in a "wide comfortable seat that cushions your body gently," and enjoy "delicious Southern-style meals served the inimitable Delta way." The promises of luxurious travel made by other airlines differed in details but not in spirit. "Only TWA offers luxurious all-sleeper service," proclaims a 1951 ad from *Time*. The accompanying black-and-white drawing shows a smiling stewardess drawing the curtains around a double berth in which a pajama-clad mother and daughter are already comfortably bedded down beneath sheets and blankets. National Airlines, in a *Newark Sunday News* ad from 1954, touted its new DC-7s as "the only aircraft on which *true* luxury is possible." Travelers to Miami were promised "foam rubber 2-abreast seating on both sides of the aisle . . . choice filet mignon . . . Starlight Cocktail Lounge . . . personalized two-stewardess service . . . music and flowers . . . red-carpet departures and arrivals!"[22]

Passenger comfort is not merely physical, however, it is also psychological. The jobs of the cabin crew have always included calming distressed passengers and reassuring anxious ones. Airline marketing in the postwar era paid close attention to mental comfort, especially that of infrequent or first-time fliers attracted by the new tourist class fares. Advertisements of the late 1940s and 1950s prominently featured such nontraditional fliers: a mother and her grown daughter traveling together, a young couple on their honeymoon, a single woman on vacation, a family of four going to grandma's house for the holidays, or grandma herself on her way to visit them. Most also showed at least one uniformed employee of the airline, smiling solicitously as if their sole responsibility was to ensure that particular passenger's comfort. One United ad from 1958, titled "Just a Little Rag Doll," describes a United pilot who discovers the worn—and clearly much beloved—doll of the title wedged between a window seat and the cabin wall. Using the airline's state-of-the-art communication and reservation systems, he identifies the family that had been seated there and reunites the doll with its grateful young owner. The ad, like Richard Nixon's career-saving "Checkers Speech" of 1952, is shamelessly manipulative and sentimental. It is also, especially for those who travel with small children, brilliantly effective.[23]

It has become commonplace, particularly since the deregulation of the airline industry in the early 1980s, for air travelers to look back on the late forties, the fifties, and even the sixties as a lost "golden age" in which passenger comfort reached a level of perfection never matched before or since.[24] Back then, according to countless misty-eyed reminiscences, the seats were more comfortable, the meals more sumptuous, and the cabin crews more solicitous. These glowing memories, like most of lost golden ages, are accurate but narrow and highly selective. They overlook, for example, the squalor, overcrowding, and inefficiency that air travelers endured in the airports and ticket offices of the era.[25] They also gloss over the casual racism that caused many flights to be "sold out" when African American travelers inquired about purchasing tickets. Most glaring, memories of the forties and fifties as a time of uniformly sumptuous cabin service overlooks the *other* postwar revolution in airline marketing: the ultracheap, no-frills ticket. Passengers who crossed the Atlantic on one of Pan Am's "tourist class" DC-6Bs in the early 1950s—dining on cold sandwiches, paying for alcoholic drinks, and sitting five-abreast in a cabin designed for four-abreast seating—would have had very different memories.[26]

Jet airliners improved the in-flight experience of all passengers. Their cabins were quieter, their engines produced less vibration, and their 600-mph cruising speeds meant substantially shorter and less fatiguing trips. Their cabins were larger than those of the Constellations and DC-7s they replaced, while those of the "jumbo jets" introduced in the late 1960s were larger still. The vast, double-aisle interiors of the new jumbos—the Boeing 747, Douglas DC-10, and Lockheed L-1011—offered passengers a freedom of movement unprecedented since the mid-1930s heyday of airships and flying boats. They also gave airlines the opportunity to indulge in customer-pleasing theatrics. Pan Am, perhaps in a nod to its 1930s heyday, used the "upstairs" section of its 747s as a restaurant for first-class passengers, giving them the opportunity to go "out to dinner" thirty thousand feet above the Earth. Continental Airlines, sacrificing several rows of coach seats, installed a bar, pianist, and lightweight piano in the main cabin of at least one 747—almost certainly the first airborne piano bar since the *Hindenburg*'s a generation earlier.[27]

The rise of spacious, quiet, smooth-riding jets also set the stage for another kind of theatrics, the temporary transformation of stewardesses from briskly efficient maternal figures to enticing sex objects. This relied more on teasing suggestiveness than on any explicit change in the stewardesses' duties, but the implication was clear: ogling the female employees was not only permitted but also expected and encouraged. Braniff, for example, offered "The Air Strip"—an impromptu floor show in which stewardesses removed pieces of their multilayered uniforms as the flight progressed, ending up in a blouse and (short) skirt. Continental, in a 1965 ad, presented an anonymous stewardess's legs and buttocks as "attractions" rivaling the first-run movies shown in the first-class cabin. Another ad, for Pacific Southwest Airlines, proclaims that while other airlines' passengers prefer window seats, PSA's passengers prefer the "aisle view." The accompanying image superimposes a photograph of a stewardess over a pen-and-ink cartoon of a cabin filled with passengers. The stewardess, blonde and smiling brightly, is balancing a small, round tray of cocktails on one upturned hand and swinging her hips as she walks. Twelve of the fourteen faces behind her are male, and all twelve are staring openly and appreciatively at her body. *Coffee, Tea, or Me?* a best-selling 1968 memoir purportedly written by Trudy Baker and Rachel Jones, reinforces the image of stewardesses as carefree "good-time girls" who might—in theory, anyway—be sexually available to any male passenger who struck their fancy.[28]

The final, and ultimately most significant, consequence of jets on cabin service was that their capacious interiors allowed airlines to institutionalize two-class service. The physical segregation of multiple classes of passengers paying different fares for different levels of comfort had been standard on trains (separate cars) and ships (separate decks, cabins, and dining facilities) for generations. Throughout the 1940s and 1950s, however, airlines had run premium- and economy-class service on different planes, each with its own suitably equipped and configured cabin. The new jetliners' cabins were large enough now to combine two (or even three) classes of service in a single airplane. They allowed airlines to simultaneously pursue both of the new marketing opportunities that had become available after World War II, offering maximum comfort for first-class passengers who were willing to pay and a basic level of comfort for economy-class passengers for whom value was the paramount consideration.[29]

Passenger comfort since the early 1970s has gradually ceased to be a factor in airlines' efforts to market their services. One reason for its disappearance is the parallel decline of ships (and in the United States trains) as viable competitors. Americans bound for distant destinations, if they are unable or unwilling to spend days on the highway, have little choice but to fly. Another reason is the gradual standardization of service. Most air travelers see one airline's first-class or economy-class service as little different from another's. A final reason is the difference between first- and economy-class ticket prices—a gulf so wide that passengers for each represent almost entirely separate markets. Few who regularly fly economy class are likely, no matter how great the upgrade in service, to pay double or triple fare in order to go first class. Indeed, airlines claim that experiments with offering modest improvements in coach service for modestly higher fares have repeatedly failed to attract passengers.[30] Passenger comfort is thus effective neither in luring customers from other modes of transportation, in siphoning business from competitors, nor in encouraging already loyal patrons to upgrade their service. Major airlines, especially, thus have little reason to use comfort as a selling point.

The principal exceptions to this pattern since the mid-1970s have been relatively small "niche" airlines operating modest fleets over limited route systems. Southwest, People Express, and ValuJet (now AirTran) used their bare-bones cabin service as a sign of their commitment to offer the lowest possible fares. Midwest Express, since it began operations in 1984, has positioned itself as the only airline to offer first-class service at economy-class fares. Its extravagantly spacious two-abreast leather seats are central to its public image, just as Southwest's peanuts-only "food service" was to its in the 1980s.[31]

Adventure

Selling air travel on the basis of convenience or comfort means offering potential travelers a better way of getting somewhere they already planned to go. The trip itself, not the destination, is the point. Selling air travel as a form of adventure means emphasizing the destination: presenting the aircraft as a gateway to someplace that would otherwise remain inaccessible.

The promise of access to exotic destinations was often used to sell overseas air travel in the 1920s and 1930s. A French poster promoting passenger and mail service to North Africa in the twenties renders in bold orange and blue a scene of a single-engine airliner swooping over an exotic Moroccan cityscape. A Belgian one shows a North African nomad gazing up at a Sabena airliner on its way (as the poster indicates in both words and graphics) to the Belgian Congo, the tiny European nation's sole African colony. British cigarette cards from the thirties show the trademark HP-42 biplanes of Imperial Airways cruising over the Dead Sea in Palestine, surrounded by Arab spectators on the shores of the Persian Gulf, and parked alongside camels in Baluchistan. A 1936 poster for Imperial Airways shows smartly dressed passengers alighting from another HP-42 at an airport that could have been located anywhere. A narrow band of words across the bottom suggests a world of possibilities: "Europe. Africa. India. China. Australia."[32]

Pan American Airways, the U.S. carrier with the most extensive overseas routes, built its corporate image around exoticism in the 1930s. On its transpacific (from 1935) and transatlantic (from 1937) routes, Pan Am competed with large shipping lines like Cunard and Canadian Pacific by appropriating the same kinds of romantic images that the shipping lines had relied on for years. Pan Am called its giant flying boats "clippers," a reference to the giant sailing ships that had carried the high-value cargoes of the middle to late nineteenth century. Its planes were laid out and decorated in ways that suggested ships' cabins, and the flight crews wore uniforms designed to resemble those of ships' officers. Long after the end of the flying boat era, the head of the cabin crew on a Pan Am flight, by company tradition, was not the "head flight attendant" but the "purser," another borrowing from the world of passenger ships. Pan Am advertising posters used the same visual elements as those printed by the cruise lines. They featured idealized images of exotic foreign ports in lush detail and vibrant color. A Pan Am plane floated or flew amid the scene, just as a ship would in a shipping line poster. Implicitly, the aircraft had replaced the ship as the viewer's gateway to the exciting world in the picture.[33]

After World War II, other U.S. airlines joined Pan Am in developing extensive overseas route systems and promoting air travel to exotic destinations. In 1940 the initials "TWA" still stood for Transcontinental and Western Air, and the airline's ads in New York newspapers highlighted such destinations as Harrisburg, Dayton, Pittsburgh, and Chicago. By 1947 "TWA" had become Trans World Airlines, and the company's ads now promoted flights to Paris, Rome, Athens, Cairo, and Bombay. Airlines aimed their postwar advertising—as Pan Am had before the war—at both business and recreational travelers. Like the market for domestic leisure travel, however, that for overseas leisure travel had been expanded by the postwar drop in ticket prices. The pool of potential travelers was larger, more middle than upper class, and more likely to be flying (or leaving the country) for the first time.

Figure 13. Pan American Airways borrowed the advertising techniques of shipping lines to promote their transpacific and transatlantic flying-boat service in the late 1930s. This 1938 advertisement shows a Pan Am "clipper" amid the traditional symbols of exotic Pacific islands: palm trees, lush jungles, a towering volcano, and a lithe young native woman. *Courtesy Library of Congress, LC-USZC4-2308.*

The content of airline advertisements for adventure travel reflected these new, postwar realities. TWA, for example, ran an elaborate series of ads in the popular weekly magazine *The Saturday Evening Post*, each introducing a different TWA destination. The full-color painting in each shows an exotic (but clean) foreign scene populated by colorful (but unthreatening) local people. The text explains, in exuberant tones aimed at the *Post*'s largely middle-American readership, the appeal of going there in person. "Stroll on the sunny Riviera, playground of princes and kings," proclaims one focusing on the Mediterranean. Come to Bombay, "where royalty rides in elephants' *howdahs* and spiked minarets mark the skyline," encourages another. "There's magic in Italy's autumn" says another, cataloging "tangy mountain lakes" in the North, "sun-drenched shores" in the South, and "ancient splendors and modern comforts" in Rome. Each ad features, amid its fine print, a globe bordered by the names of still more exotic destinations: Portugal, Iraq, Ceylon, and Indochina.[34]

Other airlines also competed, though often in less elaborate ways, for the attention of potential vacationers. TACA Airways was clearly addressing them when it advertised flights with headlines that suggested travelogue films: "El Salvador: Land of Fine Coffees, Gold and Silver" and "Costa Rica: Land of Coffee, Cacao, and Bananas." The Scandinavian Airlines System (SAS) encouraged Americans to cross the Atlantic with them for "summer in Scandinavia and Scotland," while British Overseas Airways Corporation suggested "Bermuda for Christmas." United Airlines urged travelers to fly to Hawaii for the "colorful pageantry" and the "ancient tribal rites, dances, and ceremonies" of Aloha Week. American offered vacationers a "Mid-Winter Holiday in Mexico," complete with a cartoon of a couple relaxing on the beach while two smiling Mexicans prepare coconuts for them to sample. Venezuela's national airline ran ads in the *New York Times* promising five-hour direct service to Havana—the kind of service on which hangs the plot of Frank Loesser's 1955 Broadway hit *Guys and Dolls*.[35]

Airlines' efforts to associate air travel with exotic destinations continued well into the jet age. The theme song from a Pan Am commercial of the mid-1970s, for instance, urges potential travelers: "Open up your eyes / Hey, look around you / There's a lot of world you've never seen." Hawaiian Airlines, Air India, and Singapore Airlines all dress their female flight attendants in traditional native costumes. The costumes, though perhaps less functional than typical uniforms, allow Western travelers to experience the "exotic" world of their destination from the comfort of their seat and indulge fantasies of life in a "tropical paradise" where their every whim is catered to by attentive and dutiful "native servants."[36] Singapore Airlines' consistently high rankings for customer service suggest that these theatrics still impress and appeal to significant numbers of passengers.

The exotic destinations associated with flying need not be foreign, however, and the aircraft used to reach them need not be scheduled airliners. The flying community since the 1920s has included some pilots who make (or supplement) their living by giving rides to interested passengers. The commodity being sold—whether at county fairs in the 1920s or at small-town airfields in the 1990s—is basically the same: the chance to see familiar territory from the exotic vantage point of a few thousand feet in the sky. Air tours of the Grand Canyon promise much the same thing, a view that can be obtained no other way. The bush pilots of Canada and Alaska for years have offered hunters, hikers, and anglers access to parts of the North American backwoods too distant to be easily reached by road or trail. "Helicopter skiing" promises skiers the chance to cut the first tracks into fresh snow far beyond the boundaries of crowded resorts. In all these cases—as in airline ads reaching back to the 1920s—it is the destination (and the experiences available there) being sold. The airplane is merely a gateway.

Private planes offer a different kind of access to adventure. Most of them, like most cars, are used typically for mundane purposes—short trips to and from their owner's base of operation. Just as with every car, however, every private plane comes with the promise that it could be used for something far more elaborate and adventurous. The potential is kept alive less by manufacturers' advertising campaigns—as is the case with cars—than by the first-person accounts of pilots who have gone to extraordinary places or done extraordinary things in small, private planes. Many of these accounts are among the acknowledged classics of aviation literature. Generations of pilots (and would-be pilots) have read them and, as a result, dreamt of embarking on their own adventures.

The genre emerged in the early 1930s, shortly after the appearance of the first planes expressly designed for private ownership. Francis Chichester's *Solo to Sydney* chronicles his epic trip from London to Australia in a fragile, short-range DeHavilland Gypsy Moth biplane. Anne Morrow Lindbergh's *North to the Orient* and *Listen, the*

Wind! detail the survey flights across the North Pacific and North Atlantic, respectively, that she made with her husband, Charles. Amelia Earhart's two volumes of autobiography, *The Fun of It* and *Last Flight,* are similar, though less widely read. Beryl Markham's *West with the Night* differs from the others in that Markham flew professionally as a bush pilot in East Africa, but it shares their characteristic use of flying stories as connective tissue linking personal reflection and accounts of people and places the author encountered on the ground. All these works are as much about the adventure that flying makes possible as they are about the flying itself.[37]

First-person tales of private pilots, small planes, and exotic locales continue to attract readers. Francis Chichester's autobiographical *The Lonely Sea and the Sky,* which recounted the London–Sydney flight along with later exploits, sold well in the 1960s. Paul Gahlinger's *The Cockpit,* the tale of the author's attempt to fly an aging Cessna from California to South Africa, received admiring reviews for its low-key handling of ice storms, sand storms, earthquakes, and political upheavals. Jimmy Buffett, an amateur pilot as well as a highly successful singer-songwriter, has worked his aerial adventures into songs such as "Somewhere over China," "Jimmy Dreams," and "Jamaica Mistaica." His family's three-week aerial tour of the Caribbean served as a framework for his autobiography, *A Pirate Looks at Fifty.*[38]

Gahlinger aside, most of the recent classics of the "adventures in small planes" genre focus on flights within the United States. Like the earlier works of Chichester, Lindbergh, and Markham, they devote as much attention to the people and places the pilot-author encounters as they do to the process of flying. Their shared theme, "how I saw America from the air," ties them to the rich vein of "road trip" stories that runs through American popular culture, from John Steinbeck's *The Grapes of Wrath* through Jack Kerouac's *On the Road* to William Least-Heat Moon's *Blue Highways.*

Two early works of pilot, author, and philosopher Richard Bach—*Biplane* and *Nothing by Chance*—chronicle Bach's adventures as a modern-day barnstormer in small Midwestern towns during the 1960s. Rinker Buck's *Flight of Passage*—written later (1996) but set earlier (1966)—recalls a summer when the author and his older brother, then fourteen and sixteen, flew a restored Piper Cub from New Jersey to California. Maria Gosnell traces her own solo flight from New York to the West Coast and back in *Zero Three Bravo,* and Stephen Coonts's *The Cannibal Queen* (1992) describes three months of leisurely air touring that he undertook one summer in a restored 1942 Stearman biplane. Private planes, in each of these stories, bring the pilot-authors into out-of-the-way corners of the United States that they would never have reached by driving or by flying on scheduled airlines. The new subtitle added to the paper-back edition of Coonts's book—"A Flight into the Heart of America"—emphasizes this theme. The planes (and the trips the pilots are undertaking) also act as icebreakers in their conversations with the locals. Talking to people randomly encountered on the way, each strikes up friendships with people who only moments before had been strangers.[39]

Long, loosely scheduled travels by private plane are, in these memoirs, often an occasion for the pilot-authors to reevaluate their lives or their closest personal relationships with loved ones. Richard Bach—implicitly in *Nothing by Chance* and explicitly in later works like *Illusions, Bridge across Forever*, and *Running from Safety*—intertwines physical journeys taken in airplanes with spiritual journeys.[40] Jimmy Buffett's autobiography describes how flying deepened the bonds between himself and his young son, Cameron, just as sailing helped him (as a boy) bond with his grandfather. The early chapters of Stephen Coonts's *The Cannibal Queen* dwell on the author's relationship with *his* son, a teenager who is accompanying him on the first legs of a cross-country flight. Rinker Buck, as the title of his book suggests, regards his transcontinental flight as the watershed event of his youth. It transformed him from a boy into a man, not only in his own eyes but also in the eyes of his father and brother.

All these memoirs promote the idea that the freedom granted by a private plane can change one's life. They are, in that respect, promoting the same idea as the adventure-oriented travel posters that advertised Pan Am's flying-boat service in the 1930s. Flying, they suggest, can give one a chance to step outside the familiar routine of one's life: to go places, see things, meet people, and have experiences that would otherwise remain foreign.

Image

We choose to equip ourselves with particular machines not only because of what they can do but also because of the image that they convey. A twenty-dollar watch from a discount store can tell time as well (for everyday purposes) as a thousand-dollar watch from a jewelry store. Few, however, would argue that they are interchangeable. Any properly made suit of clothes will cover enough of the body for the wearer to avoid arrest, but we choose our clothes with great care, anxious to project an image that matches our mood and intentions. Most sport-utility vehicles are never taken off-road, most pickups are never loaded to more than a fraction of their rated cargo capacity, and most "performance sedans" are never driven much above the speed of surrounding traffic. All three types of vehicle sell well, however, because they convey an image—of adventurousness, of strength, of quickness—that thousands of buyers find appealing. The appeal of the SUV lies less in the opportunity to go off-road than in the opportunity to look like you might want to do so. Television and print advertising for all three types for years has sold the image first and the vehicle second.

Aircraft too convey messages about those who fly in them. If the messages are less varied, less complex, and less subtle than those expressed by clothing or cars, it is only because aircraft are less central to everyday life. Few Americans are as attuned to the differences between types of airplane as they are to similar differences between models of cars and styles of clothing. People who might quickly form detailed opinions about the driver of a Porsche roadster or a Ford minivan would be far less likely to do so about the pilot of a Piper Cub or a Beech King Air. There are, however, exceptions to this pattern, aircraft that do convey specific, widely recognized messages about those who fly on them.

Dirigibles and the long-range flying boats that replaced them were, during their brief heyday, symbols of wealth and privilege. Like the first-rank ocean liners with which they competed—Olympic, Mauretania, Normandie, and Queen Mary—such aircraft conferred an aura of glamour on their passengers.[41] Jetliners briefly did the same but soon became too common to convey exclusivity. The Concorde, perversely, retains its prestige because it has been an economic failure. Unable to attract customers from outside the small market niche it has served since 1976, it marks everyone who flies on it as one of the very few wealthy (and busy) enough to be interested in the money-for-time exchange that it offers. The phrase "jet set," coined in the early 1960s when jetliners were new on the world's airways, gradually fell out of use as subsonic jet travel became routine. The "jet set" image—of an ultrarich elite who might casually fly to Paris for a day of shopping or the Alps for a weekend of skiing—

remains part of the culture, however. It now attaches, albeit without the label, to those who fly the Concorde or, especially, to those who own a private jet.[42]

Private jets, since Bill Lear introduced the first one in the early 1960s, have been more enduring symbols of wealth and power. The title character of the James Bond film *Goldfinger* uses one, as does secret agent Derek Flint (James Coburn) in the Bond spoofs *Our Man Flint* and *In Like Flint*. The title sequence of the television series *Hart to Hart* (1979–84) uses scenes aboard a private jet (along with images of his-and-hers Mercedes convertibles) to introduce its heroes, an ultrarich married couple (Robert Wagner, Stephanie Powers) who solve crimes in their spare time. Episodes of another television series, *The Magician* (1973–74), typically end with the title character aboard his jet, flying into the sunset. Carly Simon's 1972 song "You're So Vain," a scathing indictment of an ex-lover, uses his casual use of a personal Learjet to suggest decadence and spiritual poverty. Jimmy Buffett's "Overkill," written a quarter century later, does the same with Hollywood executives and Gulfstream G4s. In *Contact* (novel 1985, film 1997), scientist Ellie Arroway first encounters the eccentric billionaire who will help fund her research aboard a private jet whose cabin functions as his hospital room.[43]

The transatlantic "Skytrain" service, begun by upstart Laker Airways in 1977, was the antithesis of the Pan Am clipper, Concorde, or Learjet. It conveyed an image not of privilege but of populism—one in which its users reveled. Laker offered seats on its wide-bodied DC-10 jets at rock-bottom prices, but only on the day of departure. Especially during its first two years of operations, before other airlines offered comparable fares, hundreds of travelers waited for hours to buy cheap passage across the Atlantic. Skytrain tickets became, like backpacks and youth hostel cards, emblems of a generation of young travelers with ample time, a healthy sense of adventure, and limited funds. They were to air travel in the late 1970s what the hand-painted Volkswagen bus had been to road travel a decade earlier, a lifestyle statement as well as a means of transportation.[44]

Laker Airways ran its populist Skytrain service by using conventional aircraft (essentially the same as those used by the major airlines) in an unconventional way. Flying aboard unconventional *aircraft*, whether as pilot-owner or passenger, confers a different image, one of eccentricity.

The most common form of unconventional aircraft is one that

is clearly decades old. Like many heroes in 1970s and 1980s television series, Nick Ryder (Joe Penny) of *Riptide* flies a helicopter. Most such helicopters—the Hughes 500 featured in *Magnum, P.I.*, for example—were sleek, new, and immaculately painted. The fact that Ryder flies a twenty-year-old army-surplus relic named the "Screaming Mimi," painted pink, and adorned with eyes and a grinning mouth is his trademark—like the Hawaiian shirts and Detroit Tigers baseball caps that Tom Selleck wears as the title character in *Magnum*.[45] The same is true of the young pilot who, in a 1975 television commercial for Royal Crown (RC) cola, is shown dusting crops in a decades-old open-cockpit biplane. The final scene shows him at the airport, his beloved biplane parked in the shadow of a giant airliner, reflecting that (in the words of the jingle) "what's good enough for other folks ain't good enough for me." The biplane, like the RC cola in his hand, becomes a sign of his attractively offbeat personality.

Choosing a flying machine that is not a conventional aircraft at all is the ultimate way to state, "I am different." At the beginning of the 1965 film *Thunderball*, secret agent James Bond extracts a jet backpack from the trunk of his car and uses it to fly to safety. The apprentice wizards and witches in J. K. Rowling's *Harry Potter* books ride brooms—one sign of the gulf that separates them from the non-magical folk they call "muggles." Practitioners and admirers of the Wicca religion use the title "witch" proudly; some jokingly adorn their cars with bumper stickers proclaiming, "My other car is a broom!" Ned Brainerd, the eccentric title character in the 1961 film *The Absent Minded Professor*, applies his latest discovery—flying rubber, or "flubber"—to his antique Ford Model T and goes for an impromptu nighttime flight over his hometown.[46] The fact that he regards the flight as a pleasant diversion rather than a bizarre experiment that turns the laws of nature sideways is, of course, precisely what makes the scene funny. It also establishes Professor Brainerd as irredeemably, though amiably, strange. More than the RC-drinking crop duster or any real-world Concorde passenger, his choice of flying machine defines him.

5
•••

Crashes and Other Catastrophes

Sudden, unexpected catastrophes such as earthquakes, shipwrecks, and major fires leave lingering cultural echoes in their wake. The greater the trauma, the more intense, more diverse, and more lasting the echoes.[1] These can take many forms. One is the fixing of blame on a seemingly plausible scapegoat: a careless Irish immigrant in the Great Chicago Fire of 1888, a liquor-impaired captain in the *Exxon Valdez* oil spill of 1987, or violence-inducing music and video games in the Columbine High School shootings of 1998.[2] Another is the institution, with great fanfare, of measures designed to guard against future catastrophes, such as NASA's redesign of its Apollo spacecraft after an oxygen fire killed three astronauts in January, 1967.[3] A third is to focus on acts of heroism amid the catastrophe, like the resolve of the *Titanic's* radio operators and musicians, who stayed at their posts as the ship sank beneath them.[4] A fourth is making pronouncements about the larger meaning of the catastrophe. Survivors of the 1755 earthquake that devastated Lisbon saw the destruction of their city as the wrath of an angry God—a judgment on their sinful ways and a warning to repent. Survivors of the 1906 San Francisco earthquake, surveying the ruins of their own city, saw an opportunity to build it anew, a chance to make it a bigger and better city than ever before.[5]

Air crashes are, as catastrophes go, small-scale events. They often take fewer than twenty lives and seldom take more than a hundred. They kill, in any given year, only a fraction of the number killed in car accidents (roughly forty thousand annually in the United States). Air crashes, however, register differently in the public's mind than other catastrophes. High-profile accidents thus tend to draw interest—and generate cultural echoes—far out of proportion to their cost in lives or property damage.

Unlike most natural disasters, air crashes have no geographic limits. One can move away from hurricanes, tornadoes, earthquakes, and floods, but escaping the need to fly is far more difficult. Unlike most human-caused catastrophes, air crashes rarely allow those involved to save themselves through their own actions. It is possible, if not plausible, to imagine steering a car around a highway pile-up, swimming away from a sinking ship, or tackling a deranged gunman who opens fire in a crowded shopping mall. Flying accidents rarely offer even the illusion of hope. Passengers aboard a crippled aircraft can do little (beyond wearing seat belts and memorizing emergency procedures) to improve their chances of survival. Articles on "how to survive a plane crash" routinely emphasize that luck is a key factor.[6] Finally, more than most catastrophes, air crashes are likely to occur suddenly and (from the passengers' perspective) without warning—there is no ominous darkening of the sky, no rising of the river, no smoke on the horizon. All of these qualities heighten the popular perception of air accidents as random, inexplicable events. That perception, in turn, reinforces an idea as old as the myth of Icarus, that flying is a precarious, unnatural activity that could end at any moment with a sudden (and probably fatal) earthward plunge.

Air crashes are uniquely disturbing, but for most travelers, the anxiety is balanced by the realization that they are also rare—far less common, and far less lethal, than car accidents. Nonetheless, that confidence can be precarious. Reports of midair crises, high-profile crashes, and disappearances of planes and pilots upset the equilibrium by forcing images of sudden, random death into the foreground. The stories people tell about flying accidents are a means of restoring that confidence in flying. They reduce the stresses and fears accidents generate by fitting the events (real or imagined) into familiar storylines, making them familiar, comprehensible, and meaningful rather than strange, inexplicable, and random.

Midair Crises and Nonfatal Crashes

Flying accidents in the real world are not inevitably fatal.[7] Near crashes and crashes without significant loss of life are even more common in popular culture. Tales of real ones are fixtures of most pilots' memoirs, of virtually all popular biographies of fliers, and of anthologies of aviation writing. Fictional ones are staples of books, movies, and even (as framing devices for series or plots for individual episodes) in television. There are solid dramatic reasons for this. Stories about flying accidents are typically told as adventure stories, and the survival of most of the major characters is virtually a requirement of the genre. There are also cultural reasons. Stories in which crises are averted, or in which most people survive the ensuing crash, defuse anxiety about flying more effectively than those ending in outright disaster. Their message is consistent and reassuring—no matter what crisis arises, *someone* (flight crew, ground crew, or even passengers) will rise up to handle the challenge.

Pilots' tales of near catastrophes in the real world often exemplify philosopher Friedrich Nietzsche's credo, "That which does not kill us makes us stronger." The pilots telling the stories often portray themselves as nearly outmatched and only barely in control of the aircraft or the situation. For example, French airmail pilot Antoine De Saint Exupéry described an encounter with the foothills of the Andes Mountains:

> There I was, throttle wide open, facing the coast. At right angles to the coast and facing it. A lot had happened in a single minute. In the first place, I had not flown out to sea. I had been spat out to sea by a monstrous cough, vomited out of my valley as from the mouth of a howitzer. . . . The mountain range stood up like a crenelated fortress against the pure sky, while the cyclone crushed me down to the surface of the waters. How hard that wind was blowing I found out as soon as I became conscious of my disastrous mistake: throttle wide open, engines running at my maximum, which was one hundred and fifty miles an hour, my plane hanging sixty feet over the water, I was unable to budge.[8]

Saint Exupéry goes on to describe how he gradually claws his way back to shore, clears the mountains, and arrives, nearly catatonic with exhaustion, at his destination. Far from being the triumphant hero, he is glad just to have survived.

Another common theme in pilots' tales is their own inexperience, inattentiveness, or bad decisions. Ernest K. Gann describes in his classic memoir how he nearly destroyed the Taj Mahal by

overestimating the rate at which the heavily laden transport plane
he was flying could gain altitude after takeoff. Edwards Park, who
flew fighters in New Guinea during World War II, once returned
from a night mission with his windshield hopelessly fogged. He
recalled the moment—"the worst thing that ever happened to
me while flying"—in his memoir *Nanette*. "I wrenched my head inside and glared at the altimeter: 600 feet. The end was coming very
quickly, and I had a feeling of no control over it, over anything. I
wasn't flying this strange and futile aircraft, this 'it.' I was just sitting
here, waiting, all alone. And it kept right on blithely lowering itself into the pit, insensible of the imminent end when it would dash
itself—and me—against a warm hillside and light the night with
its flames." The feelings that Park describes—helplessness, frustra-
tion, and desperation—are, like Saint Exupéry's sense of impotence,
typical of such stories.[9]

The pilots narrating these stories typically describe themselves—once the crisis has passed—as exhausted, shaken, or re-
lieved, rarely triumphant. They also, however, emphasize lessons
learned and experience gained. When told by others—as when
Tom Wolfe writes about test pilot Chuck Yeager—the stories may
be celebrations of bravery and skill. When told by pilots, they are
more often about good luck, quick thinking, and the ability to learn
from past mistakes. A popular monthly column in *Flying* magazine
has provided for years a forum for pilots to share their stories of
midair crises. The column is tellingly titled "I Learned about Flying
from That."[10]

Fictional tales of near catastrophes follow a different set of conventions. Most show pilots (and others) dealing with crises in con-
ventionally heroic fashion, with complete confidence, great bravery,
and enormous skill. Most also give the pilot a small group of competent assistants—in the air, on the ground, or both.[11] Finally, most focus on spectacular problems that are initially beyond the hero's control and so not the hero's fault: hijackers, bombs, collisions, or crews
who die in flight.

Early examples of the story began to appear in the 1950s. *Breaking the Sound Barrier*, a 1952 British film about jet test pilots, focuses on the (invented) problem of pilots losing control of their aircraft at very high speeds. The hero, who has lost several colleagues
in such accidents, risks his own death in order to recreate—and
solve—the problem. Ernest K. Gann's 1953 novel *The High and the*

Mighty, filmed in 1954, takes place aboard an airliner that develops engine trouble over the Pacific en route from Honolulu to San Francisco. The pilot (atypically for such stories) is unable to cope with the problem, but the copilot coolly takes command and nurses the crippled plane to its destination. The film ends with the copilot (played by John Wayne) walking across the tarmac in San Francisco and casually whistling the main title theme. He is a study in nonchalance—a man for whom saving a planeload of people is a routine part of the job.[12]

Arthur Hailey's 1968 novel *Airport*, filmed in 1970, places similar emphasis on competence and teamwork.[13] Its central plotline involves a Rome-bound flight that is forced to turn back to its departure point—"Lincoln International" Airport—after a suicidal passenger sets off a homemade bomb in the bathroom. Lincoln International, meanwhile, is on the verge of being closed by a blizzard. Only one runway remains clear, and it is blocked by a Boeing 707 hopelessly stuck in a snow bank. All but one of the main characters have personal lives that are in complete disarray. All, however, are uniformly competent and efficient—even heroic—when on the job. Pilot Vernon Demerest comes close to apprehending the bomber, survives the explosive decompression of the cabin without a seatbelt, and lands the crippled plane while reassuring the passengers over the intercom. Airport manager Mel Bakersfield juggles snow removal, landing requests, and the press far more adroitly than he does his wife and mistress. Maintenance supervisor Joe Patroni climbs into the cockpit of the snowbound 707 and, trusting his instincts more than "the book," breaks it free with a burst of power from the engines. The main characters are so competent, in fact, that the story's suspense lies not in *whether* they will succeed but in how.

Airport is a fairly conventional story driven by two straightforward problems: an airplane that needs to land and an airport with blocked runways. Later novels, though they describe more exotic problems, also offer heroic flight crews who are well equipped to deal with them. David Graham's *Down to a Sunless Sea* takes place in the aftermath of a nuclear war aboard a commercial airship carrying a band of survivors to safety in Antarctica. Thomas H. Block's *Orbit* involves an accident that sends a hypersonic airliner hurtling out of Earth's atmosphere and into space. Unable to return the vehicle to Earth, the crew struggles to keep everyone alive and breathing until NASA can send a spacecraft to rescue them. John J. Nance's

Pandora's Clock and *Medusa's Child* take place aboard airliners with, respectively, a deadly virus loose in the cabin and an armed thermonuclear bomb in the baggage hold.[14] The members of the flight crews are, in each case, the heroes of the story: brave, highly skilled, quick witted, and resourceful. They overcome not only "routine" in-flight emergencies but also (in Graham) the end of civilization and (in Nance) powerful enemies determined to destroy them. The pilot-heroes in such stories are nearly superhuman, a reassuring, if not wholly realistic, image.

The most enduring "midair crisis" plot depends, paradoxically, on removing the flight crew from the action. The classic example is Arthur Hailey's "Flight into Danger"—a 1956 teleplay that spawned a novel in 1958 (*Runway Zero Eight*) and films in 1957 (*Zero Hour*), 1971 (*Terror in the Sky*), and 1980 (*Airplane!*).[15] Set originally aboard a chartered twin-engine airliner flying across Canada, it features a former World War II fighter pilot who must take the controls when both pilots fall victim to food poisoning. Ted Stryker, the hero, is far removed from the ultrabrave, ultracompetent professionals of *The High and the Mighty* or *Airport*. His flying skills are rusty after a decade on the ground, and his experiences in combat have left his self-confidence in tatters. Helped by ground controllers, fellow passengers, and a sympathetic flight attendant, he rediscovers both his skills and his nerve in time to save the day.

Extravagant updates of "Flight into Danger" continue to appear. The 1975 film *Airport 1975*, a spiritual though not literal sequel to *Airport,* takes place aboard a Boeing 747 that suffers a midair collision with a small private plane. The airliner's flight crew is killed, and one of the flight attendants must take over the controls until a replacement pilot can be put aboard a jet helicopter and lowered, by cable, through the gaping hole in the 747's cockpit. Thomas Block's novel *Mayday* (1979) takes place aboard a supersonic airliner crippled by an accidental missile strike. A private pilot—one of three people aboard still able to function—is left to bring the plane safely home. John J. Nance's *Blackout* (2000) involves another 747 and another incapacitated flight crew—alive this time but blinded by a mysterious flash of light. Responsibility for bringing the plane down safely falls to a small committee of passengers that, collectively, has all the skills necessary for the job. The new pilot, for example, is a teen-aged boy who honed his skills flying virtual 747s on his personal computer's flight-simulator program. Brian Lecomber's *Talk Down*

(1978) is the far-more-plausible story of a young woman with no flying experience who must land a small plane when its pilot suffers a heart attack. She quickly forms a bond with a flying instructor in another small plane who, flying in formation with her, talks her through the process.[16]

The appeal of stories about passengers taking over for dead or injured flight crews lies in the fact that they give the passengers a chance to participate in their own salvation. They turn some of the passengers, at least, from passive victims awaiting rescue into heroically active agents. Stories of (fictional) plane crashes, where most of the passengers survive only to find themselves marooned deep in the wilderness, appeal on a similar level. The survivors cannot do anything to stop their plane from crashing, but they *can* take active steps to overcome the postcrash dangers they face. The main characters of novels like Ernest K. Gann's *Island in the Sky*, Alistair MacLean's *Night without End*, or Gary Paulsen's *Hatchet*—as well as those of films like *Lost Flight*, *The Last Flight of Noah's Ark*, or *Castaway*— all have, unlike the passengers in *The High and the Mighty* or *Airport*, the chance to save themselves. Elleston Trevor's 1964 novel *The Flight of the Phoenix* (filmed in 1965) represents the ultimate variation on this story. When a transport plane crashes in the remote North African desert, the survivors build a smaller plane from the wreckage and fly to safety.[17]

Virtually all tales of midair crises do have one crucial element in common: the care they take to humanize the passengers and crew of the imperiled airplane. The process is natural and seamless in memoirs since the individual in peril is also the storyteller. It is also present in fiction, where its pedigree stretches back to novels like Thornton Wilder's *The Bridge of San Luis Rey* and movies like *Grand Hotel* and *Stagecoach,* and in nonfiction, where the obvious inspiration is Walter Lord's *A Night to Remember.* Airplane-in-crisis stories from *The High and the Mighty* onward have routinely introduced the passengers as they board the flight, using dialogue and (occasionally) flashbacks to give depth and dimension to each. Frequently, the crisis that unites all the characters in danger occurs at or after the midpoint of the story, only after the audience is sufficiently engaged in the characters lives to care about what happens to them.

The meet-the-passengers device can, of course, be reduced to the kind of stale, shallow formula used in films like *Airport 1975* and ruthlessly parodied in *Airplane!* Used thoughtfully, however, it can raise midair-crisis stories to the level of literature. Gary Pomerantz's widely praised *Nine Minutes, Twenty Seconds: The Triumph and Tragedy of ASA Flight 590*, for example, draws much of its emotional power from the fact that it is as much about people as machines.[18] The "tragedy" of the subtitle is the failure of routine safety procedures to catch the cracked propeller that failed and caused the crash. The "triumph" is the courage and determination of individual crew members, passengers, and rescuers, each of whom is portrayed as an individual.

The ways of establishing an emotional connection between the passengers and audience are, particularly onscreen, almost limitless. *Airport* uses nearly a third of its narrative to follow the intersecting paths of the main characters as they move to and through Lincoln International. *Miracle Landing* opens with a series of brief scenes showing the main characters away from their jobs, relaxing. *The Flight of the Phoenix* stops at one point while the pilot of the crashed plane tells the story of an earlier crash that still haunts him. *Slattery's Hurricane* intersperses its hero's dangerous flight into the eye of a hurricane with a series of flashbacks to earlier moments in his (mostly misspent) life. It is clear by the end of the story that Slattery's act of selfless heroism has saved not only the city of Miami but also perhaps his soul. *The Hindenburg,* a fictionalized 1975 film about the last flight of the great German airship, spends most of its running time exploring the lives of characters who, audiences know, will spend the last moments of the trip fighting for their lives when the airship catches fire. The film ends with a scene designed to underline the randomness of such disasters: a still photograph of each significant character appears in turn, and an off-screen narrator intones their fate, "Survived . . . survived . . . dead . . . dead . . . survived. . . ."[19]

Fatal Crashes

Air crashes that kill everyone aboard *do* happen, both in fiction and in fact. For obvious reasons, however, the stories told about them are very different from those told about crises—or crashes— where most survive. Occasionally, far more often in fiction than in fact, the stories about fatal accidents emphasize their senseless randomness. The Everley Brothers' song "Ebony Eyes"(1960), for instance, concerns two young lovers separated by death when the airliner carrying her to their hastily arranged wedding crashes. The films *Random Hearts* (1999) and *Bounce* (2000) reverse the story, focusing on couples brought together by the loss of loved ones in a plane crash.[20] Far more often, however, the stories attempt to find order and meaning in an event that seems disorderly and meaningless.

The most familiar of these plots involves the postcrash search for a cause and a way to prevent similar accidents in the future. The heroes of such stories are the crash investigators. They are aided by a supporting cast of witnesses, survivors, and other pilots, all of whom have a personal stake (because they will fly again in the future) in discovering and fixing the problem. The consistent message of such stories is that crashes, though tragic, ultimately make flying safer by calling attention to hidden flaws in design, maintenance techniques, or operating procedures that can then be corrected. The flaw becomes the "villain," which the heroes must first identify and then vanquish. Find-and-fix stories thus fit neatly into larger narratives about the inevitability of technological progress. They not only reassure audiences that technology gets better (specifically, less risky) over time but also show *how* the process works.

One of the first widely told find-and-fix stories emerged from the 1931 crash that killed the legendary Knute Rockne, head football coach at the University of Notre Dame. Rockne was forty-three and at the height of his considerable fame when he boarded a three-engine Fokker F-10 airliner in Kansas City for a trip to Los Angeles. Ninety minutes into the flight, the Fokker lost a wing and tumbled out of the sky, crashing in a field near Emporia, Kansas. Investigators quickly identified the cause of the crash. The F-10, like many aircraft of the time, had a wooden frame, and dry rot had developed, unnoticed, in the main wing spar. Overstressed by turbulent air encountered along the edges of a thunderstorm, the fatally weakened spar broke, causing the wing to snap off.[21]

Public opinion quickly shifted the blame from the specific Fokker F-10 that had crashed to the F-10 as a type and, from there, to wood-framed and three-engine airplanes in general. The shift destroyed the market for the once-popular F-10 and contributed to the closing of General Aircraft Corporation, the branch of General Motors that built Fokker designs under license in the United States. It also hastened the introduction of a new generation of all-metal airliners by allowing airlines to promote them as safer. Jack Frye, whose airline, Transcontinental and Western Air Transport, had operated the F-10 in which Rockne died, came under particularly intense pressure to replace his remaining F-10s with another aircraft. Unable to purchase any of Boeing's new model 247—the first of that firm's all-metal airliners—he commissioned a new design that became the Douglas DC-2.[22] Entering service in 1934, the DC-2 offered greater speed, comfort, and capacity than any other airliner, including the year-old Boeing 247. Its larger successor, the legendary DC-3, completed the revolution. The Rockne crash thus became, in the public's mind, the "cause" of the DC-2, the DC-3, and the beginnings of safe, efficient air travel in the United States.

Six years later the *Hindenburg* disaster doomed passenger airships as surely as the Rockne crash had doomed wood-framed airplanes. Most of the western powers had experimented with airships during the 1920s and 1930s, but only Germany used them to carry paying passengers. Unable to obtain sufficient supplies of helium, German engineers filled their airships with hydrogen—more buoy-

Figure 14. The DC-3 was the revolutionary successor to the DC-2, one of the first streamlined all-metal airliners. Their development was hastened by the 1931 crash of a Fokker F-10 airliner, caused by undetected rot in a wooden wing spar, that led to a public backlash against F-10s specifically and wooden airplanes in general. *Courtesy Library of Congress, LC-USZ62-95489.*

ant but highly explosive. It lifted the *Graf Zeppelin* throughout its career (1928–37) and the *Hindenburg* through ten roundtrip crossings of the Atlantic in 1936, all without incident. On May 7, 1937, however, something went terribly wrong. Approaching a mooring mast at Lakehurst, New Jersey, after the first transatlantic flight of a new season, the *Hindenburg* suddenly caught fire. Less than a minute later, she was a smoking hulk on the ground. The fact that only thirty-six of the ninety-seven people aboard died—most of them crew members working inside the hull—made only a slight impression on the public's consciousness. The memories that remained vivid were newsreel images of the giant airship engulfed in flames. The running commentary of radio reporter Herb Morrison, though recorded separately, became a soundtrack for the disaster. His anguished voice and distraught cries of "Oh, the humanity!" heightened distant listeners' sense that a uniquely terrible tragedy was unfolding.[23]

Hydrogen—over seven million cubic feet of it in the *Hindenburg*'s gas cells—quickly became the focus of the postcrash investigations. Hydrogen burned, the *Hindenburg* had burned, and the connection seemed obvious.[24] Opinions on the cause of ignition varied—a stray spark inside the ship, static charges from a just-passed thunderstorm, a saboteur's bomb—but in the end they mattered little. Passenger airships had acquired, in less than a minute, an indelible reputation as flying deathtraps. The late-1930s introduction of long-range flying boats clearly hastened the end of the dirigibles. They could match or exceed the airships' speed and, crucially, fly in the storms of winter as well as the fine weather of summer. The public, however, saw (and continues to see) the end of the passenger airship primarily as a response to the *Hindenburg*, the abandonment of an inherently unsafe technology after a horrifying demonstration of its flaws.

Since the 1930s, find-and-fix stories have been told many other times. These later retellings typically involve not an entire class of aircraft but a single type. They are typically mounted by manufacturers and operators of a troubled design in order to maintain (or restore) public confidence in their aircraft after a high-profile crash or series of crashes. Told in this form, the stories end not with the eradication of the type but with its improvement and (as a result) its resurrection. They were told about the DeHavilland Comet in the early 1950s, the Lockheed Electra in the early 1960s, and the McDonnell Douglas DC-10 in the middle to late 1970s. Partly as a result, all

Figure 15. The rapid and fiery destruction of the German dirigible *Hindenburg* in 1937 shocked Americans who saw it replayed in newsreels or heard Herb Morrison's description on the radio. The shock combined with concerns about the safety of airships to hasten the end of commercial airship travel, already threatened by the advent of long-range airplanes. *Courtesy New York World-Telegram and Sun Newspaper Photograph Collection, Library of Congress,* LC-USZ62-127529.

three types survived bad publicity, temporary loss of public confidence, and powerful but irrational suspicions that they were somehow "jinxed." British Airways and Air France, sole operators of the Concorde, deployed the storyline with great aplomb after one of the supersonic airliners crashed at Paris on July 25, 2000, killing 113. The two airlines countered serious doubts that the thirty-year-old design would ever fly again with detailed, public-friendly reports of redesigned tires, reinforced fuel tanks, and other technical improvements. The Concorde resumed passenger service on November 7, 2001.[25]

Find-and-fix tales are also popular in fiction. Novels such as Basil Jackson's *Flameout*, John J. Nance's *Final Approach,* and Michael Crichton's *Airframe* all deal with investigations of serious airliner accidents (though in Crichton's case, not a crash). The film *Fate Is the Hunter* follows a retired pilot's attempt to clear an old comrade's name by investigating the crash that killed him and left only a single survivor among his fifty-four passengers and crew. The acknowledged classic of fictional find-and-fix stories, however, is Nevil Shute's 1948 novel *No Highway*. Filmed in 1951 as *No Highway in the Sky*, it focuses on the engineer-hero's efforts to prove that a new airliner, the Reindeer, is vulnerable to metal fatigue and structural failure after a certain number of hours in the air. The protagonist finds himself, at one point, flying across the Atlantic aboard a Reindeer. Initially preoccupied, he slowly realizes that it has been flying long enough to have reached the crisis point, putting him and his fellow passengers in immediate danger. The story reflects Shute's background as an aeronautical engineer and anticipates, by a year, the real-world troubles of the DeHavilland Comet.[26]

While find-and-fix stories of problems solved and technology improved -are the most common recountings told about high-profile air crashes, they are not the only ones. A second type of story uses the crash itself as a setting for heroic actions by the crew, the passengers, or onlookers. On July 19, 1989, a United Airlines DC-10 en route from Denver to Chicago suffered an explosion in one of its engines that disabled most of its hydraulic systems and left its controls virtually useless. The plane was diverted to the airport in Sioux City, Iowa, where it made a fiery crash landing. News coverage of the crash quickly focused—with good reason—on the plane's thirty-five-year-veteran captain, Al Haynes. The skill with which Haynes landed the nearly uncontrollable plane meant that nearly two-thirds of those aboard—185 of 296 passengers and crew—survived. His postcrash interviews, mixing modesty about his extraordinary feat and sorrow over his inability to save everyone aboard, firmly established him in the public's mind as a hero.[27]

Public memories of the crash in January, 1982, of an ice-laden Air Florida 737 into the Potomac River are also tied to the heroes it produced. Lenny Skutnik, a civil service employee who witnessed the crash, dove into the river to pull an injured woman to safety. Donald Usher and Eugene Windsor—a Park Police helicopter crew—used their aircraft to lift one survivor after another from the freezing water. Five times, an initially anonymous survivor passed the helicopter's rescue harness to others clinging, along with him, to the airliner's half-submerged tail. When the helicopter returned a sixth time, he was gone. Roger Rosenblatt eulogized passenger in an essay titled "The Man in the Water." It concluded: "He could not make ice storms, or freeze the water until it froze the blood. But he could hand life over to a stranger, and that is a power of nature too. The man in the water pitted himself against an implacable, impersonal enemy; he fought it with charity, and he held it to a standoff. He was the best we can do." It was those images—not the changes in deicing procedures established as a result—that caused the Air Florida crash to linger in the public's mind.[28]

A third type of story focuses neither on the airplane nor on the survivors and their rescuers but on the dead. Its purpose is neither to reassure nor to inspire but to attach meaning to an otherwise senseless tragedy. The crash and the resulting deaths become, in these stories, part of some larger pattern of events. Treating them that way makes them at least marginally easier to bear.

Such stories typically have meaning only to those with a close connection to the victims. The death of the entire U.S. national figure skating team in a 1961 plane crash in Belgium became, for fans of the sport, part of a similar tale of triumph following tragedy. The triumph came in the team's gradual rebirth, and especially in the career of Peggy Fleming, who became its leading member. Fleming, a promising eleven-year-old unknown in 1961, lost her coach in the crash. She went on, in the seven years that followed, to five national and three world titles, reaching the climax of her amateur career when she won the sole U.S. gold medal of the 1968 Winter Olympic Games. The 1962 crash of a chartered airliner in Paris, which took the lives of 106 members of the Atlanta Arts Association, set in motion another story of death and rebirth that still resonates in the At-lanta arts community. The city's Woodruff Arts Center (originally named Memorial Arts Center) was opened in 1968 as a tribute to those killed, and their names, carved in black granite, are listed on a memorial on the front lawn. The story of the community's rebirth af-ter the crash resonates with Atlanta's image of itself as a city reborn from the ashes of the Civil War.[29]

Stories about the victims of plane crashes can also have darker shadings. The crash that killed rock musicians Buddy Holly, Richie Valens, and J. P. "The Big Bopper" Richardson in February, 1959, has been a fixture of American popular culture since Don McLean made it the centerpiece of his immensely popular 1971 song "American Pie."[30] The song's deliberately complex, symbol-laden lyrics treat the crash as a cultural watershed that separates the exuberant innocence of the 1950s from the wrenching upheavals of the 1960s. Buddy Holly's music, McLean suggests, was the spirit of the 1950s; when he died, the decade died with him. When John F. Kennedy Jr. died in a plane crash off Martha's Vineyard in July, 1999, the crash instantly became the newest chapter in a half-century-long tale of Kennedy family tragedies. News reports recited the litany of previous Kennedy deaths, believers in a "Kennedy curse" weighed in, and conspiracy theorists hinted darkly at sabotage.[31]

Postcrash tales like those told about Holly and (especially) Ken-nedy offer death without symbolic rebirth; they offer no triumph to leaven the tragedy. They do, however, ground the deaths in a larger pattern, offering an alternative to the even bleaker idea that they were simply random events.

Disappearances

Death in a plane crash is one thing. Disappearance—a (pre-sumed) crash without wreckage, bodies, or a sense of finality—is something else. Like ships that go to sea and never return, aircraft that take off and (seemingly) never land leave behind a cloud of un-resolved loose ends and uncertain outcomes. The unique nature of flying means, however, that disappearances also leave room for hope. The sky is the traditional boundary between the physical and spiri-tual realms. Heaven and all that it encompasses lies, in Western cul-ture, somewhere just beyond it. Pilots' ability to rise into the sky at will places them a step or two closer to the angels than ordinary folk.

This long association of the sky with gods, spirits, and the afterlife adds a unique dimension to the deaths of pilots—especially those whose aircraft are never found.

French pilot Georges Guynemer, leader of a crack World War I fighter squadron, disappeared somewhere over the western front in 1917. Amelia Earhart, easily the best-known American pilot after Charles Lindbergh, disappeared over the Pacific Ocean in 1937. Antoine de St. Exupéry, the internationally famous author of *Wind, Sand, and Stars* and other lyrical books about flying, disappeared over the Mediterranean in 1944 while returning from a military reconnaissance flight. All three stories have been told hundreds of times since, but all the retellings have a common thread: the use of the word "disappeared" in place of "crashed."

Rationally, "disappeared" only evades the truth. Airplanes, their pilots, and their passengers do not simply wink out of existence. "Disappeared" works as a euphemism for "crashed" because an airplane going down at sea or in the wilderness seldom leaves many traces. "Disappeared," like "lost at sea," leaves no hope that the one lost will ever return home, but it glosses over the grim details of their final moments. It even suggests, in a way that "lost at sea" does not, that those lost have departed this life for the next in the most direct way possible—flying until, somewhere beyond the sky, they reach Heaven. The verses of a popular song composed after Amelia Earhart's disappearance acknowledge that her plane had crashed at sea, but the refrain wishes her "happy landings" at a heavenly aerodrome.[32] A 1918 French painting titled *The Death of Guynemer* shows angels lifting the young ace from his doomed fighter and preparing to bear him away to Heaven.[33]

John Magee's famous poem "High Flight" taps into the same idea with exultant descriptions of flying amid towering clouds and beams of sunlight, descriptions very similar to traditional Western depictions of Heaven. The final lines make the link complete:

> And, while with silent, lifting mind I've trod
> The high untrespassed sanctity of space,
> Put out my hand, and touched the face of God.

Magee composed the poem in September, 1941, while serving as a fighter pilot in the Royal Air Force. Three months later he was dead, killed when his Spitfire descended from an overcast sky and—too low for Magee to bail out safely—collided with an Avro Oxford trainer.[34] The poem is seldom reprinted without reference to its author's youth, brief career, and death in the cockpit, all of which link him to earlier heroes like Guynemer and Ball. Readers are thus encouraged to imagine the hand of God reaching down, at the last moment, to free Magee's soul from his doomed airplane.

The climax of William Goldman's script for the 1975 adventure film *The Great Waldo Pepper* borrows freely from Magee's imagery. Waldo, an ex-barnstormer working as a stunt pilot in 1920s Hollywood, emerges from a mock dogfight with his fragile biplane too badly damaged to land safely. Having intentionally left his parachute behind, he has no means of escape. Grinning and waving at a comrade, he banks away into one of the towering cumulus clouds that has formed the backdrop for their dogfight. The cloud gradually obscures Waldo's plane until it disappears entirely. "Waldo," the stage direction reads, "never comes out of the cloud." Rationally, the direction is simply an indication of when to cut away from the shot. It hints, however, that Waldo and his plane will never actually touch the ground, that they are on their way to some aviator's Valhalla where the winds are always fair and the skies are always blue. The 1943 film *A Guy Named Joe*—fantastic where *Waldo Pepper* is realistic—begins with its pilot-hero (killed in a brave attack on an enemy warship) arriving in just such a "pilot's heaven."[35]

A Guy Named Joe is not, however, about the afterlife. Soon after his arrival, the spirit of Pete Sandige (Spencer Tracy) is ordered back to Earth by "The General" (Lionel Barrymore), his heavenly "commanding officer," who is the local avatar of Saint Peter or, perhaps, God. His new "mission" is to serve as a guardian angel to a group of young pilots training for combat. Sandige carries it out admirably, despite the fact that one of the pilots is falling in love with the late airman's former girlfriend, and in one scene even helps *her* fly a plane at a crucial moment. The idea of dead pilots reaching back from the afterlife to aid the living is also prominent in fiction such as Spencer Dunmore's *The Sound of Wings* and (purported) nonfiction like John G. Fuller's *The Ghost of Flight 401* and *The Airmen Who Would Not Die*. Frederick Forsyth uses it with particular skill in his novella *The Shepherd*, the story of a jet fighter pilot whose compass and radio fail while he is crossing the North Sea in a thick fog on Christmas Eve, 1957. Lost and low on fuel, he is guided to safety by a World War II bomber that appears out of the fog. Noting the bomber's markings, he inquires about it after he lands, only to be told that both plane and pilot disappeared over the North Sea on Christmas Eve, 1944.[36]

Disappearances of pilots and planes need not, however, have religious overtones or involve an afterlife. They are often connected, especially in fiction, to other kinds of spirits or mysterious forces that lurk in (or beyond) the skies. The disappearance of Flight 19, a formation of five U.S. Navy torpedo bombers lost off the coast of Florida in 1945, has been ascribed to magnetic anomalies, secret weapons, time warps, and the effects of the "lost continent" of Atlantis. Stephen Spielberg's 1977 film *Close Encounters of the Third Kind* suggests alien abduction as the cause. One of the first scenes shows the discovery of the planes, still intact and functional, in the middle of the Sahara Desert. One of the last shows the bewildered pilots emerging from a giant alien spaceship that has landed in Wyoming.[37] Aliens play similar roles in John Varley's 1985 science-fiction novel *Millenium* (where they kidnap passengers from doomed airliners) and in "The '37s," a 1995 episode of the television series *Star Trek: Voyager*, in which twenty-fourth-century space travelers encounter Amelia Earhart on a distant planet. "The Odyssey of Flight 33," a 1961 episode of the television series *The Twilight Zone*, concerns a jet airliner thrown, apparently by the combination of its own speed and a freak tail wind, back in time. Stephen King's short story "The Langoliers," published in the 1990 collection *Four Past Midnight*, concerns six passengers in the first-class cabin of an airliner who are somehow thrown (with the plane, though without the crew or any other passenger) into a dimension slightly *outside* of time.[38]

Visions of vanished fliers landing at Elysian airfields or, like guardian angels, watching over those who continue to fly in this world cushion the shock of air crashes in two ways. They suggest first that fliers who disappear from our world may simply have gone elsewhere and so continued to do what all fliers do, travel in exotic realms beyond the comprehension of ordinary folk. Second, for those who routinely venture into the aerial borderland between Earth and Heaven, the transition from this life to the next is seamless and natural. Even in death, fliers find the sky a warm and welcoming place.

Stories from September 11

The coordinated seizure and destruction of four airliners on September 11, 2001, was among the most devastating acts of peacetime

CRASHES AND OTHER CATASTROPHES

terrorism in history. It was also (though seldom thought of in such terms) the worst aviation disaster in history. A total of 266 passengers and crew died aboard the airliners, and nearly 3,000 others died at the crash sites in New York City and Washington. The government, media, and public have all—with good reason—treated the September 11 attacks as an act of terrorism or an act of war. The central role of commercial airliners has ensured, however, that government, media, and public alike have *also* continued to respond to the attacks *as* air disasters. The September 11 crashes have thus given rise, like earlier disasters, to a wide variety of stories told by, and for the benefit of, the witnesses and survivors. The outlines of the tales are familiar, but the details that fill in those outlines give the stories unprecedented power.

The first to emerge were those of heroism at the crash site: survivors and rescue workers who helped others to safety and, too often, lost their own lives in the process. One widely circulated photograph showed three firefighters raising an American flag on a makeshift pole amid the rubble of the World Trade Center towers, an image that echoed the famous 1945 photograph of U.S. Marines raising the flag during the Battle of Iwo Jima. A drawing by Pulitzer Prize–winning editorial cartoonist Mike Lukovich, alluding to firefighters who died trying to reach the burning upper floors of the towers, shows a small group standing atop a cloud. "We made it to the top," one observes. Beyond them, in the background, are the gates of Heaven.[39] Rick Rescorla, a British expatriate who served as chief of security for the South Tower headquarters of Morgan Stanley, directed the evacuation of thousands of his coworkers from offices spread over twenty floors. All but a handful of Morgan Stanley employees—three in some versions of the story, seven in others—escaped with their lives. Rescorla was among those lost. Like the "Man in the Water" at the 1982 Air Florida crash, Rescorla was lauded nationwide and hailed as a symbol of courage and self-sacrifice.[40]

A second, slightly later wave of stories about the September 11 crashes concerned the victims. Many of these were put forward by surviving friends and relatives either formally in postattack interviews or informally on the makeshift memorials that sprang up around the remains of the World Trade Center towers. A few came, in effect, from the victims themselves—tape recordings of final phone calls made from the airliners before they crashed or the twin towers before they collapsed. Still others came from, not just through, the news media. The *New York Times* and National Public

Radio (NPR) took the unusual step, in the days following the disaster, of composing brief obituaries—a few lines apiece—for hundreds of those who died aboard the airliners and in the buildings that the airliners struck. Such tributes were a compromise between the lists of names typical of breaking-news coverage of air disasters and the more detailed biographical sketches established through dialogue and flashback in air-disaster fiction or pages of exposition in longer nonfiction. The NPR obituaries ran only a few lines each but sought to capture the essence of their subjects' personalities in a few telling details. A typical one, read by Bob Edwards on the September 19 broadcast of NPR's *Morning Edition,* describes its subject this way: "Rhonda Sue Rasmussen, a civilian worker in the Pentagon, learned on September 10 that she had gotten her transfer to California. She and her husband thought about staying home on September 11 to celebrate, but their sense of duty led them to show up for work. When [American Airlines] Flight 77 hit the building, her husband Floyd escaped, but Rhonda did not." These profiles, memorials, and snippets of conversation did what such stories have always done: they gave faces and voices to the dead. They allowed—and encouraged—the public to see the victims not as data points in an ever changing death toll but as individuals with lives and loves that were tragically cut short by the disaster.[41]

A third, still later wave of stories about the crashes used the well-established find-and-fix "plot." They applied it, however, not to a flawed aircraft design but to the flawed security systems that had permitted four coordinated hijackings. Collectively, they did for the airline industry as a whole what earlier find-and-fix stories had done for the manufacturers of troubled airplanes, creating a strong impression of rapid, focused, coordinated efforts to identify and eliminate dangerous flaws in the system. Hijackers had smuggled lethal weapons through security checkpoints, past ill-trained private security officers? Create a new Transportation Security Agency to certify and oversee a new generation of better-trained guards. Hijackers had forced their way into airliner cockpits? Reinforce the cockpit doors and consider arming pilots with firearms or electric stun guns. Airliners were vulnerable to bombs smuggled aboard in checked luggage? Mandate the (eventual) screening of every bag by sophisticated explosives detectors. The changes, well publicized by the government and the airline industry, have unquestionably transformed air travel and produced tangible changes in the passenger's

experience. If and to what degree they have improved security remains to be seen.[42]

The most memorable story, however, to emerge from the September 11 crashes was that of United Airlines Flight 93, the fourth
to be hijacked, the last to crash, and the only one to cause no casualties on the ground. Apparently intended to strike the U.S. Capitol,
the aircraft crashed instead in rural Pennsylvania after passengers
gathered makeshift weapons and launched a counterattack against
the hijackers. The crash of Flight 93, under any other circumstances,
would have been seen as an unalloyed tragedy. Context is everything, however, and the passengers' uprising is now commemorated
as a moment of triumph within a much greater tragedy. It was to the
September 11 attacks what the abortive sortie of the battleship USS
Nevada was to the Japanese attack on Pearl Harbor, a powerful symbol of resolve and defiance at a time when such symbols were badly
needed. "Let's roll," the words that signaled the beginning of the
counterattack, became a popular rallying cry and, in the hands of
veteran rock musician Neil Young, a popular song, much as navy
chaplain Howell Forgy's exhortation to "Praise the Lord and pass the
ammunition" did after Pearl Harbor. The final moments of Flight 93
have been chronicled in four books, scores of articles, and at least a
dozen songs in addition to Young's "Let's Roll." The crash site, a re-
claimed strip mine miles from anywhere, has become a place of pil-
grimage and, like "Ground Zero" in New York, the site of makeshift
memorials.[43]

The story of Flight 93 has now become legend, a tale told and retold to illustrate important truths. What those truths are and why
the story of Flight 93 is compelling to so many are questions beyond
the scope of this book. A partial answer to both may lie, however, in
the fact that to many, those who perished aboard Flight 93 died, literally, in action. Air travel in the jet age is an inherently passive activity. Passengers are expected (and politely reminded) to remain
firmly belted in their seats except when smooth air permits brief for-
ays to the lavatory. The emphasis on passivity is redoubled in times
of crisis. Safety information cards firmly prescribe it: In the event of
an emergency landing, stay in your seat, brace against the seatback
in front of you, and listen for a crew member's instructions.[44] The
passengers of Flight 93 broke that pattern. Confronted with a midair
crisis whose outcome they *could* influence, they seized the opportunity and acted decisively. Their actions blurred the once rigid

distinction between fictional airline passengers (who could act in a crisis) and real ones (who could not). There is little doubt that, when would-be terrorist Richard Reid attempted to detonate his explosives-laden shoes on a Paris–Miami flight in December, 2001, the passengers who tackled and subdued him did so with the fresh example of Flight 93 in their minds.[45]

Few transportation disasters linger in the public mind for more than a generation. Collective memories dim as those who "witnessed" the disaster, either firsthand or through news accounts, age and die. The Fokker F-10 crash that killed Knute Rockne and reshaped commercial air travel has been forgotten by all but aviation historians and die-hard Notre Dame fans. Memories of the *Hindenburg* explosion linger, thanks to stunning newsreel footage, but memories of the other lost dirigibles of the era (*Akron, Macon, Shenandoah,* and *R-101*) have long since faded. Air travelers younger than forty board, without a second thought, DC-10s on which their parents might well have refused to buy a ticket. Public memories of the four September 11 crashes are still, at this writing, painfully fresh. Whether they will remain so (like memories of the *Hindenburg*) or fade (like memories of most other air disasters) remains to be seen.

6
· · · ·

Wings into Space

*T*he questions began in the United States almost as soon as World War II ended: What if rockets had wings and airliner-style cabins and made regularly scheduled departures from ordinary airports? What if they could take off and land horizontally as airliners do, subjecting their passengers to no more G-forces than a carnival ride? What if one could fly into space as routinely and as easily as one flies to destinations on Earth? Winged rockets that provide routine, airliner-style access to space are a distinctively American dream—and an unusually durable one. Their promise has remained fresh and bright despite the passage of decades in which reality has consistently failed to live up to expectations.

The world of post–World War II America shaped the dream of winged rockets in three important ways. First, rockets capable of reaching the upper layers of the atmosphere had become a reality. The U.S. Army had, as part of "Operation Paperclip," acquired a number of German V-2 missiles as well as much of the engineering team that designed them. Transporting both to the United States, the army began experiments with the captured equipment that led to the development of intercontinental ballistic missiles and boosters capable of putting large payloads into Earth orbit. Second, global air travel had become a fact of life. The new generation of airliners developed during the war and put into service immediately afterward allowed travelers to cross continents and oceans at unprecedented speeds and in relative comfort. The new airliners also brought lower fares, and airlines worked hard to convince Americans that any destination, no matter how distant, now lay within easy reach. Third, American optimism about technology was at a peak unequalled before or since. Technology had won the just-completed war and, with atomic bombs a U.S. monopoly, seemed likely to ensure peace for years to come. Antibiotics had begun to revolutionize medicine, and "miracle" pesticides like DDT were eradicating mosquitoes (and with them malaria). Manufacturers, eager to entice postwar buyers, offered glittering promises of the better life their products would create. The darker sides of these advances—arms races, fallout shelters, drug-resistant bacteria, smog-choked cities, and poisoned water— had yet to emerge. Technology, for the moment, seemed to offer a quick and efficient solution to every problem.[1]

The dream of winged rockets was born where these three cultural currents met and merged. Faith in the power of technology to solve any problem and overcome any obstacle made it easy to believe that the V-2 would lead to passenger- and cargo-carrying rockets, just as the bombers of 1918 led to the continent-spanning airliners of 1948. These machines, and the world of routine rocket travel they would create, became central to Americans' images of the near future.

The 1940s and 1950s

The heyday of the winged rocket in American popular culture was the decade before *Sputnik* (1947–57). Images of gleaming winged rockets and confident descriptions of the future they would soon create appeared in print, in films, on television, and on the shelves of toy stores. The dream of winged rockets was linked, to a degree it would never be again, to even larger visions—huge orbiting space stations, lunar bases, and ships built in Earth orbit for the exploration of other planets—and reflected the place, the time, and the minds in which they were formed. They embodied the postwar worldview of the American middle class: its faith in the inevitability of progress, its willingness to embrace new technology, and its conception of America as a nation shaped by its frontiers. Space, so the dream went, would be the next frontier. Spaceships would be the canoes and covered wagons, the riverboats and railroads, that would enable its exploration and eventual settlement.[2]

Hundreds of writers, illustrators, filmmakers, designers, and other artists played with the idea of winged rockets in the decade after World War II. Four, however, merit special attention. Robert Heinlein's fiction, Willy Ley's nonfiction, Chesley Bonestell's illustrations, and George Pal's films stand apart both in the clarity of their vision and in the breadth of their influence. Individually and collaboratively, they place winged rockets at the center of Americans' postwar visions of and hopes for the future.

Robert Heinlein was one of America's leading science fiction writers. He was among the first such writers in the postwar era to escape from the literary ghetto of pulp magazines and place his short stories in widely read "slick" publications like *The Saturday Evening Post*. He was also among the first to secure hardcover publication for his novels, including a dozen young-adult books for Scribners. Heinlein's stories, prominently featuring winged rockets, thus reached millions who were not regular science fiction readers. The heroes of *Rocketship Galileo* (1947), the first of the young-adult novels, make the first trip to the Moon in such a vehicle. "Space Jockey," published in 1947 and typical of Heinlein's contributions to *The Saturday Evening Post*, takes place in a future where winged rockets provide regular shuttle service between Earth and an orbiting space station. Neither story, however, is *about* winged rockets; both treat them as an ordinary and (to the characters) familiar part of life in the near future.[3]

The heroes of *Rocketship Galileo* create their moon ship by converting a cargo-carrying rocket they buy, secondhand, from its original owners. They do the conversion work themselves and learn to fly at an established school for training commercial rocket pilots. All of this suggests that winged, cargo-carrying rockets are the DC-3s of their near-future day—simple, robust machines built in quantity and used for mundane purposes. Jake Pemberton, the title character in "Space Jockey," is a pilot for a spaceship line operating between Earth and the Moon. He is at his apartment in New York City, enjoying a day off, when the line's scheduling office calls him back to work. "Going to work," for Pemberton, means riding to orbit aboard a winged shuttle that makes two round trips a day from its base in Colorado to the company's Earth-orbiting space station. He sleeps through most of the trip, which endless repetition has made routine for him, and treats the station not as a technological marvel but as a bland, austere stopover on the way to somewhere else. He is, despite his seemingly exotic job, just another white-collar worker who travels frequently. The winged rocket that carries him into Earth orbit to board a ship for the Moon is, in his world, just another kind of commuter train.

Science writer Willy Ley brought the same authoritative tone to his nonfiction writings about winged rockets that Heinlein brought to his fiction. Ley's ability to juxtapose predictions with detailed explanations of the science behind them made them even more compelling. Born in Germany, he took an active interest in rocketry during the 1920s and 1930s but fled to the United States in 1935, when the Nazis militarized all rocket research. The first edition of Ley's *Rockets* appeared in 1944 as a German team led by his old protégé, Wernher Von Braun, was preparing the world's first ballistic missile, the V-2, for use against Britain. *Rockets* quickly became the definitive English-language treatment of its subject. It appeared in a series of revised, expanded editions, the later ones under an extended title that reflected their expanded subject matter: *Rockets, Missiles, and Space Travel*. "The Rocket into Cosmic Space," chapter 10 of the 1951 edition, is typical of Ley's style. It is a dense, detailed exploration of the problems of overcoming Earth's gravity and filled with careful explanations of mass ratios, exhaust velocities, and the advantages of multistage rockets. A few pages from the end, however, it reaches this climax: "We can, therefore, confidently expect 'space rockets' in the near future, rockets which will rise high above the atmosphere but return to Earth eventually."[4]

Ley, like Heinlein, imagined spaceships with wings. "Naturally," he began, "the ship will look like a large rocket, like V-2, but taller in proportion, ten to twelve times as tall as its largest diameter. It will have short wings, placed far back; either strongly swept back or delta wings."[5] Ley took his usual care to justify these features, which became virtually standard on the designs of the 1940s and 1950s. Wings would allow the rocket to make a gliding reentry and a runway landing. A long, slender hull would facilitate the use of atomic power by maximizing the crew's distance from the engines and minimizing the area of the heavily shielded (and therefore heavy) bulkhead between them. Tail fins and a sharply pointed nose, like those of the V-2, would ease the ship's passage through Earth's atmosphere. Ley did not mention, and perhaps did not recognize, the sleek beauty of the design he so carefully described.

Architect-turned-artist Chesley Bonestell not only recognized the beauty of winged rockets but also depicted it with great skill.

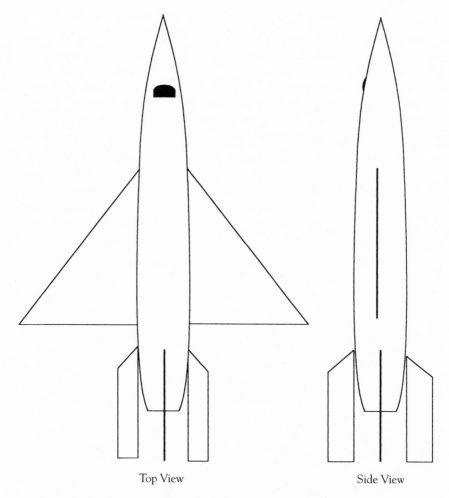

Top View   Side View

Figure 16. The classic winged rockets of the 1940s and 1950s bore a strong family resemblance to the V-2 guided missiles developed by rocket engineer Wernher Von Braun and his team for Nazi Germany during World War II. The principal differences were size and, of course, wings. *Drawn by the author.*

His illustrations of spaceships and the surfaces of other planets began to appear in 1944, the same year as Ley's *Rockets*. Bonestell prided himself on basing his works on the latest scientific knowledge, and since Ley was the preeminent authority on rocketry in the English-speaking world, Bonestell's spaceships reflected Ley's ideas. His early images of rockets (from 1946 and 1947) show "winged V-2s" virtually identical to those Ley described.[6]

The *Conquest of Space*, published in 1949, brought Bonestell's and Ley's work together for the first time.[7] The scientist's command of factual detail and the artist's ultrarealistic visual style perfectly complemented one another. Together they reinforced the idea that travel by winged rocket was not a vague "someday" possibility but a near-future certainty. *Conquest* sold briskly and became *the* key book in the self-education of many American space enthusiasts.

Conquest's images of winged spaceships are gathered in two groupings, one after each of the first two sections of text. The first, which illustrates Ley's discussion of orbits, shows the Earth as seen from two intercity transport rockets, one on its way from New York to San Francisco, the other bound across the Atlantic from North America to Europe. The views are similar to those that passengers see from the windows of conventional airliners, but because the altitude is far greater, they encompass far more. A few minutes after a rocket takes off, passengers can see the entire length of Long Island. At the apex of its trajectory, 250 miles above Nebraska, all five Great Lakes are visible as if on a map and Hudson's Bay stretches away toward a curved horizon. The second group of illustrations, which portray the exploration of the Moon, also features winged rockets prominently. For example, one shows residents of a lunar base preparing to launch the "weekly transport to Earth."[8] Both groupings reinforce the same message: winged rockets will be the routine long-range transportation of the future, linking not only distant cities and but also distant planets.

Hollywood producer George Pal put the ideas of Heinlein, Ley, and Bonestell on movie screens across the country. Intrigued, like many Americans, by rapid advances in rocketry, he set out in 1949 to make Hollywood's first realistic depiction of space travel, *Destination Moon*. Striving for technical accuracy, Pal hired Heinlein as one of the film's writers and bought a widely circulated treatment of *Rocketship Galileo* to use as the basis of the script. Heinlein, according to legend, joined the project on one condition—that Pal hire Bonestell to paint the backdrops for the scenes set on the Moon. Whether or not at the writer's urging, Pal did hire Bonestell. Released in 1950, the film shows a lunar surface looking virtually identical to that pictured in Bonestell and Ley's *Conquest of Space*. The film's spaceship, *Luna*, is a classic Ley-style machine, with a sleek, narrow hull and (naturally) wings.[9]

The climax of Americans' postwar fascination with winged rockets began to take shape in 1951, the year after *Destination Moon* premiered. Intrigued by a space-travel symposium organized by Ley,

managing editor Gordon Parks of *Collier's* magazine assigned one of
his associates, Cornelius Ryan, to investigate the possibility of an article on the subject. Ryan did so and proposed that *Collier's* devote
an entire issue to a printed version of Ley's symposium, inviting
space-travel experts to contribute articles and commissioning high-
quality illustrations of their ideas. Originally planned for a single
issue, the project eventually stretched over eight issues published between 1952 and 1954. The first, which reached newsstands in mid-
March, 1952, used a Bonestell painting of a winged rocket as its
cover illustration and carried the bold headline, "Man Will Conquer
Space *Soon*."[10]

The first article set the tone for the series. Its title asked "What
Are We Waiting For?" and its text adopted the same matter-of-fact
tone that Ley and Heinlein had used. The series, as *Collier's* estimated audience of twelve to fifteen million readers learned in the
opening paragraphs, was "the story of the inevitability of man's conquest of space. What you will read here is not science fiction. It is
serious fact."[11] An all-star cast of experts presented the facts: Ley,
Harvard astronomer Fred Whipple, astrophysicist James Van Allen,
U.N. international law expert Oscar Schachter, and—above all—
master rocket engineer Wernher Von Braun. The strategy for space
travel outlined in the series was, above all, Ley's and Von Braun's,
and winged rockets were central to it.

Ten or twelve such rockets, cycling between Earth and orbit like
the freighters of the 1948–49 Berlin Airlift, would carry aloft the
materials for a space station and the men to assemble it. Once the
station—a two-spoked wheel 250 feet across—was complete, another round of flights would bring up its food, water, air, equipment,
and first crew. Normal operations would involve a ship from Earth arriving every third day with fresh food, visitors, and other cargo. Such
a flight schedule, Ley states in his article "A Station in Space," could
readily be handled by two active rockets and two more in reserve.
Each ship's turnaround time between flights would be a week or less.
The six or eight rockets used during the construction phase (but not
needed for normal operations) then would be available for other orbital construction projects. Among them, Von Braun envisioned,
would be ships first to survey the Moon, land on the Moon, and—
the climax of the series and his vision—eventually land on Mars.
Chesley Bonestell and Fred Freeman, who provided many of the illustrations for the series, designed the winged rockets in close con-
sultation with Von Braun.[12] Their creations had shorter, broader

bodies and longer wings than the ships of the late 1940s but bore an unmistakable family resemblance.

The *Collier's* series reached millions of readers in its eight-issue run, but its influence did not stop there. The magazine's publicity staff relentlessly promoted the articles by every means imaginable: window displays, press kits, news and photo releases, and speeches by Von Braun, including an interview with John Cameron Swayze on NBC's *Camel News Caravan*. The articles themselves, expanded and repackaged, reappeared as three books published by Viking: *Across the Space Frontier* (1952), *Conquest of the Moon* (1953), and *The Exploration of Mars* (1956). George Pal's 1955 space-travel epic, *The Conquest of Space*, uses the near-future world depicted in *Collier's* as the setting for its story about the first mission to Mars. Walt Disney, intrigued by the *Collier's* series, gave his longtime collaborator Ward Kimball a million dollars to produce three hour-long film adaptations. The first two films—*Man in Space* and *Man and the Moon*—aired at least four times in 1955 on Disney's Sunday-night television series, *Disneyland*. The first airing of *Man in Space* brought the *Collier's* vision of a future built by winged rockets to a larger audience than ever before, nearly 100 million viewers.[13]

The third of the Disney films, *Mars and Beyond*, had been scheduled to air in 1956. Delayed by other work, it was completed in late 1957 and aired on December 4, exactly two months after the launch of *Sputnik* startled the world. *Sputnik* and its American rivals, *Explorer* and *Vanguard*, rode wingless rockets into orbit. Their successors, spacecraft carrying animal or human passengers, rode bigger (but still wingless) rockets and returned by falling through the atmosphere rather than gliding. The space age had arrived, but in a form very different from what Americans had imagined over the preceding decade. Just reaching and maneuvering in orbit would be formidable challenges. There would be, for the time being, no transcontinental rockets, no privately funded voyages to the moon, no orbital construction projects, and no twice-a-week shuttles to orbiting space stations. There would be spaceships, but they would not have wings—at least, not yet.

The Shuttle—Dreams

The new millennium was still a generation away when filmmaker Stanley Kubrick completed *2001: A Space Odyssey* in 1968.[14]

It is hardly surprising, with the *Collier's* series only fifteen years in the past, that his vision of space travel in 2001 reflected the dramatic conventions of the 1950s. Scientist-bureaucrat Heywood Floyd reaches the Moon in *2001* the same way pilot Jake Pemberton does in "Space Jockey," a winged shuttle to an Earth-orbiting space station where deep-space transports dock. Floyd's space station, a gleaming white wheel like the one in *Collier's,* is more comfortable than Pemberton's, but he is no more impressed by it than Pemberton was by his. Similarly, Floyd takes the wonders of space travel for granted and sleeps through his shuttle flight to orbit. Winged rockets are common in Kubrick's imagined future, and as they did in the imagined futures from the forties and fifties, they help make space travel routine.

NASA was thinking along similar lines in the late 1960s as it decided what goals to pursue after the moon landings of Project Apollo had ended.[15] The official report of its planning committee, *America's Next Decades in Space* (1969), offered a *Collier's*-style vision of the future. It proposed a space station, lunar bases, and missions to Mars, all supported by a fleet of winged rockets that would make regular trips to Earth orbit. Space enthusiasts were thrilled. Others, including Pres. Richard Nixon and most of Congress, offered tepid support at best. NASA grimly pared away one project after another until only the winged "space shuttle" was left. Even it, however, was subject to paring. Originally intended to be fully reusable, it was redesigned as a reusable winged "orbiter" launched on the back of a disposable fuel tank and two recoverable booster rockets. The appeal of this hybrid design—the system now in use— lay in its comparatively low development costs. It was the best winged spaceship that the limited money available to NASA could buy.

Determined to make a virtue of necessity, NASA promoted the shuttle as an ideal vehicle for expanding access to space. The shuttle fleet, it promised, would make twenty-four flights a year, each one capable of carrying forty thousand pounds of cargo and a crew of two pilots and up to six passengers—scientists, technicians, or anyone whose presence would enhance the mission. Each orbiter would have an operational lifetime of one hundred flights, during which each would more than pay for itself. Launching a satellite aboard the shuttle would, in time, become cheaper than launching it aboard a conventional disposable booster. Contracts for satellite launches would more than cover the shuttle's operational costs, and in time the standard rate would fall to one hundred dollars per pound. NASA thus established high expectations for its new spacecraft before it even left the drawing board.[16] Intentionally or not, the space agency revived the most optimistic late-1940s visions of winged rockets and encouraged the public to believe that the shuttle would fulfill them. It would make flights to Earth orbit cheap, easy, and frequent enough that "anyone" could take one.

NASA's relentlessly optimistic promotion of the shuttle even began before the program was approved. Wernher Von Braun, leader of the team whose rockets were putting men on the Moon, wrote in the issue of *Popular Science* for July, 1970, that shuttle operations would resemble those of an airline. His article was titled "Spaceplane That Can Put You in Orbit," and readers were clearly meant to see themselves, not a generic person, in the "you" of the title. President Nixon struck a similar note when he announced official approval of the shuttle program on January 5, 1972. The shuttle would "revolutionize" space transportation by providing routine, low-cost access to near-Earth space. It would also democratize space travel by reducing the rigors of launch and reentry, thus "making the ride safer, and less demanding for the passengers." Once the shuttle fleet became operational, Nixon told the nation, "men and women with work to do in space can 'commute' aloft, without having to spend years in training." A NASA-produced booklet published later that year explained the shuttle as a vehicle combining the best features of a rocket and an airplane, and press releases began to describe the orbiter as "about the size of a DC-9," McDonnell-Douglas's then-ubiquitous twin-engine airliner. George Mueller, head of the Office of Manned Space Flight, reached out to skeptical scientists with late-1972 articles in *Interavia* and *Aeronautics and Astronautics*. Far from draining money from NASA's science programs, he argued, the shuttle would create new opportunities to do science in Earth orbit. Scientists would now be able to go into orbit, making observations and conducting experiments firsthand.[17]

Designing, building, and testing the shuttle—first in the atmosphere, then in orbit—took most of a decade. The first orbital test flight, STS-1, lifted off from Cape Canaveral in April, 1981. A steady stream of books and articles about the shuttle kept public interest and expectations high, however, in the intervening years. Articles appeared in every category of periodical: general-interest magazines like *Smithsonian* and specialized ones like *Astronomy*, academic journals like *Technology in Society*, and science fiction monthlies like *Analog*.[18] "Are Skylab and the Space Shuttle Worth the Investment?" asked NASA administrator James Fletcher in the title of a 1974 article for *Government Executive*; not surprisingly, he concluded that they were. Another 1974 piece stated its case for the shuttle in its title, "Space Shuttle—Vital to Man's Future." James Haggerty extolled the "Space Shuttle, Next Giant Step for Mankind," a 1976 article that explicitly compared it to the first Moon landing in 1969. Invoking the democratizing effects of the Model T on the automobile, Michael O'Leary entitled a 1977 article, "Shuttling, the Ford of the Space Ways."[19]

Anticipation of the first orbital test flights in the early 1980s both raised expectations and intensified writers' optimism even further. Readers of *Science Digest*, for example, could begin the new decade with Dennis Meredith's contribution in January, 1980: "It's 1985. Come with Commander Mitty and His Crew on a Routine 'Milk Run' Flight in the Space Shuttle." The title, with its reference to James Thurber's daydreaming hero Walter Mitty, was silly; the excitement was real. John Noble Wilford, the *New York Times* science correspondent who had covered NASA for two decades, argued in 1980 that the shuttle signaled the reemergence of the U.S. space program after a decade in eclipse. Popular novelist James Michener, writing as the shuttle *Columbia* stood poised for its first flight, equated space exploration with America's westward expansion in an article tellingly titled "Manifest Destiny."[20]

The shuttle performed almost flawlessly in the four orbital test flights it made during 1981 and 1982. With the last one, Pres. Ronald Reagan declared the tests completed and the system fully operational. Speculative books and articles gave way to news coverage of actual flights—flights that had a decade's worth of towering promises to fulfill.

The Shuttle—Realities

The official purpose of the shuttle program was to create routine access to space.[21] "Routine access" from the beginning had meant two things, regular flights and seats on them for anyone with a compelling need to go. NASA planned for both capabilities long before shuttle operations began. It established twenty-four flights a year—

Figure 17. The space shuttle, first flown to orbit in April, 1981, remains the only operational winged spacecraft. Shuttles (like *Endeavor*, shown here) use an expendable fuel tank and two booster rockets in order to reach orbit and return to Earth by gliding. *Courtesy NASA.*

a flight every two weeks—as its goal and constructed a runway at Florida's Kennedy Space Center to accommodate shuttle landings and quick turnarounds. It also expanded and restructured the astronaut corps and announced its intention to allow people from outside NASA to fly on the shuttle. Hard pressed to meet its announced schedule (in the shuttle's most productive year thus far, 1985, there were nine flights), NASA focused on the human dimension of "routine access"—opening space to a wide range of travelers.

At the dawn of the shuttle era, NASA reorganized the astronaut corps into two distinct groups. Pilots, two of whom would fly on each shuttle mission, would be astronauts as the public had always known them, ex-military jet pilots chosen for their flying skills and ability to master complex systems. Mission specialists, also NASA employees and also professional astronauts, would be chosen for their expertise in science and medicine. They would take primary responsibility for accomplishing the mission's objectives: satellite launch or repair, on-board experiments, or other scientific projects. NASA also created a third designation specifically with the capabilities of the shuttle in mind. Payload specialists would be one-time passengers from outside the agency who would apply their specialized expertise to a particular objective on a particular flight. They would be the first space travelers who were not professional astronauts.[22]

Bill Lenoir and Joe Allen, the first mission specialists to fly, went into space on STS-5 in November, 1982, the fifth shuttle flight and the official beginning of "normal" operations. Four missions later, in November, 1983, Bryon Lichtenberg and Ulf Merbold became the first payload specialists to go into orbit. Merbold, a citizen of Germany, also became the first foreign national to go into space aboard an American ship. The press paid close attention to such "firsts," which injected a welcome element of human interest into the shuttle program, and the first five years of operations provided a steady supply. Guion Bluford and Ellison Onizuka became, respectively, the first African American and Asian American to fly in space. Sally Ride, a physicist, became the first American woman in space in 1983; a year later, geologist Kathryn Sullivan became the first woman to walk in space. Rhea Seddon, a physician, became the first mother in space in 1985; a widely reprinted photograph showed her young son, Paul, joyfully running to greet her on her return to Kennedy Space Center. Sen. Jake Garn of Utah flew as a payload specialist aboard *Discovery* in 1985, and Rep. Bill Nelson of Florida did the same aboard *Columbia* in 1986.[23]

The teacher-in-space program, which drew eleven thousand applications, was a natural extension of the process.[24] It was also a powerful symbolic statement. Most of the nonpilot crew members on the first twenty-four shuttle flights had been scientists and engineers; the rest, like Garn and Nelson, owed their seats to political clout. American culture not only reveres scientists and engineers but also treats them as "different," set apart in popular stereotype by their towering intellect and deficient social skills. Politicians too are "different," set apart, again in popular stereotype, by their towering ambition and deficient moral compass. The first "teacher in space" would "the first ordinary American" to leave the Earth.

Christa McAuliffe was not, strictly speaking, "ordinary." She was physically fit, highly intelligent, educated, and ambitious—chosen by distinguished judges from a field of eleven thousand others. On a deeper and more significant level, though, the description was true. She embodied many citizens' idealized images of an "ordinary American." She was smart, enthusiastic, charming, funny, and clearly beloved by her students, colleagues, and family. She also *looked* the part—not movie-star beautiful but girl-next-door pretty. Her selection meant that more Americans than ever before could look at a prelaunch photograph of a shuttle crew and see someone like themselves.

McAuliffe's selection was not a literal promise by NASA to start flying "ordinary Americans" into space on a regular basis. Many saw it, however, as a promise that such a time was coming. If a Christa McAuliffe could fly on the shuttle today, and other individual "ordinary Americans" (whether teachers or journalists) could fly on it in years to come, then truly democratic access to space was only a matter of time. The shuttle itself might not have room to accommodate everyone who wanted to go into space, but its successors would. The shuttle was, as Ben Bova casually observed during the year of its first orbital flights, "only the *first* reusable spacecraft to be flown." Others, soon to be built, would offer more seats and lower the "ticket price" in the bargain.[25]

The destruction of the *Challenger* and the death of McAuliffe and her six crewmates permanently altered the shuttle's public image. Addressing the nation on the night of the disaster, Pres. Ronald Reagan eulogized the *Challenger* astronauts as brave explorers. They had blazed a trail into the unknown for others to follow and, as trailblazers sometimes do, paid with their lives.[26] It was stirring rhetoric, widely repeated in the public mourning that followed the disaster, but it marked a shift in public attitudes toward the program. Voyages of exploration are never "routine," and pathfinders do not "commute" into the unknown.

NASA and the shuttle program survived the *Challenger* disaster and the long hiatus in shuttle operations that followed, but the image of the orbiter as a vehicle for routine, even casual, space flight did not. When it resumed operations in September, 1988, NASA promoted the shuttle's reliability, versatility, and ability to undertake missions that would otherwise go undone: in-flight satellite repair, maintenance of the Hubble telescope, and the assembly of the International Space Station. Quality rather than quantity became the new measure of the vehicle's effectiveness. Twenty-four flights a year, once the Holy Grail of shuttle operations, quietly vanished from NASA's public statements. The fleet settled, during the 1990s, into a comfortable routine of five to six flights a year. Scientists and engineers continue to fly on such missions, and retired Project Mercury astronaut John Glenn flew in 1998, but there are no plans for other "ordinary Americans" to follow Christa McAuliffe. Barbara Morgan, McAuliffe's backup, declared herself "ready to fly" soon after the explosion. NASA accepted her offer twelve years later, concurrent with (and perhaps because of) its decision to fly John Glenn. Significantly, when Morgan rejoined the space program in 1998, it was as NASA's first "Educator Mission Specialist"—that is, as a professional astronaut and full-time NASA employee. She was, until the loss of *Columbia* in February, 2003, scheduled to fly to the International Space Station sometime in 2004.[27]

The destruction of *Columbia* threw NASA's ambitious flight schedule for 2003 and 2004 into disarray. It also cast doubt on the agency's decision, announced the previous year, to suspend the search for a vehicle to replace the shuttle. The disaster reduced the shuttle fleet from four vehicles to three, and the fact that *Columbia* had been the oldest of the four orbiters raised serious questions about the wisdom of NASA's plans to keep the fleet operating for fifteen to twenty more years. Like the *Challenger* disaster seventeen years earlier, it was both an occasion for mourning and a license to dream.

Variations on a Dream, 1986–2003

The loss of both *Challenger* and *Columbia* shattered any remaining hope that the shuttle was or could ever become the "space airliner" Americans had dreamed of since the 1940s. The loss of two shuttles and fourteen astronauts did not, however, diminish the intensity of the dream itself and may, in fact, have given it new life by freeing (or forcing) even those who cherished it to think beyond the shuttle. The plans for "next generation" American spacecraft that emerged after the loss of *Challenger* and drew new attention after the loss of *Columbia* took a variety of forms. Some proposed vehicles were designed to take off and land vertically, others horizontally. Some had wings, others had bodies shaped to provide lift, and some had no lifting surfaces at all. Some, using a combination of rockets and air-breathing engines, were designed to double as intercity transports. Most of the designs shared a common element, however: they were single-stage-to-orbit (SSTO) vehicles, capable of going from ground to orbit and back without jettisoning any parts.

The SSTO designs lay at or beyond the cutting edge of aerospace technology but came wrapped in familiar promises: They would cut travel time between major cities to an hour or two. They would make access to low Earth orbit routine and inexpensive, creating lucrative opportunities for manufacturing and tourism. They would enable humankind to create a permanent presence in space, revolutionizing everyday life. SSTOs would, in other words, fulfill the promises made for winged rockets in the late 1940s and the space shuttle in the late 1970s.

The idea of such a successor to the shuttle made its spectacular public debut only days after the *Challenger* disaster. President Reagan, in a State of the Union address originally scheduled for the night of *Challenger*'s launch, assured Congress and the American people: "[T]his nation remains fully committed to America's space program. We're going forward with our shuttle flights, we're going forward to build our space station, and we are going forward with research on a new Orient Express that could, by the end of the next decade, take off from Dulles Airport, accelerate up to 25 times the speed of sound, attaining low earth orbit and flying to Tokyo within two hours."[28] The project was officially the National Aero-Space Plane, but "Orient Express" was the name that stuck. Once the name of a legendary luxury train that linked Paris to Istanbul, it had irresistible connotations. "Orient" (mostly replaced by "Asia" in everyday usage) still suggests exotic, faraway places. "Express" (long gone from railroading but resurrected by the delivery company Federal Express) connoted fast, dependable transport. The new project's name perfectly captured the promise of SSTO spaceships: reliable access to exotic places, whether on Earth or off.

Pioneering the Space Frontier, the final report of the National Commission on Space, appeared shortly after Reagan's address and reinforced his call for an SSTO spaceship. It lent an air of validity to the project. The commission, appointed early in Reagan's second term, had credibility to spare. Nobel Prize–winning physicist Luis Alvarez, space-colony designer Gerard O'Neill, and former NASA administrator Thomas Paine were all members, joining a half-dozen leading figures in the aerospace industry, astronauts Neil Armstrong and Kathryn Sullivan, and retired test pilot Chuck Yeager. Charged by Congress to "formulate a bold agenda to carry America's civilian space enterprise into the 21st century," the commission did just that. Their report became the *Conquest of Space* of a new generation, with space artist Robert McCall bringing the future to life as Chesley Bonestell once had. The report outlined a fifty-year plan filled with space stations, lunar and Martian bases, and a fleet of deep-space transports that maintained a "bridge between worlds." It was, with minor adjustments, the future as it had been envisioned many times before: by Heinlein in "Space Jockey," by Von Braun in *Collier's*, by Kubrick in *2001*, and by countless writers on the eve of the shuttle's 1981 debut. Like them, this vision depended on "flexible, routine access to orbit" at low cost.[29]

The commissioners saw SSTO ships as the key to providing such access for passengers and high-value cargo, outlining two basic designs for the vehicles. The first was a winged rocket. It would look like a smaller version of the shuttle orbiter—blunt-nosed and thick-bodied with rocket engines clustered in its tail. Like the shuttle, it would take off vertically and glide to a landing. Like the largest airliners, it would have modular systems for ease of maintenance and modular cargo containers for ease of loading. Preparations for launch would be handled by automated systems overseen from the cockpit by the pilots. The SSTO rocket would, like airliners but unlike the shuttle, be capable of "all-weather" operations, grounded only by the worst storms. The second design, preferred by the commissioners but requiring more-advanced technology, was a "space plane." It would look like a supersonic airliner—needle nosed and slender bodied, with engines carried beneath narrow delta wings—and would operate like one. Taking off and landing horizontally from conventional airstrips, it would function as a hypersonic jet (capable of operating above Mach 5) in Earth's atmosphere and a rocket beyond it. The same aircraft, differently configured, could also serve as an intercity transport—the president's "Orient Express."[30]

A private group, the Citizens' Advisory Council on National Space Policy, also joined the push for SSTO spaceships in the spring of 1986. The council was a diverse, loosely affiliated group of aerospace experts and professional writers—Jerry Pournelle, Larry Niven, Dean Ing, and (fittingly) an aging Robert Heinlein. Many of the council's conclusions echoed those of the National Commission on Space. The shuttle, they argued, was too old, too fragile, and too expensive to serve as America's principal means of access to Earth orbit. Something better was needed, specifically, an SSTO spaceship developed, at least initially, with government money but built and operated by private corporations.

The council's 1986 report was published as an eighty-four-page pamphlet titled "America: A Spacefaring Nation Again." Distributed by the pro-space L5 Society, it reached an audience that, though modest in size, was highly educated, scientifically literate, and deeply committed to space exploration. G. Harry Stine, coeditor of the pamphlet, reached a similar audience in monthly articles he wrote for *Analog*, a leading science fiction magazine. Many dealt with SSTO spacecraft, and titles like "Comes the Revolution . . ." and "Will They Let the Spaceships Fly?" reflected the council's thesis: SSTO spaceships are the natural next step into space but are opposed by NASA and other entrenched interests. Stine elaborated on his ideas in his book *Halfway to Anywhere*, in which he urged development of a wingless, gumdrop-shaped vehicle called the DC-X as a first step toward more ambitious SSTO projects. Pournelle, Ing, Niven, and other author-members of the council also published articles in support of SSTO vehicles. Like Stine, their status as science and science fiction writers gave them instant credibility with their intended audience.[31]

The National Space Commission and the Citizens' Advisory Council on Space Policy were not alone. *Space: The Next 100 Years*, a lavishly illustrated 1990 book by journalist Nicholas Booth, shows a two-page, three-dimensional cutaway view of an SSTO space plane under the title "Australia in an Hour." Two pages later, another space plane is shown docking at "Tokyo Orbital International," an imagined Japanese-run tourist hotel, sometime in the mid-2020s. Engineering professor Thomas McDonough's 1987 book *Space: The Next Twenty-Five Years*, more restrained in both the scope and presentation of its predictions, exults over "wonderful" and "brilliant" designs for space planes. The accompanying illustration depicts a proposed Boeing design for such a machine. It carries U.S. Air Force insignia on its wings, but its silver, white, and blue paint scheme suggests the livery of a civilian airliner. In 1997 T. K. Mattingly, who flew on Apollo 16 and two early space-shuttle missions, wrote in *Scientific American*'s "Future of Transportation" issue of "A Simpler Ride into Space." The key to such rides, he argues, is the SSTO ships, like those in development under Lockheed's "Venturestar" project, applying new technologies tested by NASA in its (then) ongoing X-33 and X-34 programs.[32]

Figure 18. Single-stage-to-orbit (SSTO) spacecraft, capable of reaching Earth orbit using only their onboard engines and fuel tanks, are widely regarded as the natural successors to the shuttle. The X-33, a NASA pilot project designed to pioneer the SSTO concept, was cancelled in 2001. It was intended to lead to the development of the full-sized spacecraft shown here, to be built by Lockheed-Martin and called "Venturestar." *Courtesy NASA/Dryden Flight Research Center.*

The article's introductory blurb, probably written by *Scientific American* editors based on Mattingly's text, is remarkable for its blend of old promises and new caution. "Technological advances may allow rockets of the next century to operate much as aircraft do today," it begins. "That change might cut the cost of reaching orbit by 10-fold." The qualifying "may" and "might" reflect the unsettled state of the U.S. space program in the late 1990s. The abrupt end of the Cold War had stalled the Strategic Defense Initiative, which would have created a huge demand for space launches. The X-30 project, from which the "Orient Express" would have evolved, had been cancelled in 1996. NASA had concluded that the existing shuttle fleet would still be flyable and adequately meet U.S. needs in the first decades of the new millennium.[33]

At this writing, five years later, the skepticism seems fully war-
ranted. The X-33 program has been cancelled, eliminated from the
federal government's 2002 budget. The X-34, a smaller rocket plane
designed to test engines that might one day drive an SSTO space
plane, has also been scrapped along with the X-38 "crew return vehicle" for the International Space Station. Of the five major programs introduced since 1986 to pave the way for SSTO flight, only
one now remains, the X-43. It is a small, wedge-shaped test vehicle
designed to fit over the nose of a Pegasus rocket that will accelerate
it past Mach 8 in order to test the X-43's aerodynamics at hypersonic
speeds. Its fuselage, twelve feet long, is shorter than some cars; its
wingspan, five feet, is shorter than a man's outstretched arms. The
initial flight test in July, 2001, ended seconds after it began when the
Pegasus rocket propelling the first of three X-43s went out of control
and had to be destroyed for safety reasons. Flight tests of the two remaining aircraft have not yet been scheduled.[34]

At best, the X-43 is a small first step down the road toward airliner-like access to Earth orbit. At worst, it is another dead end. Like
all its predecessors, however, it is the focus of great expectations. A
Popular Mechanics article in July, 2001, assessed the failed flight test
as a minor setback and the X-43 as "an aircraft . . . with a remarkable
pedigree and a promising future." Three of the article's four illustrations show the real X-43. The fourth, the largest and most prominent illustration, though, is an artist's conception of a full-size, operational space plane clearly meant to be a descendent of the X-43.
It is shown dressed in the distinctive red, white, and blue livery of
American Airlines and parked at Gate 35 of an unspecified airport.
A jetway connects it to the terminal, fuel and baggage trucks service
it, and a tow vehicle stands ready to pull it toward the runway. Except for its distinctive shape, it is just another airliner—little different than the Boeing 767 parked at Gate 34. The article's point of
view is evident in its title, "Two Hours to Tokyo," and reinforced in
its subtitle, "The 'Orient Express' Lives."[35]

Whether or not the "Orient Express" lives on in the X-43 is de-
batable. What *is* clear is that the dream of a spaceship that operates
like an airliner is alive and well. It has persisted for more than half a
century, outlasting all the forecasts, predictions, and spacecraft (real
or imagined) that have sprung from it. The winged rockets envisioned by Ley and Bonestell faded away as the real "conquest of
space" began in 1957. We have seen 2001 and found that it was not

like *2001*. The space shuttle, extraordinary achievement though it is, has failed to usher in the bright new future its promoters hoped for. Trips to Earth orbit are more frequent and less expensive than they once were, but they are neither cheap nor routine. Seventeen years after the 1986 State of the Union Address, it still takes thirteen hours to fly from Washington to Tokyo. Despite it all, however, the dream of airliner-like access to space endures.

Conclusion

*T*echnology is, in the end, a symbol of power. The shovel, axe, and plow give us power over the land. The spear, bow, and gun give us power over our enemies and our prey. The ship, train, and automobile give us power over time and distance, as do (by other means) the telephone and television. The electric light gives us power over the daily cycle of light and dark, and our heated, cooled, insulated homes give us power over the yearly cycle of the seasons. Networked computers, in the century just ended, have given us unprecedented power over the building blocks of knowledge. Genetic engineering, in the century just begun, is poised to give us unprecedented power over the building blocks of life itself.

The power that our technology confers on us, both as individuals and as societies, is a source of pride and a basis for hope. We eat better, live longer, and know more than our ancestors. We live in comfort beyond their wildest dreams, knowing that we have less to fear from disease, little to fear from storms, and virtually nothing to fear from wild beasts. We envision a future shaped by further improvements and marvel at technology's power to enhance our lives.

That power is also, however, a source of anxiety and a cause for concern. The tools that clear the land for productive use can, if used unwisely, leave the soil ravaged and desolate. The weapons that keep us safe can also be turned against us. The highways and parking lots that serve our cars are built over green space and once-thriving neighborhoods. The rise of computerized information gathering has eroded our privacy. The rise of genetic engineering, many fear, will erode our humanity. We envision a future shaped by further technological changes and worry about what will be lost in the process.

This double-edged view of technology is deeply rooted in Western culture. We delight in the power that technology gives us but fear being rendered powerless by it. The stories we tell about technology often feature both themes, which are often intertwined so tightly that they cannot be fully teased apart. The 1932 film *Frankenstein*—more familiar and thus more central to our view of technology than Mary Shelley's 1819 novel—is famous for its scenes of the Monster running amuck. It is nearly as famous, however, for its equipment-stuffed castle laboratory and for Dr. Frankenstein's delight in what technology has enabled him to achieve. The film's most famous line of dialogue is not fearful but ecstatic: "It's alive! It's alive!" The 1992 film *Jurassic Park*, a direct cinematic descendent of *Frankenstein*, treads the same thematic ground. Audiences shake their heads at the folly of using genetic engineering to resurrect *Tyrannosauruses* and *Velociraptors* and gasp at the beasts' effortless pursuit of the human heroes. The key to the film's box-office success was not the story or the characters, however, but the dinosaurs themselves. Director Stephen Spielberg portrays John Hammond, his Dr. Frankenstein, as a misguided fool—but still invites the audience to marvel at his creations.

Popular perceptions of aviation, as a group, display a similar ambivalence toward technology. Typically, however, the relationship of the two themes is the reverse of that in *Frankenstein* and *Jurassic Park*. Optimism is the dominant tone, but a dark undertone of caution runs beneath it.

Many visions of the future from the early years of the air age emphasize the inevitability of aeronautical progress and its potential to transform the lives of individuals and societies. Rudyard Kipling imagined a twenty-first century in which "Britannia rules the waves" and, with her great fleets of commercial dirigibles, the skies as well. American progressives saw aviation as a universal solvent for railway monopolies and other intractable economic problems. Students of foreign affairs—amateurs and professionals alike—hoped that aircraft would make war, and perhaps even national boundaries, obsolete. Alfred W. Lawson and Charlotte Perkins Gilman imagined that the human race itself would be transformed by the act of flight. Others, however, saw the coming of aircraft as a dire threat to lives, property, and established ways of life. Years before the first zeppelins released their bombs over London, scores of writers offered dark pictures of cities laid waste and citizens fleeing in panic. H. G. Wells described the destruction of New York City by a German air fleet, and Jack London the extermination of the "Asiatic race" by a Western airborne armada (though London, admittedly, saw his fictional genocide as a triumph). Harold Frazer Wyatt warned his British readers that Britain's failure to build an air fleet left both the home islands and the empire in jeopardy. A 1914 issue of *Sunset* featured, as its cover, a seaplane preparing to release its load of bombs onto the just-completed Panama Canal. All these dark prophecies emphasized a common theme: the invulnerability of aircraft to any force but other aircraft and the abject helplessness of ground dwellers in the face of an aerial attack.

The business of aviation produced heroes, living symbols of national greatness and embodiments national character, in numbers out of proportion to its size. To thousands who followed World War I from the home front, Georges Guynemer *was* France, Oswald Boelcke *was* Germany, and Eddie Rickenbacker *was* America. The glider pilots of post-1918 Germany became a symbol of German resistance to the crushing burdens (real and imagined) imposed by the Treaty of Versailles. The fighter pilots of the Battle of Britain became symbols of British resistance to Nazi aggression. Chuck Yeager embodied the resurgent American nationalism of the 1980s, and his willingness to ignore inconvenient regulations (by flying the X-1 with cracked ribs, for example) seemed cut from the same cloth as the unconventional business dealings of Wall Street traders and the shadowy politics of the Reagan administration's Iran-Contra scheme. But aviation destroys heroes almost as readily as it creates them. Guynemer and Boelcke died in the cockpit, as did Albert Ball, Mick Mannock, Manfred von Richthofen, and countless other World War I aces. Amelia Earhart never returned from her last, greatest adventure, and Lindbergh was feted in Paris by a nation simultaneously grieving for its own heroes, Charles Nungesser and Francois Coli, killed in their attempt to win the Ortieg Prize. The last image of Chuck Yeager in *The Right Stuff* embodies this tension: he is triumphantly alive, having cheated death at the last instant, but horribly injured by his dying aircraft.

The bomber's appeal as a weapon has always been starkly clear. It allows a nation to strike its enemies from a safe distance while putting only a handful of its own warriors in the line of fire. Attacking forces of a few thousand aviators can—and by the end of World War II repeatedly did—kill tens of thousands of the enemy, injure or render homeless tens of thousands more, and tear at a city's physical and social fabric. The grim assessment Stanley Baldwin delivered to Britons in 1932 was right: the bomber—that is, *some* bombers from an attacking force—would always get through, and if they got through, there was little that the ordinary citizen could do but find shelter and wait for the bombs to stop falling. Operational lessons learned in World War II raised doubts about the efficacy of the bomber, though not about Baldwin's central premise. The bomber *had* always gotten through, often at great cost, and Germany's use of the V-2 missile in 1944–45 suggested that a day was coming when aerial bombardment would be literally unstoppable. Citizens of every nation—including by 1950 the United States—were thus obliged to confront the dark side of the bomber's rapid development. Their nation's defenses were no more proof against aerial attack than the enemy's. Their cities and their homes were no more robust. Their friends, families, and loved ones would be just as vulnerable as the enemy's. And they, as individuals, would be just as helpless to prevent it.

Air travel allows individual travelers unprecedented mobility for business or pleasure, mobility that airlines enthusiastically promoted for decades. It shortens trips that once took days or even weeks to a matter of hours and creates opportunities that would be inconceivable without it. One-day out-of-state business trips, two-week overseas vacations, and major-league baseball on the West Coast were all made possible by air travel. More prosaically, so were holiday visits to distant friends and holiday reunions of scattered extended families. Air travel also makes the exotic accessible. The Great Wall of China, the Great Barrier Reef, the beaches of Rio, and the streets of Paris are now less than a day's journey from any major city on Earth. The winged, single-stage-to-orbit spaceships anticipated for more than fifty years will, when they become operational, add Earth orbit to that list of destinations. Gaining the freedom to cross continents or oceans in a matter of hours has come, however, at a cost higher than that printed on the ticket. Air travelers surrender much of their autonomy when they board their flight. Their needs, from the time they enter the airport, are subordinated to those of the technological system that will move them. Many such sacrifices are modest and tangible: limits on the size, weight, number, and contents of bags; limits on anonymity (now that positive identification is required at boarding); and limits on movement within the aircraft cabin. The greatest sacrifice of autonomy, however, is intangible, for passengers, in order to enjoy the extraordinary benefits of air travel, must depend on the near-perfect performance of an imperfect machine. Their options should it fail are limited: no steering wheels to grab (as in a car), no platforms to leap from (as on a train), and no lifeboats to board (as on a ship). The passenger's fate, in the end, cannot be separated from the airliner's.

Aviation in the century since the Wright brothers' first powered flights has been the focus of an extraordinary range of emotions and the subject of an extraordinary body of stories. Many of them have been told by observers whose business is the telling of tales: novelists, filmmakers, songwriters, journalists, and advertisers. Many more, however, are the work of pilots, passengers, and onlookers who, for reasons of their own, were captivated by aviation and felt a need to share what they thought and felt. Even in our machine-laden world, few other technologies have the power to evoke such a diversity of responses from such a wide range of people. It is this power that, a century after the invention of flight, keeps us looking up.

Notes

Introduction

1. James Thurber and E. B. White, *Is Sex Necessary?* (Garden City, N.Y.: Blue Ribbon, 1929), p. ix.

2. Roger Bilstein, *Flight in America: From the Wrights to the Astronauts,* 3d ed. (Baltimore: Johns Hopkins University Press, 2001), chap. 2.

3. *Wings,* dir. William Wellman, writ. John Monk Saunders, Louis Lighton, and Hope Loring (Paramount, 1927); *Hell's Angels,* dir. Howard Hughes et al., writ. Harry Behn et al. (United Artists, 1930); *Air Mail Pilot,* dir. Gene Carroll, writ. Harriet Virginia (Superlative Pictures, 1928); *The Air Legion,* dir. Bert Glennon, writ. Randolph Bartlett et al. (Film Booking Offices of America, 1929); *The Air Circus,* dir. Howard Hawks and Lewis Seiler, writ. C. Graham Baker et al. (Fox, 1928); *Won in the Clouds,* dir. Bruce M. Mitchell, writ. Gardner Bradford and Karl Crusada (Universal, 1928).

4. Dorothy L. Sayers, *Clouds of Witness* (New York: Harper and Row, 1928). Nevil Shute, *The Mysterious Aviator* (New York: Grosset and Dunlap, 1928). Later U.S. reprints of Shute's novel generally use its British title, *So Disdained.*

5. Histories of pulp magazines typically pay little attention to aviation-related titles. Doug Ellis, John Locke, and John Gunnison, *The Adventure House Guide to the Pulps* (Silver Spring, Md.: Adventure House, 2000), includes issue-by-issue checklists for virtually every significant aviation pulp. Jeff Rovin, *Adventure Heroes: Legendary Characters from Odysseus to James Bond* (New York: Facts on File, 1994), includes entries on "G-8" and other pulp aviator-heroes, as does Robert Sampson, *Yesterday's Faces: A Study of Series Characters in the Early Pulp Magazines* (Bowling Green, Ohio: Popular, 1983).

6. For one view of toolmaking and its role in human evolution, see Kathy D. Shick and Nicholas Toth, *Making Silent Stones Speak: Human Evolution and the Dawn of Technology* (New York: Simon and Schuster, 1993). Clive Ponting, *A Green History of the World* (New York: St. Martin's, 1992), and Jared Diamond, *Guns, Germs, and Steel* (New York: Norton, 1997), take the long view of human efforts to adapt the Earth to their needs.

7. A useful single-volume overview is Donald Cardwell, *The Norton History of Technology* (New York: Norton, 1995). Ruth Schwartz Cowan, *A Social History of American Technology* (New York: Oxford University Press, 1997), and Arnold Pacey, *Technology in World Civilization* (Cambridge: MIT

Press, 1990), offer less breadth and less nuts-and-bolts detail but place the technologies they describe in a social and cultural context.

8. On the social and cultural meaning of medieval cathedrals, see David Macaulay, *Cathedral* (New York: Houghton Mifflin, 1973); on electric lighting, see David E. Nye, *Electrifying America: Social Meanings of a New Technology, 1880–1940* (Cambridge: MIT Press, 1990); on the Panama Canal, see David McCullough, *The Path between the Seas* (New York: Simon and Schuster, 1977); on the telephone, see Claude S. Fischer, *America Calling* (Berkeley and Los Angeles: University of California Press, 1992); on the automobile, see Wolfgang Sachs, *For Love of the Automobile*, trans. Don Reneau (Berkeley and Los Angeles: University of California Press, 1992); and David Gartman, *Auto Opium* (London: Routledge, 1994).

9. For a deeper exploration of these themes, see Bayla Singer, *Sex with Gods: A Cultural History of Flying* (College Station: Texas A&M University Press, 2003).

10. On the history of migrations, see Robert P. Clark, et al., *The Global Imperative: An Interpretive History of the Spread of Humankind* (Boulder, Colo.: Perseus/Westview, 1992).

11. Bilstein's *Flight in America* covers the pioneering flights and the expansion of scheduled air service. On bush pilots, see, for example, Gerry Bruder, *Heroes of the Horizon: Flying Adventures of Alaska's Legendary Bush Pilots* (Portland, Ore.: Graphic Arts Center Publishing/Alaska Northwest Books, 1991); and William J. Wheeler, ed., *Skippers of the Sky: The Early Years of Bush Flying* (Markham, Ontario: Fitzhenry and Whiteside, 2000).

12. First published as the third of "Clarke's Laws" in Arthur C. Clarke, "Technology and the Future," *Report on Planet Three and other Speculations* (New York: Harper and Row, 1972).

Chapter 1. Imagining the Air Age

1. For general treatments of the changing pace of technological change, see George Basalla, *The Evolution of Technology* (New York: Cambridge University Press, 1988); and Thomas P. Hughes, *American Genesis: A Century of Invention and Technological Enthusiasm, 1870–1970* (New York: Viking, 1989).

2. See, for example, Joseph J. Corn, ed., *Imagining Tomorrow: History, Technology, and the American Future* (Cambridge: MIT Press, 1986); and Joseph J. Corn and Brian Horrigan, *Yesterday's Tomorrow: Past Visions of the American Future* (New York: Summit, 1984). I. F. Clarke, *Voices Prophesying War: Future Wars, 1763–3749*, 2d ed. (New York: Oxford University Press, 1992), discusses tales of future wars and, by extension, the future technologies they depicted.

3. The best-known examples from the pre-1900 era are Jules Verne's *Clipper of the Clouds* (1885) and its sequel, *Master of the World* (which,

though published in 1904, uses the same giant airship described in *Clipper*). Forecasts of the future were staples of popular nonfiction books about aviation during the 1920s and 1930s and flourished in magazines such as *Popular Science* and *Mechanix Illustrated* after World War II. For a book-length, jet-age example of the genre, see Bernt Balchen and Erik Bergaust, *The Next Fifty Years of Flight* (New York: Harper, 1954).

4. On the history and symbolic role of electricity in the United States, see Thomas P. Hughes, *Networks of Power: Electrification in Western Society, 1880–1930* (Baltimore: Johns Hopkins University Press, 1993); and Nye, *Electrifying America.* On the transformation of domestic life by electricity, see Ruth Schmartz Cowan, *More Work for Mother: The Ironies of Household Technology from the Open Hearth to the Microwave* (New York: Basic, 1983); and Ronald C. Tobey, *Technology as Freedom: The New Deal and the Electrical Modernization of the American Home* (Berkeley and Los Angeles: University of California Press, 1996).

5. Compare, for example, Col. F. N. Maude, "Airships and their Value in War, *Contemporary Review* 94 (1908): 605–609; and T. G. Tulloch, "The Aërial Peril," *Nineteenth Century* 65 (1909): 800–809.

6. Folke T. Kihlstedt, "Utopia Realized: The Worlds Fairs of the 1930s," in Corn, *Imagining Tomorrow*, pp. 97–118; Robert W. Rydell, *World of Fairs: The Century of Progress Expositions* (Chicago: University of Chicago Press, 1993). The sixty-second Apple commercial can be downloaded at <http://www.apple-history.com/gallery.html>. For a Macintosh-centered case study of the computer industry's change-the-world ethos, see Stephen Levy, *Insanely Great: The Life and Times of Macintosh, the Computer that Changed Everything* (New York: Penguin, 2000).

7. Wilbur Wright, "The Aeroplane: What It Will Be Like in Five Years' Time—What Wilbur Wright Thinks," *Motor*, Nov. 17, 1908, pp. 457–58 (quote, p. 457) (reprinted in Peter L. Jakab and Rick Young, eds., *The Published Writings of Wilbur and Orville Wright* [Washington, D.C.: Smithsonian Institution Press, 2000], pp. 196–99 [quote, p. 196]); Joseph J. Corn, *The Winged Gospel: America's Romance with Aviation, 1900–1950* (New York: Oxford University Press, 1983), p. 44; Louis Paulhan, "The Future of Flying," in Claude Grahame-White and Harry Harper, *The Aeroplane: Past, Present, and Future* (Philadelphia: Lippincott, 1911), pp. 294–310 (quote, p. 294).

8. Wilbur Wright, "Flying from London to Manchester," *London Magazine*, Feb., 1909, pp. 617–25 (quote, p. 625) (reprinted in Jakab and Young, *Published Writings*, pp. 201–205 [quote, p. 205]); Paulhan, "Future of Flying," p. 298; Henri Farman, "The Constructional Future of the Aeroplane," in ibid., pp. 262–71 (quote, p. 265).

9. Farman, "Constructional Future," pp. 262–63; Paulhan, "Future of Flying," p. 299; Wilbur Wright, "Wright Considers High Speed Too Dangerous," *Fly Magazine*, Aug., 1911, p. 9 (reprinted in Jakab and Young,

Published Writings, pp. 211–12 [quote, p. 212]); Wilbur Wright, "Wilbur Wright Favors Reliability Tests," *Aero*, Mar. 30, 1912, p. 514 (reprinted in Jakab and Young, *Published Writings*, p. 213); Orville Wright, "Wright Finds Ocean Crossing Risky Just Now," *Aero & Hydro*, Feb. 21, 1914, p. 261 (reprinted in Jakab and Young, *Published Writings*, pp. 213–14).

10. Claude Grahame-White, *The Story of the Aeroplane* (Boston: Small, Maynard, 1911), pp. 378–79; Paul Beck, "Flying Men-o'-War," *Sunset* 24 (Mar., 1910): 253–57 (quote, p. 257); S. F. Cody, ["The Future of Flying"], in Grahame-White and Harper, *The Aeroplane*, p. 314. Mervyn O'Gorman, ["The Future of Flying"], in ibid., pp. 310–13 (quote, p. 311); Paulhan, "Future of Flying," p. 306; A. V. Roe, ["The Future of Flying"], in Grahame-White and Harper, *The Aeroplane*, pp. 316–17 (quote, p. 317). The comments of Cody, O'Gorman, and Roe, as well as those of McClean and Moore-Brabazon (below), are brief, untitled discussions solicited by Grahame-White and printed as appendixes to Paulhan's article.

11. F. K. McClean, ["The Future of Flying"], in Grahame-White and Harper, *The Aeroplane*, pp. 315–16(quote, p. 315); J. T. C. Moore-Brabazon, ["The Future of Flying"], in ibid., p. 314; Farman, "Constructional Future," pp. 263–64; Paulhan, "Future of Flying," pp. 308–309.

12. McClean, ["Future of Flying"], p. 315; Glenn Curtiss, "Flying in an Aeroplane," *Review of Reviews* 40 (Nov., 1909): 609; Farman, "Constructional Future," pp. 265–67 ;Wilbur Wright, "Airship Safe: Air Motoring No More Dangerous Than Land Motoring," *Cairo Bulletin*, Mar. 25, 1909 (reprinted in Jakab and Young, *Published Writings*, pp. 205–206).

13. Orville Wright and Fred C. Kelly, "Flying Machines and the War," *Collier's Weekly*, Jul. 31, 1915, pp. 24–25 (reprinted in Jakab and Young, *Published Writings*, pp. 214–19).

14. Paulhan, "Future of Flying," pp. 300–301.

15. Beck, "Flying Men-o'-War," p. 257 (emphasis added).

16. Rudyard Kipling, *With the Night Mail: A Story of 2000 A.D.* (New York: Doubleday, 1909). The story originally appeared in magazine form in 1905.

17. T. R. MacMechen and Carl Dienstbach, "The Greyhounds of the Air," *Everybody's Magazine* 27 (Sept., 1912): 290–304 (quotes, pp. 291, 294, 304).

18. Harold F. Wyatt, "The Future of Aviation," *The Nineteenth Century and After* 73 (Apr., 1913): 741–48; (May, 1913): 1040–47.

19. [Alberto] Santos-Dumont, "The Future of Air-Ships," *Fortnightly Review* 83 (1905): 443–54 (quote, p. 447).

20. Corn, *Winged Gospel*, pp. 32–34.

21. The case for 1908 as a pivotal year is elegantly stated in Robert Wohl, *A Passion for Wings: Aviation and the Western Imagination* (New Haven: Yale University Press, 1994), pp. 5–30.

22. Explorations of military technology and global politics in the de-

cade before World War I can be found in Paul M. Kennedy, *The Rise and Fall of British Naval Mastery* (London: Allen Lane, 1976); William McNeill, *The Pursuit of Power* (Chicago: University of Chicago Press, 1982); Robert K. Massie, *Dreadnought: Britain, Germany, and the Coming of the Great War* (New York: Random House, 1991); and Kenneth Wimmel, *Theodore Roosevelt and the Great White Fleet* (Dulles, Va.: Brassey's, 1998).

23. Carl Dienstbach and T. R. MacMechen, "The Aërial Battleship," *McClure's Magazine* 34 (Aug., 1909): 342–54 (quote, p. 249); Henry B. Hersey, "The Menace of Aërial Warfare," *The Century Magazine* 77 (Feb., 1909): 627–30 (quote, p. 628); Wyatt, "Future of Aviation," p. 1042.

24. H. G. Wells, *The War in the Air* (London: George Bell and Sons, 1908), p. 207; Jack London, "The Unparalleled Invasion," *McClure's Magazine* 35 (July, 1910): 308–15.

25. Edmund Clarence Stedman, "The Prince of Power of the Air," *The Century Magazine* 76 (May, 1908): 18–26; Harold F. Wyatt, "The Wings of War," *The Nineteenth Century and After* 66 (Sept., 1909): 450–56; Wyatt, "Future of Aviation," pp. 747–48, 1040–46; Hersey, "Menace of Aërial Warfare," p. 627.

26. Alfred Gollin discusses the airplane's emergent role in British defense policy (and politics) in *No Longer an Island: Great Britain and the Wright Brothers, 1902–1909* (Stanford, Calif.: Stanford University Press, 1984); and *The Impact of Air Power on the British People and Their Government, 1909–1914* (London: Macmillan, 1989). On "future war" fiction, see Clarke, *Voices Prophesying War*, for the British; and H. Bruce Franklin, *War Stars: The Superweapon and the American Imagination* (New York: Oxford University Press, 1988), for the Americans.

27. Corn, *Winged Gospel*, pp. 29–50. Most Quimby biographies are aimed at young adult readers, but see Henry M. Holden, *Her Mentor Was an Albatross: The Autobiography of Pioneer Pilot Harriet Quimby* (Rolling Meadows, Ill.: Black Hawk, 1993); and The Harriet Quimby Research Center Web site <http://www.harrietquimby.org>.

28. Corn, *Winged Gospel*, p. 37.

29. Franklin, *War Stars*, p. 84; Corn, *Winged Gospel*, p. 37.

30. Corn, *Winged Gospel*, p. 38.

31. Ibid., pp. 37–43. For a detailed discussion of Lawson's ideas, see Lyell D. Henry Jr., *Zig-Zag-and-Swirl: Alfred W. Lawson's Quest for Greatness* (Iowa City: University of Iowa Press, 1991), pp. 60–78.

Chapter 2. Pilots as National Heroes

1. Paul Brickhill, *Reach for the Sky* (1954; Annapolis, Md.: Naval Institute Press, Bluejacket Books, 2001) is an admiring, uncritical study of Bader and one of the foundations of the Bader legend. More-recent treatments of Bader's life and legend are John Frayn Turner, *Douglas Bader: The*

Biography of the Legendary World War II Fighter Pilot (Shrewsbury, UK: Airlife, 2002); Robert Jackson, *Douglas Bader: A Biography* (London: Arthur Barker, 1983); and Laddie Lucas, *Flying Colours: The Epic Story of Douglas Bader* (London: Hutchinson, 1981).

2. Dominick A. Pisano et al., *Legend, Memory, and the Great War in the Air* (Seattle: University of Washington Press, 1992), pp. 11–41. Scholarly treatments of the fighter's (and fighter pilot's) role in the war, many of which also address the popular image of the ace, include Lee Kennett, *The First Air War, 1914–1918* (New York: Free Press, 1991); Richard P. Hallion, *The Rise of Fighter Aircraft, 1914–1918* (Annapolis, Md.: Nautical and Aviation, 1984); Denis Winter, *The First of the Few: Fighter Pilots in the First World War* (Athens: University of Georgia Press, 1993); and Peter Liddle, *The Airman's War, 1914–1918* (New York: Blanford, 1987).

3. "Frequently Asked Questions," *Old Rhinebeck Aerodrome Home Page*, Sept., 2002 <http://www.oldrhinebeck.org/FAQ's.htm>.

4. Pisano, *Legend, Memory, and the Great War*, p. 29.

5. Fictionalized examples include "Snoopy's Christmas," a 1967 novelty song recorded by Barry Winslow and the Royal Guardsmen as the second sequel to their "Snoopy vs. Red Baron," and *The Great Waldo Pepper*, a 1974 film about American barnstormers and stunt pilots of the 1920s.

6. Wohl, *Passion for Wings*, pp. 229–38 (quotes, p. 235).

7. Quoted in ibid., p. 236. Bourdeaux's biography appeared as *Vie Héroïque de Guynemer* ([The] Heroic Life of Guynemer) in 1918; the most recent English-language edition is *Georges Guynemer: Knight of the Air* (North Stratford, N.H.: Ayer, 1972).

8. Ball's life and career are covered in Walter Alwyn Briscoe, *Captain Ball, V.C.* (London: Jenkins, 1918); and Chaz Bowyer, *Albert Ball, VC* (London: Kimber, 1977). The initials "V.C." denote a winner of the Victoria Cross, the British armed forces' highest decoration for valor.

9. For a short account of Boelcke's career, see Wohl, *Passion for Wings*, pp. 211–23; and Peter Fritzsche, *A Nation of Fliers: German Aviation and the Popular Imagination* (Cambridge: Harvard University Press, 1992), pp. 67–82.

10. Johannes Werner, *Knight of Germany: Oswald Boelcke, German Ace*, trans. Claud W. Sykes (1932; reprint, New York: Presidio, 1991) (also available online, along with the autobiographies of Rene Fonck and Ernst Udet, in the untitled books section of *Pilots and Planes of the First Air War* <http://www.pilots-n-planes-ww1.com/Books/Books-3.htm>); Fritzsche, *Nation of Fliers*, pp. 76–78, 80 (quote, p. 78).

11. Fritzsche, *Nation of Fliers*, pp. 90–94. William E. Burrows, *Richthofen: A True History of the Red Baron* (New York: Harcourt, 1969), stands out among more recent biographies for its simultaneous attention to the man and the legend that grew around him.

12. Fritzsche, *Nation of Fliers*, pp. 81, 99. For a color reproduction of the Richthofen cover, see Wohl, *Passion for Wings*, p. 251.

13. Fritzsche, *Nation of Fliers*, pp. 86–95; Kennett, *First Air War*, pp. 63–82. For detailed analyses of Richthofen's tactics, see Leon Bennett, *Three Wings for the Red Baron: Von Richthofen, Strategy, Tactics, and Airplanes* (Shippensburg, Pa.: White Mane, 2001); and Norman Franks, Hal Giblin, and Nigel McCrery, *Under the Guns of the Red Baron: The Complete Record of Von Richthofen's Victories and Victims* (London: Grub Street, 1995).

14. For a brisk summary of Rickenbacker's life, see Walter J. Boyne, "Rickenbacker," *Air Force Magazine* 83 (Sept., 2000): 68–74. See also Edward V. Rickenbacker, *Fighting the Flying Circus* (1919; reprint, Garden City: Doubleday, 2001) (also available online through the *War Times Journal* Web site <http://www.wtj.com/wars/greatwar>). Edward V. Rickenbacker, *Rickenbacker* (New York: Prentice Hall, 1967), though an autobiography, remains the best full-length account of his life. Finnis Farr's fawning, error-ridden *Rickenbacker's Luck: An American Life* (New York: Houghton Mifflin, 1979) is best avoided.

15. Davy Crockett is the classic example of this American archetype. Frank Luke, the second leading American ace of World War I, reflected a very different (but equally potent) archetype: a taciturn cowboy-loner like the heroes of *The Virginian* (novel 1902; film 1929), *Shane* (novel 1949, film 1953), and *The Man Who Shot Liberty Valence* (film 1962).

16. Mannock's career is covered briefly in virtually every history of World War I aviation. For a deeper, more nuanced view, see Adrian Smith, *Mick Mannock: Myth, Life, and Politics* (London: St. Martin's, 2001).

17. The narrative and analysis in this section follows, and is distilled from, that presented in Fritzsche, *Nation of Fliers*, pp. 103–131, 190–96.

18. Pictured in ibid., p. 105.

19. Ibid., p. 111.

20. Ibid., p. 196.

21. The details of Lindbergh's life and career have been recorded many times. The definitive biography is A. Scott Berg, *Lindbergh* (New York: Putnam's, 1998). Other useful treatments include Von Hardesty, *Lindbergh: Flight's Enigmatic Hero* (New York: Harcourt, 2002); Dominick A. Pisano and F. Robert Van Der Linden, *Charles Lindbergh and the Spirit of St. Louis* (New York: Harry N. Abrams, 2002); and Walter L. Hixson, *Charles A. Lindbergh: Lone Eagle*, 2d ed. (New York: Longman, 2001).

22. Charles A. Lindbergh, *We* (New York: Grossett and Dunlap, 1927). Not satisfied with the account of the flight he gave in *We*—written under deadline pressure and with the help of a collaborator, Fitzhugh Green—Lindbergh returned to the subject in *The Spirit of St. Louis* (New York: Scribners, 1955). His second book won the Pulitzer Prize and

became the basis for a 1956 movie of the same title starring James Stewart as an overage but otherwise convincing Lindbergh.

23. Fitzhugh Green, "A Little of What the World Thought of Lindbergh," appendix to Lindbergh, *We*, pp. 241, 277, 313. All three quotations are from speeches by Herrick, Coolidge, and Hughes wholly or partly reprinted by Green.

24. Earhart, like Lindbergh, has been well-served by biographers. The standard works are Doris L. Rich, *Amelia Earhart: A Biography* (Washington, D.C.: Smithsonian Institution Press, 1989); and Mary S. Lovell, *The Sound of Wings: The Life of Amelia Earhart* (New York: St. Martin's, 1989). Also useful are Susan Butler, *East to the Dawn: The Life of Amelia Earhart* (Reading, Mass.: Addison-Wesley, 1997); and Donald M. Goldstein and Katherine V. Dillon, *Amelia: The Centennial Biography of an Aviation Pioneer* (Dulles, Va.: Brassey's, 1997).

25. Goldstein and Dillon, *Amelia*, p. 41; Railey quoted in Rich, *Amelia Earhart*, pp. 46–47.

26. On Earhart as a public figure, see Susan Ware, *Still Missing: Amelia Earhart and the Search for Modern Feminism* (New York: Norton, 1993).

27. Rich, *Amelia Earhart*, p. 97.

28. A brief, penetrating analysis of the contest is Richard Overy, *The Battle of Britain: The Myth and the Reality* (New York: Norton, 2001). A more detailed narrative is Stephen Bungay, *The Most Dangerous Enemy: A History of the Battle of Britain* (London: Aurum, 2002). Other valuable studies of the Battle of Britain include Phil Craig and Tim Clayton, *The Finest Hour: The Battle of Britain* (New York: Simon and Schuster, 2000); Richard Townshend Bickers, *The Battle of Britain: The Greatest Battle in the History of Air Warfare* (London: Salamander, 1999); Richard Hough and Denis Richards, *The Battle of Britain* (New York: Norton, 1989); Len Deighton, *Fighter: The True Story of the Battle of Britain* (New York: Knopf, 1978); Telford Taylor, *The Breaking Wave: German Defeat in 1940* (London: Weidenfeld and Nicholson, 1967); and Derek Wood and Derek Dempster, *The Narrow Margin: The Battle of Britain and the Rise of Air Power, 1930–1940* (New York: McGraw Hill, 1961).

29. *The Battle of Britain, August–October 1940* (London: His Majesty's Stationery Office, 1941); a 150-page facsimile edition, edited by Peter Coates and including additional information, was published by the Stationery Office in 2001. On the pamphlet's success and effect, see Overy, *Battle of Britain*, pp. 130–31. Churchill offered his own account of the battle in book 2, chap. 1 of *Their Finest Hour*, vol. 2 of *The Second World War* (New York: Houghton Mifflin, 1949).

30. Leonard Mosley, *The Battle of Britain: The Making of a Film* (London: Pan, 1969).

31. For images of the battle, see Leonard Mosley, *The Battle of Britain*,

vol. 3 of *The Time-Life History of World War II* (Alexandria, Va.: Time-Life, 1977); and Philip Kaplan and Richard Collier, *Their Finest Hour: The Battle of Britain Remembered* (London: Artabras, 1991).

32. Patricia A. Turner, *Ceramic Uncles and Celluloid Mammies: Black Images and Their Influence on Culture*, 2d ed. (Charlottesville: University of Virginia Press, 2002); Karen Ross, *Black and White Media: Black Images in Popular Film and Television* (Cambridge, U.K.: Polity, 1995); Donald Bogle, *Toms, Mulattoes, Coons, Mammies, and Bucks: An Interpretive History of Blacks in American Film*, 3d ed. (New York: Continuum, 1994). On the "scientific" basis of racism, see Stephen Jay Gould, *The Mismeasure of Man*, rev. ed. (New York: Norton, 1996); and Pat Shipman, *The Evolution of Racism: Human Differences and the Use and Abuse of Science* (New York: Simon and Schuster, 1994).

33. Charles E. Francis and Adolph Caso, *The Tuskegee Airmen: The Men Who Changed a Nation*, 4th ed. (Boston: Branden, 1997), pp. 130, 394; Patricia and Fredrick McKissack, *The Red-Tail Angels: The Story of the Tuskegee Airmen of World War II* (New York: Walker, 1995), pp. 92, 116.

34. Francis and Caso, *Tuskegee Airmen*, pp. 168–69, 194–95.

35. For one example, see John B. Dendy IV, "A Fateful Mission: Chance Meeting with Tuskegee Airmen Changes B-24 Crew," *Airman*, Web ed. (Feb., 2002), Oct. 2002 <http://www.af.mil/news/airman/0202/crew.html>.

36. McKissack and McKissack, *Red-Tail Angels*, pp. 79–82, 100, 106.

37. *The Tuskegee Airmen*, dir. Robert Markowitz; writ. Robert Williams, et al. (HBO Studios, 1995).

38. On nationalism during the Cold War era, see Stephen J. Whitfield, *The Culture of the Cold War*, 2d ed. (Baltimore: Johns Hopkins University Press, 1996); John Fousek, *To Lead the Free World: American Nationalism and the Cultural Roots of the Cold War* (Chapel Hill: University of North Carolina Press, 2000); and Peter J. Kuznick and James Burkhart Gilbert, eds., *Rethinking Cold War Culture* (Washington, D.C.: Smithsonian Institution Press, 2001).

39. Charles Williams, *The Last Great Frenchman: A Life of General De Gaulle* (New York: Wiley, 1995); Eric J. Evans, *Thatcher and Thatcherism*, 2d ed. (London: Routledge, 1997); Garry Wills, *Reagan's America* (Garden City, N.Y.: Doubleday, 1987); *Stripes*, dir. Ivan Reitman; writ. Len Blum, Daniel Goldberg, and Harold Ramis (Columbia, 1981).

40. *Airwolf*, created by Donald P. Bellisario (CBS Television, 1984–87); *Top Gun*, dir. Tony Scott; writ. Jim Cash and Jack Epps Jr. (Paramount, 1986); *Iron Eagle*, dir. Sidney J. Furie; writ. Kevin Elders and Sidney J. Furie (Tristar, 1986); Dale Brown, *Flight of the Old Dog* (New York: Dutton, 1987).

41. The basic source of information on Yeager remains his autobiography: Chuck Yeager and Leo Janos, *Yeager* (New York: Bantam, 1985). For other perspectives on Yeager's career as a test pilot and role in studying supersonic flight, see Louis C. Rotundo, *Into the Unknown: The X-1 Story* (Washington, D.C.: Smithsonian Institution Press, 2001); and Chuck Yeager et al., *The Quest for Mach One: A First-Person Account of Breaking the Sound Barrier* (New York: Penguin Studio, 1997).

42. Tom Wolfe, *The Right Stuff* (New York: Farrar, Straus, and Giroux, 1979), 24, 44–78.

43. Ibid., pp. 44–46; *The Right Stuff*, dir. Philip Kauffman; writ. Philip Kauffman and Tom Wolfe (Warner Brothers, 1983).

44. Wolfe, *The Right Stuff*, pp. 54–57.

45. On the handling qualities of the F-104 at extreme altitude, see George J. Marrett, "Sky High: My Climb to the Top in the F-104," *Air & Space* (Oct./Nov., 2002), pp. 62–70. On the accident, see Wolfe, *The Right Stuff*, pp. 410–31; and Yeager and Janos, *Yeager*, pp. 278–84. The movie's exchange between ground crewmen appears in neither printed account. Wolfe ends his version of the story with one onlooker being violently sick at the sight of Yeager's injuries and the other telling the pilot: "My God! . . . you look awful!"

Chapter 3. Death from Above

1. On the relationship between technology and war generally, see Martin Van Creveld, *Technology and War*, rev. ed. (New York: Free Press, 1991); and Robert L. O'Connell, *Arms and Men: A History of War, Weapons, and Aggression* (New York: Oxford University Press, 1989). On the longbow, see Robert Hardy, *Longbow*, rev. ed. (London: Patrick Stephens, 1992); and John Keegan, *The Face of Battle: A Study of Agincourt, Waterloo, and the Somme* (New York: Viking, 1976), chap. 2. On the influence of gunpowder, see McNeill, *Pursuit of Power*; Geoffrey Parker, *The Military Revolution* (New York: Cambridge University Press, 1988); and John Ellis, *The Social History of the Machine Gun* (New York: Pantheon, 1975).

2. Franklin, *War Stars*, pp. 19–53.

3. Gollin, *No Longer an Island*; Gollin, *Impact of Air Power on the British*.

4. Clarke, *Voices Prophesying War*; Franklin, *War Stars*. On the prewar airship-induced panics of 1909 and 1913, see Gollin, *Impact of Air Power on the British*, pp. 49–63, 230–60.

5. For a brief, reliable overview of World War I bombing campaigns, see Kennett, *First Air War*, pp. 41–62. See also Tami Davis Biddle, *Rhetoric and Reality in Air Warfare: The Evolution of British and American Ideas about Strategic Bombing, 1914–1945* (Princeton: Princeton University Press, 2002).

6. James L. Stokesbury, *A Short History of Air Power* (New York: Morrow, 1988); Robin Higham, *Air Power: A Concise History* (New York: St. Martin's, 1972); Kennett, *First Air War*, pp. 60–62; John Buckley, *Air Power in the Age of Total War* (Bloomington: Indiana University Press, 1999), pp. 59–62. For additional details, see Andrew P. Hyde, *The First Blitz: The German Bomber Campaign against Britain in the First World War* (London: Leo Cooper, 2001).

7. Biddle, *Rhetoric and Reality*, pp. 11–68.

8. Franklin, *War Stars*, pp. 91–100; Michael Sherry, *The Rise of American Air Power: The Creation of Armageddon* (New Haven: Yale University Press, 1987), pp. 22–46. A balanced, critical account of Mitchell's life and career is James J. Cooke, *Billy Mitchell* (Boulder, Colo.: Lynne Rienner, 2002).

9. Buckley, *Air Power in the Age of Total War*, pp. 102–106; Franklin, *War Stars*, pp. 81–90; Sherry, *Rise of American Air Power*, pp. 61–62; Philip M. Taylor, "War and the Media" (keynote address, Conference on Military-Media Relations, Royal Military Academy, Sandhurst, UK, 1995), Philip M. Taylor home page, Oct. 2002 <http://www.leeds.ac.uk/ics/arts-pt2.htm>; Stokesbury, *Short History of Air Power*, pp. 141–47. On the genesis of Pablo Picasso's famous painting depicting the bombing, see Russell Martin, *Picasso's War: The Destruction of Guernica and the Masterpiece That Changed the World* (New York: Dutton, 2002).

10. Buckley, *Air Power in the Age of Total War*, pp. 111–12; Sherry, *Rise of American Air Power*, pp. 23–33, 44–46, 61–69; Franklin, *War Stars*, pp. 95–97; Hector C. Bywater, *The Great Pacific War: A History of the American Japanese Campaign of 1931–33* (1925; Bedford, Mass.: Applewood, 2002); William H. Honan, *Visions of Infamy: The Untold Story of How Journalist Hector C. Bywater Devised the Plans That Led to Pearl Harbor* (New York: St. Martin's, 1991); Stanley Baldwin, Address to the House of Commons, Nov. 10, 1932, in *The Impact of Air Power*, ed. Eugene M. Emme (Princeton, N.J.: Van Nostrand, 1959), pp. 51–52; Winston S. Churchill, Address to the House of Commons, July 20, 1934, in ibid., pp. 53–54. For essential context in understanding these dire forecasts, see Biddle, *Rhetoric and Reality*, pp. 69–127.

11. Reliable histories of British and American bomber operations are Biddle, *Rhetoric and Reality*, pp. 176–213; Max Hastings, *Bomber Command* (New York: Dial, 1979); and Ronald Schaffer, *Wings of Judgment: American Bombing in World War II* (New York: Oxford University Press, 1985).

12. Constantine Fitzgibbon, *The Blitz* (1957; reprint, London: MacDonald, 1970); Angus Calder, *The People's War: Britain, 1939–1945* (New York: Pantheon, 1969), chap. 6; Tom Harisson, *Living through the Blitz* (New York: Schocken, 1989).

13. The standard narratives listed above generally emphasize this theme, as do first-person accounts such as Barbara Marion Nixon, *Raiders*

Overhead: A Diary of the Blitz (London: Scolar, 1980). For an alternate and critical view, see Clive Ponting, *1940: Myth and Reality* (Chicago: Ivan R. Dee, 1991); and Angus Calder, *The Myth of the Blitz* (London: Jonathan Cape, 1991).

14. Quentin Reynolds, *The Wounded Don't Cry* (New York: Dutton, 1941) (also available online at <http://www.ku.edu/~hisite/AFS/library/Wounded/ReynoldsTC.html>); Edward R. Murrow, *This Is London* (1941; reprint, New York: Schocken, 1989); *Mrs. Miniver*, dir. William Wyler, writ. George Froeschel et al. (MGM, 1942).

15. Hastings, *Bomber Command*, app. A; Sherry, *Rise of American Air Power*, pp. 204–206.

16. John Steinbeck, *Bombs Away: The Story of a Bomber Team* (New York: Viking, 1942); *Memphis Belle: A Story of a Flying Fortress*, dir. William Wyler (U.S. Army Air Corps/Paramount, 1944); *Target for Tonight*, dir. Harry Watt ([UK] Ministry of Information, 1941); *Air Force*, dir. Howard Hawks, writ. Dudley Nichols and William Faulkner (Warner Brothers, 1943); *Desperate Journey*, dir. Raoul Walsh, writ. Arthur T. Horman (Warner Brothers, 1942). For a comprehensive survey of World War II "bomber crew" movies, see Michael Paris, *From the Wright Brothers to Top Gun: Aviation, Nationalism, and Popular Cinema* (New York: St. Martin's, 1995), pp. 127–72.

17. On the evolution of saturation bombing as a conscious Allied policy, see Biddle, *Rhetoric and Reality*, chap. 5; Sherry, *Rise of American Air Power*, chaps. 5–6; Schaffer, *Wings of Judgment*, chaps. 6–7; and Hastings, *Bomber Command*, chap. 14. On Dresden, see Alexander McKee, *Dresden 1945: The Devil's Tinderbox* (New York: Dutton, 1984); and David Irving, *The Destruction of Dresden* (New York: Holt, 1964) (but note that Irving's estimate of 130,000 dead has been criticized as too high). On the U.S. firebombing of Japan, see Kenneth Werrell, *Blanket of Fire* (Washington, D.C.: Smithsonian Institution Press, 1996). A balanced, judicious introduction to its still-contentious subject is J. Samuel Walker, *Prompt and Utter Destruction: Truman and the Use of Atomic Bombs against Japan* (Chapel Hill: University of North Carolina Press, 1997).

18. *Command Decision*, dir. Sam Wood, writ. George Froeschel, William Wister Haines, and William R. Laidlaw (MGM 1948); Sy Bartlett and Beirnie Lay Jr., *Twelve O'Clock High!* (New York: Harper, 1948); *Twelve O'Clock High*, dir. Henry King; writ. Sy Bartlett and Beirnie Lay Jr. (Twentieth Century Fox, 1949); *Above and Beyond*, dir. Melvin Frank and Norman Panama, writ. Melvin Frank, Norman Panama, and Beirnie Lay Jr. (MGM, 1952); James A. Michener, *The Bridges at Toko-Ri* (New York: Random House, 1953); *The Bridges at Toko-Ri*, dir. Mark Robson, writ. Valentine Davies and James Michener (Paramount, 1955). *Strategic Air Command*, dir. Anthony Mann, writ. Valentine Davies and Beirnie Lay Jr. (Para-

mount, 1955); *Bombers B-52*, dir. Gordon Douglas, writ. Sam Rolfe and Irving Wallace (Warner Brothers, 1957).

19. John Hersey, *The War Lover* (New York: Knopf, 1959); *The War Lover*, dir. Philip Leacock, writ. John Hersey and Howard Koch (Columbia, 1962); Eugene Burdick and Harvey Wheeler, *Fail-Safe* (New York: McGraw-Hill, 1962); *Fail-Safe*, dir. Sidney Lumet, writ. Eugene Burdick, Harvey Wheeler, and Walter Bernstein (Columbia, 1964); *Dr. Strangelove, or: How I Learned to Stop Worrying and Love the Bomb*, dir. Stanley Kubrick, writ. Peter George, Stanley Kubrick, and Terry Southern (Hawk Films/ Columbia, 1964); Joseph Heller, *Catch-22* (New York: Simon and Schuster, 1961); *Catch-22*, dir. Mike Nichols, writ. Joseph Heller and Buck Henry (Filmways Productions/Paramount, 1970).

20. *Panic in the Year Zero!* dir. Ray Milland, writ. Ward Moore, John Morton, and Jay Simms (American International Pictures/Santa Clara Productions, 1962); Robert A. Heinlein, *Farnham's Freehold* (New York: Putnam, 1964). Studies of fictional nuclear wars include Paul Brians, *Nuclear Holocausts: Atomic War in Fiction, 1895–1984* (Kent, Ohio: Kent State University Press, 1987); Joyce A. Evans, *Celluloid Mushroom Clouds: Hollywood and the Atomic Bomb* (Boulder, Colo.: Westview, 1998); and Kim Newman, *Apocalypse Movies: End of the World Cinema* (New York: St. Martin's, 2000).

21. John Hersey, *Hiroshima* (New York: Knopf, 1946); John Lear, "Hiroshima USA," *Collier's*, Aug. 5, 1950, pp. 180 ff; Kurt Vonnegut, *Slaughterhouse-Five, or: The Children's Crusade, a Duty-Dance with Death* (New York: Delacorte, 1969).

22. George R. Stewart, *Earth Abides* (New York: Random House, 1949); Walter M. Miller, *A Canticle for Leibowitz* (Philadelphia: Lippincott, 1959); *The Bed-Sitting Room*, dir. Richard Lester, writ. John Antrobus, Spike Milligan, and Charles Wood (Oscar Lewenstein Productions, 1969); Nevil Shute, *On the Beach* (New York: Morrow, 1957); *On the Beach*, dir. Stanley Kramer, writ. Nevil Shute, John Paxton, James Lee Barrett (Lomitas Productions, 1959).

23. *The War Game*, dir. Peter Watkins, writ. Peter Watkins (British Broadcasting Corporation, 1965).

24. *The Day After*, dir. Nicholas Meyer, writ. Edward Hume (ABC Circle Films, 1983); *Twelve O'Clock High*, created by Quinn Martin (ABC, 1964–67); Frederick E. Smith *633 Squadron* (New York: Signet, 1964). Five sequels with titles of the form *633 Squadron: Operation* ——— followed, beginning in 1975.

25. On U.S. press coverage of Vietnam, see William Hammond, *Reporting Vietnam: Media and Military at War* (Lawrence: University Press of Kansas, 1998); and Daniel C. Hallin, *The "Uncensored War": The Media and Vietnam* (New York: Oxford University Press, 1986).

26. See Wayne Thompson, *To Hanoi and Back: The U.S. Air Force and North Vietnam, 1966–1973* (Washington, D.C.: Smithsonian Institution Press, 2000).

27. Tom Clancy, *Red Storm Rising* (New York: Putnam's, 1986); Dale Brown, *Flight of the Old Dog* (New York: D. I. Fine, 1987); Larry Bond, *Red Phoenix* (New York: Warner, 1989). Richard P. Hallion, *Storm over Iraq: Air Power and the Persian Gulf War* (Washington, D.C.: Smithsonian Institution Press, 1992), places Gulf War air operations in the context of the U.S. military's evolving ideas of how to use air power. Rick Atkinson, *Crusade: The Untold Story of the Persian Gulf War* (Boston: Houghton Mifflin, 1993), offers a different, less air force–centric perspective on the war.

28. Viorst quoted in Hallion, *Storm over Iraq*, pp. 197–99. On media coverage of the Gulf War, see W. Lance Bennett and David L. Paletz, *Taken by Storm: The Media, Public Opinion, and U.S. Foreign Policy in the Gulf War* (Chicago: University of Chicago Press, 1994).

29. Frederick Forsyth, *The Fist of God* (New York: Bantam, 1994); *Saving Private Ryan*, dir. Steven Spielberg, writ. Robert Rodat (Amblin/Dreamworks/Paramount, 1998). Historians have observed that even the single airplane that *does* appear is itself inaccurate—P-47s, not P-51s, carried out "tank-busting" missions during the Normandy campaign.

30. On the Chinese embassy bombing, see Steven Lee Myers, "Chinese Embassy Bombing: A Wide Net of Blame," *New York Times*, Apr. 17, 1999, p. A1; and Norman Friedman, "U.S. Bombs Hit Chinese Embassy," *United States Naval Institute Proceedings* 125 (July, 1999): 107–109.

31. Jack Olsen, *Aphrodite: Desperate Mission* (New York: Putnam, 1970).

32. *Telefon*, dir. Don Siegel, writ. Peter Hyams, Walter Wager, and Sterling Silliphant (MGM, 1977); Stephen King, *The Running Man* (New York: New American Library, 1982); Dean Ing, *Soft Targets* (New York: Tom Doherty, 1986); Tom Clancy, *Debt of Honor* (New York: Putnam, 1994); Ridley Pearson, *Hard Fall* (New York: Delacorte, 1992); Dale Brown, *Storming Heaven* (New York: Putnam, 1994).

33. Chip Cummins, "Pentagon Avoids Subject of Civilian Deaths— Estimating Afghan Casualties Is Difficult, Officials Say," *Wall Street Journal*, Dec. 4, 2001, p. A20; Michael Massing, "Grief without Portraits," *The Nation* 274 (Feb. 4, 2002): 6–8; "Hold the Applause," *The Progressive* 66 (Feb., 2002): 8–10; Thom Shanker, "Rumsfeld Calls Civilian Deaths Relatively Low," *New York Times*, July 23, 2002, p. A9.

Chapter 4. The Allure of Air Travel

1. The definitive history of the airline industry's relationship with the public (through advertising, marketing, and customer service) has yet to be

written. Three works, however, stand out from the vast, diffuse literature on the subject: Kenneth Hudson and Julian Pettifer, *Diamonds in the Sky: A Social History of Air Travel* (London: Bodley Head/British Broadcasting Corporation, 1979); Roger Bilstein, "Air Travel and the Traveling Public: The American Experience, 1920–1970," in *From Airships to Airbus: The History of Civil and Commercial Aviation*, vol. 2, ed. William F. Trimble (Washington, D.C.: Smithsonian Institution Press, 1995), pp. 91–111; and Carl Solberg, *The Conquest of the Skies: A History of Commercial Aviation in America* (Boston: Little, Brown, 1979).

2. Oliver E. Allen, *The Airline Builders* (Alexandria, Va.: Time-Life, 1981), pp. 72–73.

3. Hudson and Pettifer, *Diamonds in the Sky*, pp. 24–25.

4. Ibid., pp. 32–33. For a map of Quantas's early route structure, see Allen, *Airline Builders*, p. 33.

5. Hudson and Pettifer, *Diamonds in the Sky*, p. 79; Solberg, *Conquest of the Skies*, pp. 74–90; Allen, *Airline Builders*, p. 152. On the history of Pan American, see Marilyn Bender and Selig Altschul, *The Chosen Instrument* (New York: Simon and Schuster, 1982); and Lynn M. Homan and Thomas Reilly, *Pan Am* (Charleston, S.C.: Arcadia Tempus, 2000).

6. Allen, *Airline Builders*, pp. 92–93, 7.

7. Transcontinental and Western Airlines, "Your Competitors Fly TWA," 1940, ad number T1939, J. Walter Thompson Company Competitive Advertisements Collection, John W. Hartman Center for Sales, Advertising, and Marketing History; Rare Book, Manuscript, and Special Collections Library, Duke University, Durham, N.C. [Subsequent citations to this collection cited as "Thompson Collection, T####." All Thompson Collection advertisements cited herein are available online: Hartman Center for Sales, Advertising, and Marketing History, *Ad*Access* <http://scriptorium.lib.duke.edu/adaccess/>].

8. Pan American Airways, "'Roll-Top Desk Thinking Won't Do in Selling Latin America!" 1941, Thompson Collection, T1576; Transcontinental and Western Airlines, "Be There Today!" 1941, Thompson Collection, T1949; Transcontinental and Western Airlines, "Commuter Convenience to Cincinnati and Dayton," 1941, Thompson Collection, T1950.

9. Capital Airlines, "Home again . . . same day . . . 1000 miles later," 1951, Thompson Collection, T1079; British Overseas Airways Corporation, "Called to Calcutta?" 1952, Thompson Collection, T0871.

10. Trans World Airlines, "Daddy will be back tonight," 1951, Thompson Collection, T2060; Trans World Airlines, "Here today . . . there today . . . home today, too," 1952, Thompson Collection, T2081; Trans World Airlines, "Dad's Favorite Chair," 1951, Thompson Collection, T2070.

11. T. A. Heppenheimer, *Turbulent Skies: The History of Commercial Aviation* (New York: Wiley, 1995), pp. 72, 124–27.

12. Trans World Airlines, "It's a long way from the office—or is it?" 1951, Thompson Collection, T2058; American Airlines, "How to have a 'Big' time in a short time," 1949, Thompson Collection, T0368; Capital Airlines, "Time is a girl's best friend," 1954, Thompson Collection, T1093; Heppenheimer, *Turbulent Skies*, p. 128.

13. Heppenheimer, *Turbulent Skies*, p. 193.

14. Robert J. Serling, *The Jet Age* (Alexandria, Va.: Time-Life, 1982), p. 82.

15. Southwest Airlines, "How do we love you? Let us count the ways?" 1971, *Southwest Airlines—Historical Advertising Gallery*, Sept., 2002 <http://www.iflyswa.com/images/p_ad01.jpg>; Southwest Airlines, "We're spreading love all over Texas," 1977, *Southwest Airlines—Historical Advertising Gallery*, Sept., 2002 <http://www.iflyswa.com/images/p_ad03.jpg>. On the history of Southwest, see Thomas Petzinger Jr., *Hard Landing: The Epic Contest for Power and Profits That Plunged the Airlines into Chaos* (New York: Random House/Times Business, 1995), pp. 23–46; and Lamar Muse, *Southwest Passage: The Inside Story of Southwest Airlines' Formative Years* (Austin: Eakin, 2002). For reproductions of both Pacific Southwest advertisements, see Kevin Trinkle, *The PSA History Page*, Sept., 2002 <http://www.iflypsa.com/museum/ads.htm>.

16. Heppenheimer, *Turbulent Skies*, pp. 191–94; Anthony Sampson, *Empires of the Sky: The Politics, Contests, and Cartels of World Airlines* (New York: Random House, 1984), pp. 105–114, 123–46. On the Concorde as an economic failure, see R. E. G. Davies, *Fallacies and Fantasies of Air Transport History* (McLean, Va.: Paladwr, 1994), pp. 106–119; and R. E. G. Davies, "SST Market Limitations: A Simple Matter of Arithmetic," in *From Airship to Airbus: The History of Civil and Commercial Aviation*, vol. 1, ed. William M. Leary (Washington, D.C.: Smithsonian Institution Press, 1995), pp. 190–99.

17. John Maxtone-Graham, *The Only Way to Cross* (New York: Macmillan, 1972); Hudson and Pettifer, *Diamonds in the Sky*, pp. 29–51; Solberg, *Conquest of the Skies*, pp. 100–121. For trains, see Mike Schafer et al., *The American Passenger Train* (St. Paul, Minn.: Motorbooks International, 2001); and James D. Porterfield, *Dining by Rail: The History and Recipes of America's Golden Age of Railroad Cuisine* (New York: St. Martin's, 1993). For examples of luxuriously appointed airliner cabins from 1919–21, see Allen, *Airline Builders*, pp. 22–23.

18. Hudson and Pettifer, *Diamonds in the Sky*, pp. 90–110; Solberg, *Conquest of the Skies*, pp. 207–224; Ernest K. Gann, *Fate Is the Hunter* (New York: Simon and Schuster, 1961), p. 57. For images of cabin service during this period, see Allen, *Airline Builders*, pp. 129–31, 136–43.

19. On the airships, see Hudson and Pettifer, *Diamonds in the Sky*, pp. 58–64; and Solberg, *Conquest of the Skies*, pp. 90–99. On the flying

boats, see Hudson and Pettifer, *Diamonds in the Sky*, pp. 71–88; Solberg, *Conquest of the Skies*, pp. 223–48; Stan Cohen, *Wings to the Orient: Pan American Clipper Planes, 1935 to 1945—A Pictorial History* (Missoula, Mont.: Pictorial Histories, 1985); and Robert L. Gandt, *China Clipper: The Age of the Great Flying Boats* (Annapolis, Md.: Naval Institute Press, 1991).

20. Reprinted in Cohen, *Wings to the Orient*, pp. 30–31.

21. On wartime air travel, see Hudson and Pettifer, *Diamonds in the Sky*, pp. 111–29; and Solberg, *Conquest of the Skies*, pp. 259–84. For a concise account of the technological development of U.S. airliners during this period, see Roger E. Bilstein, *The Enterprise of Flight: The American Aviation and Aerospace Industry* (Washington, D.C.: Smithsonian Institution Press, 2001), pp. 55–62, 135–41.

22. Delta Air Lines, "No Queen Could Have it Better," 1949, Thompson Collection, T1271; Trans World Airlines, "Only TWA Offers Luxurious All-Sleeper Service," 1951, Thompson Collection, T2057; National Airlines, "D.C.-7 Star," 1954, Thompson Collection, T1922.

23. On cabin service from this period, see Hudson and Pettifer, *Diamonds in the Sky*, 130–52; and Solberg, *Conquest of the Skies*, pp. 333–42, 377–84.

24. See, for example, Rick Marin, "When Flying Tourist Meant Going in Style," *New York Times*, Mar. 28, 1999, p. G1; and Michelene Maynard, "When Pilots Were Stars and Airlines Glamorous," *[Sunday] New York Times*, Feb. 2, 2003, sec. 2, p. 24.

25. Heppenheimer, *Turbulent Skies*, pp. 130–33. Most major-city airports of the era, built when the twenty-one-passenger DC-3 was a large airliner, where overwhelmed by the fifty-to-sixty-seat cabins and expanding schedules of the postwar era. The immense airports of the jet age—Chicago's O'Hare, Atlanta's Hartsfield, and Washington's Dulles—lay a decade in the future. For the history of U.S. airports, see Janet R. Daly Bednarek, *America's Airports: Airfield Development, 1918–1947* (College Station: Texas A&M University Press, 2001).

26. Bilstein, "Air Travel," p. 103; Heppenheimer, *Turbulent Skies*, pp. 128, 191–92; Solberg, *Conquest of the Skies*, pp. 345–52.

27. Serling, *Jet Age*, p. 139.

28. Lee Kolm, "Stewardesses' 'Psychological Punch': Gender and Commercial Aviation in the United States, 1930–1978," in *From Airships to Airbus: The History of Civil and Commercial Aviation*, vol. 2, ed. William F. Trimble (Washington, D.C.: Smithsonian Institution Press, 1995), pp. 112–27; Bruce Handy, "Glamour with Attitude," *Vanity Fair*, Oct., 2002, pp. 220–27; "PSA Aisle Seats $13.50—While They Last," Pacific Southwest Airlines, *The PSA History Page*, Sept., 2002 <http://www.iflypsa.com/museum/ads.htm>; Trudy Baker and Rachel Jones, *Coffee, Tea, or Me?: The Uninhibited Memoirs of Two Airline Stewardesses* (New York: Bantam, 1968).

The book and its two sequels (which collectively sold seventeen million copies) were, in fact, the work of veteran ghostwriter Donald Bain, who invented the women and their stories. See "For Ghost Author Bain, Writing Is a Craft," *Jam!* Sept. 23, 2002 <http://www.canoe.ca/JamBooksFeatures/bain_donald.html>.

29. The intertwining of culture and commerce in this era of air travel are explored in Hudson and Pettifer, *Diamonds in the Sky*, pp. 153–70, 193–233; Sampson, *Empires of the Sky*, pp. 123–46, 209–223; Petzinger, *Hard Landing*; and Heppenheimer, *Turbulent Skies*.

30. Heppenheimer, *Turbulent Skies*, pp. 191–95. On the broader cultural significance of airline class distinctions, see Mark Dery, "Memories of the Future: Excavating the Jet Age at the TWA Terminal," in *Prefiguring Cyberculture: Informatics from Plato to Haraway*, ed. Darren Tofts et al. (Sydney: Power, 2001).

31. On People Express and other early examples of low-fare niche airlines, see Petzinger, *Hard Landing*, pp. 95–153; and Heppenheimer, *Turbulent Skies*, pp. 319–25. On Southwest, see Muse, *Southwest Passage*. On Midwest Express, see, for example, Daniel Pedersen, "Cookies and Champagne," *Newsweek*, Apr. 27, 1998, p. 60; and Perry Flint, "Milwaukee's Best," *Air Transport World* 34 (May, 1997): 79–80.

32. Allen, *Airline Builders*, p. 10.

33. On the culture of the Pan American flying boats, see Cohen, *Wings to the Orient*. M. D. Klaas, *Last of the Flying Clippers: The Boeing B-314 Story* (Atglen, Pa.: Schiffer, 1998), is a rich source of images, but the text is poorly edited and (according to reviewers) error ridden. For a debunking of the flying boats' romantic reputation, see Davies, *Fallacies and Fantasies*, pp. 51–62, 87–93.

34. Trans World Airlines, "High Moments over the Mediterranean," 1947, Thompson Collection, T2327; Trans World Airlines, "High Speed, High Way to Bombay," 1947, Thompson Collection, T2325; Trans World Airlines, "The Old Greets the New in Italy . . . As Near as Tomorrow by TWA," 1948, Thompson Collection, T2330.

35. TACA Airways System, "El Salvador: Land of Fine Coffees, Gold and Silver," 1948, Thompson Collection, T1727; TACA Airways System, "Costa Rica: Land of Coffee, Cacao, and Bananas," 1948, Thompson Collection, T1728; Scandinavian Airlines System, "There's So Much to See This Summer in Scandinavia and Scotland," 1948, Thompson Collection, T1655; British Overseas Airways Corporation, "Bermuda for Christmas," 1948, Thompson Collection, T0744; United Airlines, "Fly United to Hawaii for 'Aloha Week,'" 1949, Thompson Collection, T2186; American Airlines, "That Mid-Winter Holiday in Mexico," 1949, Thompson Collection, T0341; Linea Aeropostal Venezolana, "Lowest Fare: New York Non-Stop to Havana in Only 5 Hours," 1947, Thompson Collection, T1379.

36. Hudson and Pettifer, *Diamonds in the Sky*, pp. 164–66; the practice was still in place on all three airlines in late 2001.

37. Francis Chichester, *Solo to Sydney* (New York: Stein and Day, 1930); Anne Morrow Lindbergh, *North to the Orient* (New York: Harcourt, 1935); and *Listen, the Wind!* (New York: Harcourt, 1938); Amelia Earhart, *The Fun of It: Random Records of My Own Flying and of Women in Aviation* (New York: Harcourt, 1932); and *Last Flight* (New York: Harcourt, 1937); Beryl Markham, *West with the Night* (Boston: Houghton Mifflin, 1942).

38. Francis Chichester, *The Lonely Sea and the Sky* (New York: Coward-McCann, 1964); Paul Gahlinger, *The Cockpit: A Flight of Escape and Discovery* (Salt Lake City: Sagebrush, 2000); Jimmy Buffett, *A Pirate Looks at Fifty* (New York: Random House, 1998); "Somewhere over China," *Somewhere over China* (MCA, 1982); "Jimmy Dreams," *Barometer Soup* (MCA, 1995); and "Jamaica Mistaica," *Banana Wind* (MCA, 1996).

39. Richard Bach, *Biplane* (New York: Harper and Row, 1966); and *Nothing by Chance: A Gypsy Pilot's Adventures in Modern America* (New York: Morrow, 1969); Rinker Buck, *Flight of Passage* (New York: Hyperion, 1997); Maria Gosnell, *Zero Three Bravo: Solo across America in a Small Plane* (New York: Knopf, 1993); Stephen Coonts, *The Cannibal Queen: An Aerial Odyssey across America* (New York: Pocket, 1992).

40. Richard Bach, *Illusions: The Adventures of a Reluctant Messiah* (New York: Delacorte, 1977); *Bridge across Forever: A Lovestory* (New York: Morrow, 1984); and *Running from Safety: An Adventure of the Spirit* (New York: Morrow, 1994).

41. Novels like Richard Doyle's *Imperial 109* (New York: Bantam, 1977) and Ken Follett's *Night over Water* (New York: Morrow, 1991), for example, use flying boats in the same way that Agatha Christie used a train in *Murder on the Orient Express* (1934), as a luxurious, self-contained setting for romance, intrigue, and the occasional crime.

42. Solberg, *Conquest of the Skies*, pp. 405–410; Hudson and Pettifer, *Diamonds in the Sky*, pp. 201–204.

43. *Goldfinger*, dir. Guy Hamilton, writ. Ian Fleming, Richard Maibaum, and Paul Dehn (United Artists, 1964); *Our Man Flint*, dir. Daniel Mann, writ. Hal Fimberg and Ben Starr (Twentieth Century Fox, 1966); *In Like Flint*, dir. Gordon Douglas, writ. Hal Fimberg (Twentieth Century Fox, 1967); *Hart to Hart*, created by Aaron Spelling (ABC, 1979–84); *The Magician* (NBC, 1973–74); Carly Simon, "You're So Vain," *No Secrets* (Elektra/Asylum, 1972); Jimmy Buffett, "Overkill," *Banana Wind* (MCA, 1996); Carl Sagan, *Contact* (New York: Simon and Schuster, 1985); *Contact*, dir. Robert Zemeckis, writ. Carl Sagan, Ann Druyan, James V. Hart, and Michael Goldenberg (Warner Brothers, 1997).

44. The rise and fall of Laker Airways is chronicled from a business and regulatory standpoint in Sampson, *Empires of the Sky*, pp. 147–62.

Hudson and Pettifer (*Diamonds in the Sky*, pp. 195–97) focus on Laker's customers.

45. *Riptide*, created by Stephen J. Cannell (NBC, 1984–86); *Magnum, P.I.* (CBS, 1980–88). Other television series of the era that prominently featured helicopters (though without using them to define a lead character's personality) include *Chase* (1973–74), *Chopper One* (1974), *240-Robert* (1979–81), *Blue Thunder* (1984), and *Airwolf* (1984–88).

46. *Thunderball*, dir. Terence Young, writ. Kevin McClory et al. (United Artists, 1965); J. K. Rowling, *Harry Potter and the Sorcerer's Stone* (New York: Arthur Levine, 1997); *Harry Potter and the Chamber of Secrets* (New York: Scholastic, 1998); *Harry Potter and the Prisoner of Azkaban* (New York: Scholastic, 1999); and *Harry Potter and the Goblet of Fire* (New York: Scholastic, 2000); *The Absent-Minded Professor,* dir. Robert Stevenson, writ. Samuel Taylor and Bill Walsh (Walt Disney Studios, 1961).

Chapter 5. Crashes and Other Catastrophes

1. See, for example, Ann Larrabee, *Decade of Disaster* (Urbana: University of Illinois Press, 2000); and Steven Biel, *Down with the Old Canoe: A Cultural History of the* Titanic *Disaster* (New York: Norton, 1996).

2. On the Chicago Fire, see Chicago Historical Society, "The O'Leary Legend," in *The Great Chicago Fire and the Web of Historical Memory* (last rev., Oct. 8, 1996) <http://www.chicagohs.org/fire/oleary/>. On the *Exxon Valdez*, see Larrabee, *Decade of Disaster,* pp. 82–116. On Columbine, see John M. Broder, "Clinton Orders Study on Selling of Violence," *New York Times,* June 2, 1999, p. A20; and Angie Cannon, "The Loud Echo of Littleton's Gunfire," *U.S. News and World Report,* June 21, 1999, pp. 24–25.

3. Charles Murray and Catherine Bly Cox, *Apollo: The Race to the Moon* (New York: Simon and Schuster, Touchstone,1989), pp. 189–225; Andrew Chaikan, *A Man on the Moon: The Voyages of the Apollo Astronauts* (New York: Penguin, 1994), pp. 11–26. Typical of the fire's treatment in the memoirs of NASA personnel is Chris Kraft, *Flight: My Life in Mission Control* (New York: Dutton, 2001), pp. 269–78. For a (rare) dissenting view from the standard progress-from-tragedy narrative, see Betty Grissom and Henry Still, *Starfall* (New York: Thomas Crowell, 1974), pp. 174–248.

4. Walter Lord, *A Night to Remember* (New York: Holt, Rinehart, and Winston, 1955) remains the classic narrative of such stories. For an analysis of Lord's book and its role in shaping the popular memory of the *Titanic* disaster, see Biel, *Down with the Old Canoe,* pp. 149–60.

5. Philip L. Fradkin, *Magnitude 8: Earthquakes and Life along the San Andreas Fault* (New York: Henry Holt, 1998), pp. 19–22, 98–139.

6. See, for example, Marilyn Achiron, "Sitting Aft: Is It Really Safer?" *Newsweek,* Aug. 26, 1985, p. 16.

7. Comprehensive, regularly updated databases of air crashes are avail-

able on the Web sites *AirDisaster.com* <http://www.airdisaster.com> and *PlaneCrashInfo.com* <http://www.planecrashinfo.com>.

8. Antoine de St. Exupéry, *Wind, Sand, and Stars*, trans. Lewis Galantière (1939; reprint, New York: Harcourt/Harbrace Paperbound Library, 1967), pp. 60–61.

9. Ernest K. Gann, *Fate Is the Hunter* (1961; reprint, New York: Simon and Schuster/Touchstone 1986), pp. 256–60; Edwards Park, *Nanette: Her Pilot's Love Story* (1977; reprint, Washington, D.C.: Smithsonian Institution Press, 1989), pp. 152–60 (quote, p. 159).

10. Three books of the columns have been published by the editors of *Flying* magazine: *I Learned about Flying from That!* (New York: Delacorte, 1976); *More I Learned about Flying from That!* (New York: Macmillan, 1984); and *I Learned about Flying from That, Volume 3* (New York: McGraw Hill Professional, 1993).

11. The 1980 film *Airplane!* a spoof of "midair crisis" movies, plays with this convention by giving the mentally unstable pilot-hero assistants who are even less sane than he is. The chief air traffic controller deals with on-the-job stress by sniffing glue, his assistant unplugs the runway lights as a practical joke, and the lead flight attendant has a brief (but evidently satisfying) sexual encounter with the airliner's "automatic pilot"—a full-sized inflatable doll.

12. *Breaking the Sound Barrier*, dir. David Lean, writ. Terence Rattigan (London Film Productions, 1952); Ernest K. Gann, *The High and the Mighty* (New York: William Sloane, 1953); *The High and the Mighty*, dir. William Wellman, writ. Ernest K. Gann (Warner Brothers, 1954).

13. Arthur Hailey, *Airport* (Garden City, N.Y.: Doubleday, 1968); *Airport*, dir. George Seaton and Henry Hathaway, writ. Arthur Hailey and George Seaton (Universal, 1970).

14. David Graham, *Down to a Sunless Sea* (New York: Simon and Schuster, 1981); Thomas H. Block, *Orbit* (New York: Howard, McCann, and Geoghegan, 1982); John J. Nance, *Pandora's Clock* (Garden City, N.Y.: Doubleday, 1995); and *Medusa's Child* (Garden City, N.Y.: Doubleday, 1997).

15. Arthur Hailey and John Castle, *Runway Zero Eight* (Garden City, N.Y.: Doubleday, 1958); *Zero Hour!* dir. Hall Bartlett, writ. Arthur Hailey, Hall Bartlett, and John C. Champion (Paramount, 1957); *Terror in the Sky*, dir. Bernard L. Kowalski, writ. Arthur Hailey et al. (Paramount [made for CBS TV], 1971); *Airplane!* dir. Jim Abrahams, David Zucker, and Jerry Zucker, writ. Arthur Hailey, Jim Abrahams, David Zucker, and Jerry Zucker (Paramount, 1980).

16. *Airport 1975*, dir. Jack Smight, writ. Don Ingalls (Universal, 1974); Thomas Block, *Mayday* (New York: Marek, 1979); John J. Nance, *Blackout* (New York: Putnam, 2000); Brian Lecomber, *Talk Down* (New York: Coward, McCann, and Geoghegan, 1978).

17. Ernest K. Gann, *Island in the Sky* (New York: Viking, 1944); Alistair MacLean, *Night without End* (Garden City, N.Y.: Doubleday, 1960); Gary Paulsen, *Hatchet* (New York: Bradbury, 1987); *Lost Flight*, dir. Leonard Horn, writ. Dean Riesner (Universal TV, 1969); *The Last Flight of Noah's Ark*, dir. Charles Jarrott, writ. George Arthur Bloom et al. (Walt Disney Pictures, 1980); *Cast Away*, dir. Robert Zemeckis (Twentieth Century Fox, 2000); Elleston Trevor, *The Flight of the Phoenix* (New York: Harper and Row, 1964); *The Flight of the Phoenix*, dir. Robert Aldrich, writ. Ada Hall [Elleston Trevor] and Lukas Heller (Twentieth Century Fox, 1965).

18. Gary M. Pomerantz, *Nine Minutes, Twenty Seconds: The Tragedy and Triumph of ASA Flight 590* (New York: Crown, 2001).

19. *Miracle Landing*, dir. Dick Lowery, writ. Garner Simmons (CBS TV, 1990); *The Hindenburg*, dir. Robert Wise, writ. Nelson Gidding et al. (Universal, 1975); *Slattery's Hurricane*, dir. André de Toth, writ. Richard Murphy and Herman Wouk (Twentieth Century Fox, 1949).

20. *Random Hearts*, dir. Sydney Pollack, writ. Warren Adler, Darryl Ponicsan, and Kurt Luedtke (Columbia, 1999); *Bounce*, dir. Don Roos, writ. Don Roos (Miramax, 2000).

21. Dominick Pisano, "The Crash That Killed Knute Rockne," *Air & Space Smithsonian* (Dec., 1991/Jan., 1992): 88–93; William Least Heat-Moon, *PrairyErth* (Boston: Houghton-Mifflin, 1991), pp. 386–99.

22. Eric Schatzberg, *Wings of Wood, Wings of Metal: Culture and Technological Choice in American Airplane Materials, 1914–1945* (Princeton: Princeton University Press, 1998), pp. 132–34, 168–74.

23. Harold G. Dick and Douglas H. Robinson, *The Golden Age of the Great Passenger Airships: Graf Zeppelin and Hindenburg* (Washington, D.C.: Smithsonian Institution Press, 1985); Douglas Botting, *Dr. Eckener's Dream Machine: The Great Zeppelin and the Dawn of Air Travel* (New York: Henry Holt, 2001); Guillaume de Syon, *Zeppelin!: Germany and the Airship, 1900–1939* (Baltimore: Johns Hopkins University Press, 2002), pp. 172–210. Michael M. Mooney, *The Hindenburg* (New York: Dodd, Mead, 1972), is a detailed account of the final flight and crash, but Mooney's argument that the airship was sabotaged is a minority position. For Herb Morrison's broadcast, see Joe Garner, *We Interrupt This Broadcast*, 3d ed. (Naperville, Ill.: Sourcebooks Trade, 2002), pp. 2–6, CD 1, track 2. Recordings of Morrison's broadcast are also widely available online.

24. Recent studies suggest that the fire may actually have started in the aluminum-rich "dope" used to tighten and waterproof the fabric covering of the hull. See, for example, Malcolm W. Browne, "Hydrogen May Not Have Caused *Hindenburg*'s Fiery End," *New York Times*, May 6, 1997, p. C4; Richard G. Van Treuren, "Odorless, Colorless, Blameless," *Air & Space Smithsonian* 12 (Apr.–May, 1997): 14–16; Mariette de Christina, "What Really Downed the *Hindenburg*," *Popular Science*, Nov., 1997, pp. 70–78.

25. For a comprehensive bibliography on crashes and their aftermaths,

see Kenneth G. Madden, "Single Types or Events," *Madden's Air Transport Safety Resources* (last rev., June 23, 2001), Oct. 2002 <http://courses.unt.edu/madden/WWW/bib3d.html>. On the Comet, see Timothy Hewatt and W. A. Waterton, *The Comet Riddle* (London: Frederick Muller, 1955); and Derek D. Dempster, *The Tale of the Comet* (New York: David MacKay, 1958). On the Electra, see Robert J. Serling, *The Electra Story: Aviation's Greatest Mystery* (Garden City, N.Y.: Doubleday, 1963; reprint, New York: Bantam, 1991). The definitive source on the DC-10 is John H. Fielder and Douglas Birsch, eds., *The DC-10 Case: A Study in Applied Ethics, Technology, and Society* (Albany: State University of New York Press, 1992). For a brief but authoritative synopsis, see John Newhouse, *The Sporty Game* (New York: Knopf, 1982), pp. 88–109. On the Concorde, see *Guardian Unlimited*, "Special Report: The Concorde Crash" (last rev., Jan. 17, 2002) <http://www.guardian.co.uk/concorde/0,7368,347037,00.html>; BBC News, "In Depth: The Concorde Crash" (last rev., July 21, 2002), Oct., 2002 <http://news.bbc.co.uk/1/hi/in_depth/europe/2000/concorde_crash/>.

26. Basil Jackson, *Flameout* (New York: Norton, 1976); John J. Nance, *Final Approach* (New York: Crown, 1990); Michael Crichton, *Airframe* (New York: Knopf, 1996); *Fate Is the Hunter*, dir. Ralph Nelson, writ. Ernest K. Gann and Harold Medford (Twentieth Century Fox, 1964); Nevil Shute, *No Highway* (New York: Morrow, 1948); *No Highway in the Sky*, dir. Henry Koster, writ. Nevil Shute, R. C. Sherriff, Oscar Millard, and Alex Coppell (Twentieth Century Fox, 1951).

27. Emily Dee, *Souls on Board: Responses to the United 232 Tragedy* (Sioux City, Iowa: Loess Hills, 1990). For a transcript of an extensive post-crash interview with Haynes (source and date unknown), see "Crash of United Flight 232 as Described by the Pilot, Captain Al Haynes," May 24, 1991, Oct., 2002 <http://www.snowcrest.net/marnells/haynes.htm>.

28. Josh Eppinger, "The Most Amazing Rescue of '82: Air Florida 737 Potomac River Crash," *Popular Science*, Jan., 1983, pp. 80–82; Michael Paterniti, "The American Hero in Four Acts: J. Matus, L. Skutnik, S. Mohammed, and G. Littrell," *Esquire*, Nov., 1998, pp. 96–103; "Lenny Skutnik: A Bystander's Quick Leap Saves a Life," *People*, Mar. 15–22, 1999, p. 84; Roger Rosenblatt, "The Man in the Water," *Time*, Jan. 25, 1982, p. 86 (reprinted in *The Man in the Water: Essays and Stories* [New York: Random House, 1994]).

29. See, for example, E. M. Swift, "Peggy Fleming," *Sports Illustrated*, Sept. 19, 1994, pp. 134–35 (part of a commemorative issue on the forty most significant sports figures of the preceding forty years); Ann Uhry Abrams, *Explosion at Orly: The Disaster That Transformed Atlanta* (Avion, 2002).

30. For the song's status as a cultural landmark, see David Browne, "American Pie: 25 Years Ago, America Listened," *New York Times*, Feb. 9,

1997, sec. 2, p. 40. For a polished interpretation of the consensus view of the lyrics, see Rich Kulawiec, "FAQ: The Annotated American Pie," Oct., 2002 <http://www.faqs.org/faqs/music/american-pie/>. For McLean's (brief) commentary on the song and links to other interpretations, see "American Pie: Analysis," *Don McLean Online*, Oct. 2002 <http://www.don-mclean.com/DonMcLean/analysis.asp>.

31. "The Death Race: *Talk* and *Vanity Fair* Cover the Death of J. F. Kennedy, Jr.," *Time*, Aug. 9, 1999, p. 63; Kelly Heyboer, "Shifting into Overdrive: Newsmagazines' Coverage of the Death of JFK, Jr.," *American Journalism Review* 21 (Sept., 1999): 24–30; John Corporon, "The JFK, Jr. Coverage: It's as if Nothing Else Was Going On," *Television Quarterly* 30 (winter, 2000): 4–9.

32. David McEnery, "Amelia Earhart's Last Flight," 1937.

33. Wohl, *Passion for Wings*, p. 234.

34. For the basic facts of Magee's short life, see Alan Fotheringham, "And Touched the Face of God," *Macleans* 99 (Mar. 24, 1986): 60; and Hermann Hagedorn, *Sunward I've Climbed: The Story of John Magee, Poet and Soldier, 1922–1941* (New York: Macmillan, 1944). Dwayne Linton, a squadron-mate of Magee, describes the fatal crash in Michael F. Jerram, "The Last High Flight," *Flying* 120 (Jan., 1993): 36. The popularity and public-domain status of "High Flight" ensure its ubiquity; as of this writing, it appears on well over one thousand Web sites.

35. William Goldman and George Roy Hill, *The Great Waldo Pepper* (New York: Dell, 1975); *The Great Waldo Pepper*, dir. George Roy Hill, writ. William Goldman (Universal Pictures, 1975); *A Guy Named Joe*, dir. Victor Fleming, writ. David Boehm et al. (MGM, 1943).

36. Spencer Dunmore, *The Sound of Wings* (New York: Macmillan, 1984); John G. Fuller, *The Ghost of Flight 401* (New York: Berkley, 1976); and *The Airmen Who Would Not Die* (New York: Putnam, 1979); Frederick Forsyth, *The Shepherd* (New York: Viking, 1976).

37. *Close Encounters of the Third Kind*, dir. Stephen Spielberg, writ. Stephen Spielberg et al. (Columbia, 1977). The disappearance of Flight 19 is one of the cornerstones of the "Bermuda Triangle" legend, a decades-old idea that enjoyed a brief vogue (a dozen books, two made-for-television movies, and a short-lived television series) in the mid-1970s. Credulous accounts of the story are thus readily available; Charles Berlitz, *The Bermuda Triangle* (Garden City, N.Y.: Doubleday, 1974) is the most famous. Lawrence David Kusche, *The Bermuda Triangle Mystery Solved* (New York: Harper and Row, 1975), the definitive debunking of the legend, attributes the loss of Flight 19 to navigational errors and inexperience.

38. John Varley, *Millennium* (New York: Berkely, 1983); "The '37s," *Star Trek: Voyager*, dir. James L. Conway, writ. Jeri Taylor and Brannon Braga (broadcast Aug. 28, 1995); "The Odyssey of Flight 33," *The Twilight*

Zone, dir. Justus Addiss, writ. Rod Serling (broadcast Mar. 3, 1961); Stephen King, "The Langoliers," in *Four Past Midnight* (New York: Viking, 1990).

39. Mike Luckovich, "Firemen Reach the Top," *Atlanta Journal-Constitution*, Sept. 13, 2001.

40. See, for example, Sean D. Naylor, "The Bravest Man I Ever Knew," *The Officer* 77 (Dec., 2001): 46; Michelle Malkin, "Rick Rescorla, True American Hero," *Human Events* 58 (Mar. 11, 2002): 12; and especially Robert Bateman, "British-born Rick Rescorla was a Hero of the Ia Drang and Both Terrorist Attacks on the World Trade Center," *Vietnam* 15 (June, 2002): 12–13. Rescorla's wartime heroism at the 1965 battle of the Ia Drang Valley is discussed at length in Harold G. Moore and Joseph Galloway, *We Were Soldiers Once . . . and Young* (New York: Random House, 1992).

41. Howell Raines et al., *Portraits: 9/11/01* (New York: Times, 2002), is a collection of the *New York Times* profiles. Audio files of some of the NPR profiles can be found on the NPR Web site (<http://www.npr.org>) by using the search keyword "obituaries."

42. For a representative selection of the coverage, see Karen Tumulty, "The Feds Take on Airport Security," *Time,* Nov. 26, 2001, p. 77; Harry Hutchinson, "Technology vs. Terrorism," *Mechanical Engineering* 124 (Jan., 2002): 48–52; James Trebilcock, "New Ground Rules for Air Travelers," *Good Housekeeping,* Mar., 2002, pp. 177–78; Barbara S. Peterson, "Airports: The New Anatomy," *Conde Nast's Traveler* 37 (Sept., 2002): 93–104; and Adele C. Schwartz, "Second-Generation Security," *Air Transport World* 39 (Sept., 2002): A20–A21. On the potential pitfalls of the "find-and-fix" mentality, see Brendan I. Koerner, "The Security Traders," *Mother Jones* 27 (Sept.–Oct., 2002): 42–47; and H. George Frederickson, "Airport Security, High Reliability, and the Problem of Rationality," *Public Administration Review* 62 (Sept., 2002): 33–43.

43. Jere Longman, *Among the Heroes: United Flight 93 and the Passengers and Crew Who Fought Back* (New York: HarperCollins, 2002), is, to date, the definitive reconstruction of the story. On the crash site and its role as a memorial, see Louis Jacobson, "A 9/11 Memorial in Pennsylvania," *Planning* 68 (June, 2002): 33–34; Francis X. Clines, "Pilgrims Flock to Site of Crash, Near Rural Hill," *New York Times,* Sept. 9, 2002, p. A1; and Samantha Levine, "Honoring Lives Lost on Flight 93," *U.S. News and World Report,* Sept. 16, 2002, p. 40 ff.

44. A familiar joke about emergency-landing procedures plays on the average passenger's sense of helplessness by rewriting the familiar safety-card instructions: Remove all sharp objects from your pockets, tighten your seat belt, bend over, put your head between your knees . . . and kiss your ass goodbye.

45. Pam Belluck, "Crew Grabs Man, Explosive Feared," *New York Times*, Dec. 23, 2001, p. A1.

Chapter 6. Wings into Space

1. Standard works include Frederick I. Ordway III and Mitchell R. Sharpe, *The Rocket Team: From the V-2 to the Saturn Moon Rocket* (1979; reprint, Cambridge: MIT Press, 1982); and Clarence G. Lasby, *Project Paperclip: German Scientists and the Cold War* (New York: Athenaeum, 1971). For a sharply critical view, see Linda Hunt, *Secret Agenda: The United States Government, Nazi Scientists, and Project Paperclip, 1945–1990* (New York: St.. Martin's, 1991). On post-1945 visions of the technological future, including transportation, see Corn and Horrigan, *Yesterday's Tomorrows*; and Corn, *Imagining Tomorrow*. On technological optimism as an enduring theme in American culture, see David E. Nye, *American Technological Sublime* (Cambridge: MIT Press, 1994).

2. The definitive work on these never-built designs (and much else) is Ron Miller, *The Dream Machines: An Illustrated History of the Spaceship in Art, Science, and Literature* (Melbourne: Krieger, 1993). Generous collections of images from the pre-*Sputnik* era are also reprinted in Ron Miller and Frederick C. Durant, *The Art of Chesley Bonestell* (London: Paper Tiger, 2001); Frederick I. Ordway III, *Visions of Spaceflight: Images from the Ordway Collection* (New York: Four Walls, Eight Windows, 2001); and Jack Hagerty and John C. Rogers, *The Spaceship Handbook* (Livermore, Calif.: ARA, 2001); On space as a frontier, see Howard E. McCurdy, *Space and the American Imagination* (Washington, D.C.: Smithsonian Institution Press, 1997).

3. Robert A. Heinlein, *Rocketship Galileo* (New York: Scribners, 1947); and "Space Jockey," *Saturday Evening Post*, Apr. 26, 1947, pp. 32–33 (reprinted in Heinlein, *The Green Hills of Earth* [1951], and *The Past through Tomorrow* [1967]). Studies of Heinlein's work include Alexei Panshin, *Heinlein in Dimension: A Critical Analysis* (Chicago: Advent, 1968); H. Bruce Franklin, *Robert A. Heinlein: America as Science Fiction* (New York: Oxford University Press, 1980); and James Gifford, *Robert A. Heinlein: A Reader's Companion* (Sacramento, Calif.: Nitrosyncretic, 2000). All treat, though to varying degrees, his life as well as his work.

4. Willy Ley, *Rockets: The Future of Flight beyond the Stratosphere* (New York: Viking, 1944); and *Rockets, Missiles, and Space Travel* (New York: Viking, 1951), p. 277. The publishing history of *Rockets*, which defies easy summary, is detailed in "Willy Ley Bibliography," *University of Alabama–Huntsville, Salmon Library, Special Collections Department*, Aug., 2002 <http://www.uah.edu/library/archives/download.html>.

5. Ley, *Rockets, Missiles, and Space Travel*, pp. 304–316 (quote, p. 304).

6. Miller and Durant, *Art of Chesley Bonestell*. For a comprehensive list

of Bonestell's space-related work, see Melvin H. Schuetz, *A Chesley Bonestell Space Art Chronology* (Parkland, Fla.: Universal, 1999).

7. Chesley Bonestell and Willy Ley, *The Conquest of Space* (New York: Viking, 1949).

8. Ibid., pp. 33–40, 73–88; the "weekly transport" picture appears on p. 80.

9. Robert A. Heinlein, "Shooting Destination Moon," *Astounding Science Fiction* (July, 1950) (reprinted in Robert A. Heinlein, *Requiem: New Collected Works by Robert A. Heinlein and Tributes to the Grandmaster,* ed. Yoji Kondo [New York: Tor, 1992], pp. 117–31); *Destination Moon,* dir. Irving Pichel, writ. Rip Van Ronkel, Robert A. Heinlein, and James O'Hanlon (George Pal Productions, 1950).

10. The following discussion is based on Randy Liebermann, "The *Collier's* and Disney Series," in *Blueprint for Space: Science Fiction to Science Fact,* ed. Frederick I. Ordway III and Randy Liebermann (Washington, D.C.: Smithsonian Institution Press, 1992), pp. 135–46. The original series appeared in *Collier's* as follows: Mar. 22, 1952, pp. 22–36, 38–39, 65; Oct. 18, 1952, pp. 51–58, 60; Oct. 25, 1952, pp. 38–40, 42, 44–48; Feb. 28, 1953, pp. 40–48; Mar. 7, 1953, pp. 56–63; Mar. 14, 1953, pp. 38–44; June 27, 1953, pp. 33–35, 38, 40; and Apr. 30, 1954, pp. 21–29. See also David R. Smith, "They're Following Our Script: Walt Disney's Trip to Tomorrowland," *Future,* May, 1978, p. 55; and Mike Wright, "The Disney–Von Braun Collaboration and Its Influence on Space Travel" (a paper presented at the Southern Humanities Conference, 1993), *Marshall Space Flight Center History Office,* Aug., 2002 <http://history.msfc.nasa.gov/special/disney.html>.

11. Liebermann, "*Collier's* and Disney Series," pp. 136–37.

12. Ibid., pp. 139–41.

13. Ibid., pp. 142–46. See also Wright, "Disney–Von Braun Collaboration."

14. *2001: A Space Odyssey,* dir. Stanley Kubrick, writ. Stanley Kubrick and Arthur C. Clarke (MGM, 1968). On the production of the film, see Stephanie Schwam, ed., *The Making of 2001: A Space Odyssey* (New York: Modern Library, 2000); and Piers Bizony, *2001: Filming the Future* (1994; reprint, London: Aurum, 2001).

15. The following discussion of the shuttle is drawn largely from the works of T. A. Heppenheimer, especially *Countdown: A History of Space Flight* (New York: Wiley, 1997), chap. 9, which offers a useful overview of the period. For additional, more detailed sources, see the bibliographic essay at the end of this volume.

16. These high expectations are reflected even in the work of veteran aerospace engineers. See, for example, G. Harry Stine, *Shuttle into Space: A Ride in America's Space Transportation System* (Chicago: Fawcett, 1979); and Jerry Grey, *Enterprise* (New York: Morrow, 1979).

17. Wernher Von Braun, "Spaceplane That Can Put You in Orbit: Space Shuttle," *Popular Science*, July, 1970, pp. 37–39; "President Nixon's Announcement on the Development of the Space Shuttle," Jan., 5, 1972; National Aeronautics and Space Administration, *Key Documents in the History of Space Policy* <http://history.nasa.gov/stsnixon.htm>; George F. Mueller, "The Benefits of Space Exploration Related to the Space Shuttle," *Interavia* 27 (Dec., 1972): 1335–36; and "Space Shuttle: Beginning a New Era in Space Cooperation," *Astronautics & Aeronautics*, Sept., 1972, pp. 20–25.

18. For a discussion in detail of the first orbital test flight, see T. A. Heppenheimer, *The Development of the Space Shuttle: 1972–1981* (Washington, D.C.: 2002). For a comprehensive guide to books, articles, and other printed material on the shuttle published before 1992, see at the NASA Web site Roger D. Launius and Aaron K. Gillette, *Toward a History of the Space Shuttle: An Annotated Bibliography* <http://www.hq.nasa.gov/office/pao/History/Shuttlebib/contents.html>. Chapter 8, "Shuttle Promotion," includes the works cited in this and subsequent paragraphs along with scores of others like them.

19. James C. Fletcher, "Are Skylab and the Space Shuttle Worth the Investment?" *Government Executive*, Jan., 1974, pp. 38–40, 42; "Space Shuttle—Vital to Man's Future," *Space World*, Mar., 1974, pp. 4–35; James J. Haggerty, "Space Shuttle, Next Giant Step for Mankind," *Aerospace* 14 (Dec., 1976): 2–9; Michael O'Leary, "Shuttling, the Ford of the Spaceways," *Air Progress* 39 (Dec., 1977): 38–44.

20. Dennis Meredith, "It's 1985: Come with Commander Mitty and His Crew on a Routine 'Milk Run' Flight in the Space Shuttle," *Science Digest* 87 (Jan., 1980): 52–59; John Noble Wilford, "Riding High," *Wilson Quarterly* 4 (autumn, 1980): 56–70; James A. Michener, "Manifest Destiny," *Omni*, Apr., 1981, pp. 48–50, 102–104.

21. Jenkins, *Space Shuttle*, provides a detailed chronology of the first one hundred shuttle missions (roughly the first twenty years of shuttle operations, 1981–2001). Alex Roland, "The Shuttle: Triumph or Turkey?" *Discover*, Nov., 1985, pp. 14–24, is a detailed critique of the shuttle's failure to live up to NASA's extravagant promises.

22. David J. Shayler, "NASA Astronauts," in Michael Cassutt, *Who's Who in Space: The First 25 Years* (Woodbridge, Conn.: G. K. Hall, 1987), pp. 5–10, on pp. 9–10.

23. For brief biographies of all astronauts named in this paragraph, see Cassutt. For a book-length case study of a single shuttle crew and mission, see Henry S. F. Cooper, *Before Liftoff: The Making of a Space Shuttle Crew* (Baltimore: Johns Hopkins University Press, 1987).

24. Colin Burgess and Grace George Corrigan, *Teacher in Space: Christa McAuliffe and the Challenger Legacy* (Lincoln: University of Nebraska Press, Bison Books, 2000) is the only book-length history of the

program. McAuliffe's "everywoman" quality is amply documented in an impressionistic memoir by her mother; see Grace George Corrigan, *A Journal for Christa: Christa McAuliffe, Teacher in Space* (Lincoln: University of Nebraska Press, 1993). Robert T. Hohler, *I Touch the Future: The Story of Christa McAuliffe* (New York: Random House, 1986), is a more conventional biography.

25. Ben Bova, "The Shuttle, Yes," *New York Times*, Jan. 4, 1982, p. A23.

26. The full text of the speech is available at *The Ronald Reagan Home Page*, Aug., 2002 <http://reagan.webteamone.com/speeches/challenger.cfm>. Peggy Noonan, the White House speechwriter responsible for the text, gives a detailed account of its origins in *What I Saw at the Revolution: A Political Life in the Reagan Era* (New York: Random House, 1990), pp. 252–59. For a literary analysis, see Charles Garton, "Slipping the Surly Bonds," *ANQ*, n.s., 7 (July, 1994): 54–62.

27. Morgan's official biography is available at NASA's Johnson Space Center Web site , Aug., 2002 <http://www.jsc.nasa.gov/Bios/htmlbios/morgan.html>. For the NASA administrator's announcement that Morgan will fly in 2004, see Sean O'Keefe, "Pioneering the Future" (address delivered at Maxwell School of Citizenship and Public Affairs, Syracuse University, Apr. 12, 2002), NASA Web site, Aug., 2002 <http://www.nasa.gov/newsinfo/pioneering_the_future.html>. For an outside observer's perspective on Morgan and the retooled Educator in Space Program, see Keith Cowing, "An Hour with Educator-Astronaut Barbara Morgan," May 18, 2002, *SpaceRef.com*, Aug., 2002 <http://www.spaceref.com/news/viewnews.html?id=450>.

28. Ronald Reagan, "State of the Union Address," Feb. 4, 1986, *ThisNation.com* <http://www.thisnation.com/library/sotu/1986rr.html>.

29. National Commission on Space, *Pioneering the Space Frontier* (New York: Bantam, 1986).

30. Ibid, pp. 107–115.

31. G. Harry Stine, "Comes the Revolution . . . ," *Analog Science Fiction and Science Fact*, mid-Dec., 1993 (reprinted in *Islands in the Sky*, ed. Stanley Schmidt and Robert Zubrin [New York: Wiley, 1996], pp. 7–25); "Will They Let the Spaceships Fly?" *Analog Science Fiction and Science Fact*, May, 1996, pp. 58–64; and *Halfway to Anywhere: Achieving America's Destiny in Space* (New York: M. Evans, 1996). For an insider's account of one of the meetings of the Citizens' Advisory Council and some of its results, see Larry Niven, "Space," in *N-Space* (New York: Tor, 1990), pp. 650–68.

32. Nicholas Booth, *Space: The Next 100 Years* (New York: Orion, 1990), pp. 80–81, 84–85; Thomas McDonough, *Space: The Next Twenty-Five Years* (New York: Wiley, 1987), pp. 41–43; Thomas K. Mattingly, "A Simpler Ride into Space," *Scientific American*, Oct., 1997, pp. 120–25.

33. Mattingly, "Simpler Ride into Space," p. 120; Andrew J. Butrica,

"'La force motrice' of Reusable Launcher Development: The Rise and Fall of the SDIO's SSTO Program, from the X-Rocket to the Delta Clipper," Aug., 2002 <http://www.hq.nasa.gov/office/pao/History/x-33/nasm.htm>.

34. Frank Morning Jr., "NASA Kills X-33, X-34, Trims Space Station," *Aviation Week and Space Technology*, Mar. 5, 2001, pp. 24–25; Jim Wilson, "Space Plane Grounded," *Popular Mechanics*, Feb., 2002, p. 28; Mark Alpert, "Has the Space Age Stalled?" *Scientific American*, Apr., 2002, pp. 18–20; Warren E. Leary, "Test of Revolutionary Jet Promises to Transform Flight," *New York Times*, May 22, 2001, p. F4; Bruce A. Smith, "Evelon Failure Precedes Loss of First X-43A," *Aviation Week and Space Technology*, June 11, 2001, pp. 50–51; Peter Grier, "Hypersonic Aircraft Test Fails," *Air Force Magazine*, Aug., 2001, pp. 17–18.

35. Jim Wilson, "Two Hours to Tokyo," *Popular Mechanics*, July, 2001, pp. 64–67.

Bibliographic Essay

The sources used in the writing of this book are fully documented in the endnotes. The purpose of this essay is neither to recapitulate nor to summarize those notes but to present a compact guide to the most important works on the cultural history of aviation. It echoes the structure of the book, with two sections devoted to general works followed by one for each of the chapters. The contents of such a guide inevitably reveal not only the boundaries of the existing literature but also the boundaries of the author's knowledge. This essay should, therefore, not be taken as an exhaustive list. It is offered instead as an answer to the question that every author hopes to elicit: "Where can I go to find out more?"

General Works: Technology, Society, and Culture

The underlying premise of *Looking Up* is that a two-way relationship, equally influential in both directions, links technology with society and culture. Arnold Pacey, *The Maze of Ingenuity*, 2d ed. (Cambridge: MIT Press, 1992), is an unconventional survey that places selected technological innovations firmly in their social and cultural context. Ruth Schwartz Cowan, *More Work for Mother: The Ironies of Household Technology from the Open Hearth to the Microwave* (New York: Basic, 1983), and Edward Tenner, *Why Things Bite Back: Technology and the Revenge of Unintended Consequences* (New York: Knopf, 1996), explore the unintended social consequences of technological change. George Basalla, *The Evolution of Technology* (New York: Cambridge University Press, 1988); Donald A. Norman, *The Design of Everyday Things* (Garden City, N.Y.: Doubleday, 1988); and Henry Petroski, *The Evolution of Useful Things* (New York: Vintage, 1994), examine the role of users (individually and collectively) in shaping new technologies. Wiebe Bijker, *Of Bicycles, Bakelites, and Bulbs: Toward a Theory of Sociotechnical Change* (Cambridge: MIT Press, 1995), uses case studies to illustrate the mutual influences of technology and society.

General Works: Cultural Histories of Aviation

Comprehensive surveys of aviation in particular branches of popular culture are scarce. The two key exceptions are Michael Paris, *From the Wright Brothers to Top Gun: Aviation, Nationalism, and Popular Cinema* (New York: St. Martin's, 1995), and Lawrence Goldstein, *The Flying Machine and Modern Literature* (Bloomington: Indiana University Press, 1986).

Studies of specific themes in the cultural history of aviation are also rare. Two important exceptions are Dominick A. Pisano et al., *Legend, Memory, and the Great War in the Air* (Seattle: University of Washington Press, 1992), which contrasts the realities and the popular image of World War I aviation, and Eric Schatzberg, *Wings of Wood, Wings of Metal: Culture and Technological Choice in American Airplane Materials, 1914–1945* (Princeton: Princeton University Press, 1998), which deals with the cultural "coding" of different aircraft-construction materials.

Cultural histories of aviation in particular countries are more numerous. Robert Wohl, *A Dream of Wings: Aviation and the Western Imagination, 1908–1918* (New Haven: Yale University Press, 1994), is a comprehensive and lavishly illustrated study of early responses to aviation in European high culture (for the most part). Peter Fritzsche, *A Nation of Fliers: German Aviation and the Popular Imagination* (Cambridge: Harvard University Press, 1992), and Guillaume de Syon, *Zeppelin!: Germany and the Airship, 1900–1939* (Baltimore: Johns Hopkins University Press, 2002), explore the relationship between aviation and German nationalism. David Egerton, *England and the Airplane: Essays on a Militant and Technological Nation* (London: Macmillan, 1991), and Joseph J. Corn, *The Winged Gospel: America's Romance with Aviation, 1900–1950* (New York: Oxford University Press, 1983), are episodic rather than comprehensive, but both treat topics that receive little attention elsewhere.

Technological Forecasting

Joseph J. Corn and Brian Horrigan, *Yesterday's Tomorrows: Past Visions of the American Future* (New York: Summit, 1984), remains the best introduction to the cultural history of technological forecasting. It is also the only book on the subject that touches in any depth on aviation. Joseph J. Corn, ed., *Imagining Tomorrow: History, Technology, and the American Future* (Cambridge: MIT Press, 1986), and Robert W. Rydell, *World of Fairs: The Century of Progress Expositions* (Chicago: University of Chicago Press, 1993), while not specifically concerned with aviation, provide important background. Post-1945 issues of periodicals such as *Popular Science* and *Popular Mechanics* are rich in primary-source material, breathless descriptions of technological "tomorrows" thought to be just around the corner.

Pilots as Heroes

Any comprehensive biography of a renowned individual inevitably touches on the breadth, depth, and effects of its subject's fame. A. Scott Berg, *Lindbergh* (New York: Putnam's, 1998), and Doris L. Rich, *Amelia Earhart: A Biography* (Washington, D.C.: Smithsonian Institution Press, 1989), are excellent examples of this.

A few biographies, however, go further. Tom Wolfe, *The Right Stuff* (New York: Farrar, Straus, and Giroux, 1979), in effect a "group biography" of the Project Mercury astronauts, uses their transformation from obscure test pilots into national icons as its central motif. Susan Ware, *Still Missing: Amelia Earhart and the Search for Modern Feminism* (New York: Norton, 1993), sets Earhart's image and public career against the backdrop of women's changing role in American society and culture. Ware's analysis of Earhart's lead-by-example feminism and her comparison of the aviator with other iconic "independent women" of the 1930s are especially valuable.

The ongoing controversy over William Avery "Billy" Bishop, officially the second-highest-scoring Allied fighter pilot of World War I, provides a fascinating case study of how pilot-heroes are made and, perhaps, unmade. Bishop won the Victoria Cross, Britain's highest military honor, for a heroic single-handed attack on a German airfield. A 1982 Canadian documentary film, *The Kid Who Couldn't Miss*, raised a firestorm of controversy by suggesting that Bishop, a Canadian national hero, had systematically inflated his wartime exploits. H. Clifford Chadderton, *Hanging a Legend: The NFB's Shameful Attempt to Discredit Billy Bishop, VC* (Ottawa: War Amputations of Canada, 1986), and Dan McCaffrey, *Billy Bishop, Canadian Hero* (Toronto: Lorimer, 1988), defend the Bishop legend. Brereton Greenhous, *The Making of Billy Bishop: The First World War Exploits of Billy Bishop, VC* (Toronto: Dundurn, 2002), sides with the filmmakers in questioning it.

Bombing

The literature on the development of the bomber, bomber operations, and air-power doctrine is vast. John Buckley, *Air Power in the Age of Total War* (Bloomington: Indiana University Press, 1999), stands out as a brief, accessible introduction to the subject and offers a useful bibliography.

Work on the cultural history of aerial bombing, though modest by comparison, is still substantial. H. Bruce Franklin, *War Stars: The Superweapon and the American Imagination* (New York: Oxford University Press, 1988), and I. F. Clarke, *Voices Prophesying War: Future Wars, 1763–3749*, 2d ed. (New York: Oxford University Press, 1992), discuss the bomber's (often decisive) role in fictional wars. Michael S. Sherry, *The Rise of American Air Power: The Creation of Armageddon* (New Haven: Yale University Press, 1987), traces the emergence of the *idea* of bombing as a central part of U.S. strategy. Ronald Schaffer, *Wings of Judgment: American Bombing in World War II* (New York: Oxford University Press, 1985), is both a detailed operational history and an in-depth study of contemporary views on the moral issues involved. Tami Davis Biddle, *Rhetoric and Reality in Air Warfare: The Evolution of British and American Ideas about Strategic Bombing, 1914–1945* (Princeton: Princeton University Press, 2002), offers a valuable comparative perspective on the two nations that pursued strategic bombing most enthusiastically. Sven Lindqvist, *A History of Bombing*, trans. Linda Haverty Rugg (New York: New Press, 2001), uses a mosaiclike arrangement of diverse materials to create a cultural history of bombing largely from the perspective of those bombed.

The cultural history of nuclear warfare—experienced, imagined, prepared for, and feared—is the subject of a substantial literature of its own. Allan M. Winkler, *Life under a Cloud: American Anxiety about the Atom* (Urbana: University of Illinois Press, 1993), is an excellent one-volume introduction. Paul Boyer, *By the Bomb's Early Light: American Thought and Culture at the Dawn of the Atomic Age* (New York: Pantheon, 1985); Spencer Weart, *Nuclear Fear: A History of Images* (Cambridge: Harvard University Press, 1988); and Margot A. Henriksen, *Dr. Strangelove's America* (Berkeley and Los Angeles: University of California Press, 1997), are all worthwhile follow-ups to Winkler. J. Samuel Walker, *Prompt and Utter Destruction: Truman and the Use of Atomic Bombs against Japan* (Chapel Hill: University of North Carolina Press, 1997), discusses the use of atomic bombs against Japan concisely and evenhandedly, while Philip Nobile, ed., *Judgment at the Smithsonian* (New York: Marlowe, 1995), discusses the 1995 controversy over the National Air and Space Museum's planned exhibit on the fiftieth anniversary of the bombings. The centerpiece of Nobile's book is an (unauthorized) verbatim reprint of the script that triggered the controversy and a congressional vote of disapproval.

Air Travel

Three articles in William F. Trimble, ed., *From Airships to Airbus: The History of Civil and Commercial Aviation*, vol. 2 (Washington, D.C.: Smithsonian Institution Press, 1995), repay the work of tracking down the volume. Roger Bilstein, "Air Travel and the Traveling Public: The American Experience, 1920–1970" (pp. 91–111), is the best passenger-centered view of the history of air travel yet written. It makes up for its (clearly indicated) geographic and chronological limits with a clear narrative line, persuasive analysis, and an abundance of details. Lee Kolm, "Stewardesses' 'Psychological Punch': Gender and Commercial Aviation in the United States, 1930–1978" (pp. 112–27), and William F. Trimble, "The Collapse of a Dream: Lightplane Ownership and General Aviation in the United States after World War II" (pp. 128–48), are broad, authoritative treatments of important but neglected topics. Keith Lovegrove, *Airline: Identity, Design, and Culture* (New York: Te Neues, 2000), concerns itself with the ephemera of airline culture: aircraft color schemes, crew uniforms, tableware, and the like. Though brief and selective rather than comprehensive, its design-oriented approach is unique.

Beyond these few sources, the cultural history of air travel remains a do-it-yourself project. Kenneth Hudson and Julian Pettifer, *Diamonds in the Sky: A Social History of Air Travel* (London: Bodley Head/British Broadcasting Company, 1979), is a deeply flawed but still essential overview. Its global scope and passenger-centered focus are unique, but its brevity means that few of the subjects it treats are covered in depth or followed across multiple decades. Carl Solberg, *The Conquest of the Skies: A History of Commercial Aviation in America* (Boston: Little, Brown, 1979), and T. A. Heppenheimer, *Turbulent Skies: The History of Commercial Aviation* (New York: Wiley, 1995), offer more depth and greater narrative coherence but focus more on machines and business practices than on passengers and their experiences. Histories of individual airlines and aircraft types are a valuable source of specific cultural details for readers willing to extract them bit by bit from narratives largely concerned with other topics. The works of R. E. G. Davies and Robert J. Serling are excellent starting points for such an enterprise.

Crashes

The best historical work on the cultural legacies of technological disasters has, for better or worse, focused on technologies other than aircraft.

Henry Petroski, *To Engineer Is Human: The Role of Failure in Successful Design*, rev. ed. (New York: Vintage, 1992), is a series of brief case studies that illuminate the nature of technological failures and, in passing, some of their cultural dimensions. Ann Larrabee, *Decade of Disaster* (Urbana: University of Illinois Press, 2000), deals with four major technological disasters of the 1980s in greater depth and with more attention to cultural issues. Paul Heyer, Titanic *Legacy: Disaster as Media Event and Myth* (New York: Prager, 1995), and Steven Biel, *Down with the Old Canoe: A Cultural History of the* Titanic *Disaster* (New York: Norton, 1996), are full-length studies of one of the two best-known technological disasters of the century. Klaus Jensen, *No Downlink: A Dramatic Narrative about the* Challenger *Accident and Our Time*, trans. Barbara Haveland (New York: Farrar, Straus, and Giroux, 1996), is a thought-provoking exploration of the other.

Spaceflight

The three standard overviews of the history of spaceflight—T. A. Heppenheimer, *Countdown: A History of Space Flight* (New York: John Wiley, 1997); William E. Burrows, *This New Ocean: The Story of the First Space Age* (New York: Random House, 1999); and Tom D. Crouch, *Aiming for the Stars: The Dreamers and Doers of the Space Age* (Washington, D.C.: Smithsonian Institution Press, 1999)—each devote substantial space to the *Collier's* articles of the 1950s and to the origins of the space shuttle. Howard E. McCurdy, *Space and the American Imagination* (Washington, D.C.: Smithsonian Institution Press, 1997) places the American fascination with space travel, including routine access to space aboard winged rockets, in its cultural context (particularly that provided by myths of the frontier). Ron Miller, *The Dream Machines: An Illustrated History of the Spaceship in Art, Science, and Literature* (Melbourne: Krieger, 1993), provides an encyclopedic history of spaceships both real and imagined, including many with wings.

Index

Pages with illustrations are indicated in **bold** type.